In *Encounters in Faith: Christianity in Interreligious Dialogue*, Peter Feldmeier opens the discipline of comparative theology, often seen as the provenance of a few scholars with expertise in more than one religion, to a broad audience. Focusing on certain selective themes, he draws other religions into dialogue with Christianity, carefully explaining the meaning and place of a particular topic (mysticism, mediators, etc.) within a particular religion, and subsequently suggesting ways in which Christians might learn from the other. This book thus forms a welcome complement to the vast literature in both theology of religions and history of religions. It will be a useful handbook for undergraduate teaching as well as for disseminating the fruit of comparative theology and interreligious dialogue to the wider public.

Catherine Cornille
Associate Professor of Comparative Theology
Boston College

This engaging, informative textbook leads students quickly into interreligious inquiry and encounter. With its clear focus on religious practice, it will be a most helpful teaching tool.

Leo D. Lefebure, Matteo Ricci, SJ
Professor of Theology
Georgetown University

There is something fresh and distinctive about Feldmeier's approach to religions that serves as a timely corrective to so many textbooks on the same themes. Religions are too often presented as some exotic doctrinal system for conceptual analysis or some curious relic for historical investigation. Rather, for Feldmeier, religions are to be encountered and experienced. In his hands, religions no longer appear as so many isms but as living, evolving, and above all, mystical realities that expand and transform one's spiritual perspective and way of life. Professors and students who are bored to tears by bone-dry religion textbooks that every year swamp college campuses will rejoice in having Feldmeier's book at their disposal. They can now have a cor ad cor [heart to heart] conversation with the religious Other they encounter.

Dr. Peter C. Phan,
Ignacio Ellacuria Chair of Catholic Social Thought
Georgetown University

Author Acknowledgments

There are several people I'd like to recognize and thank. First, I'd like to thank Leslie Ortiz who helped me think about this book out loud for the last several years and who supported and advocated the proposal for Anselm Academic. I'd also like to thank Donna Crilly, whose careful reading, corrections, and many suggestions made the editing process so much smoother. I am also grateful to the University of St. Thomas, whose MAXI grant offered me the space for research and writing I needed to address such a bold project. Above all, I'd like to thank Laura Stierman, who worked through this manuscript several times with extraordinary skill and wisdom. Her criticisms were always spot on, and her support always particularly uplifting and gratifying.

Publisher Acknowledgments

Thank you to the following individuals who reviewed this work in progress.

Scott Edgar, *University of Phoenix*

Ariel Glucklich, *Georgetown University, Washington, DC*

Regina Pfeiffer, *Chaminade University of Honolulu*

Louise Prochaska, *Notre Dame College, South Euclid, Ohio*

ENCOUNTERS IN FAITH

Christianity in Interreligious Dialogue

Peter Feldmeier

Created by the publishing team of Anselm Academic.

Cover art royalty-free from iStock

Printed in the United States of America

7032

ISBN 978-1-59982-031-6

For Marie,
Beautiful wife,
Soul mate,
Companion on our spiritual journey

———

Contents

Introduction ix

How to Use This Book xii

1. Christianity in a Multireligious World 1

A Starting Point 1
The History of Christian Thought about Non-Christians 5
The Modern Theology of Religions 8
Holding a Postmodern Creative Tension 16
Hopes and Postures in Encountering the Other 19

2. Mysticism 23

What Is Mysticism? 23
Mysticism as Apophatic 27
Mysticism as Kataphatic 33
Conclusions 43

3. Masters and Mediators 47

The Role of a Mediator 47
Mediation and Cosmology 50
Spiritual Guides as Mediators 56
Lessons 65
Conclusions 67

4. The Jewish Vision 71

Entering the Jewish Imagination 71
Jewish Vision of Time 76
Torah Study: An Intersection between Time and Space 85
Jewish Vision of Space 88

5. Islam: The Surrendering Soul 95

What Makes a Muslim? 95
Muhammad and the Human Condition 98
The Qur'an 106
Salat: Before the Throne of God 108

6. Hinduism's Many Layers 119

From Sacrifice to Brahman 119
Finding God and Self 124
Passionately Loving God 129
Witnessing an Untamable God 136

7. Buddha's Revision 142

Buddha's Biography 142
Meditation 153
Two Confounding Questions: The Self and Nirvana 156
Shifts in Buddhism and Their Meanings 161

8. Zen Mind, Ordinary Mind 170

Introducing Zen 170
Spiritual Progress in Zen 185

9. The Chinese Spirit 196

Chinese Religiosity 196
The Daoist Contribution 201
The Confucian Contribution 209

10. Indigenous Traditions: The Primal Voice 219

Why Native Traditions Matter 219
Spirits and Shamans 228

11. The New Age Message 239

What Is New Age? 239
Interesting Contributions and Strange Permutations 243

12. Interreligious Encounters: Backward and Forward 261

Looking Back 261
Looking Forward: The Future of Interreligious Dialogue 267
Does What You Believe Matter? 272
Personal Last Word by the Author: Why I Am a Christian 278

Glossary 285

Index 295

Introduction

Most approaches to and presentations of religions focus on two things: doctrine and history. Far and away, doctrine dominates. It is as though the purpose of a given religion is to provide a set of metaphysical claims. History is also emphasized, as typically one traces the organizational development of a religious community, its historic spread, and its theological progressions. There are good reasons for emphasizing these two dimensions. One is that doctrine and history are indeed important aspects of a religion, and they play formative roles in the development of worship, leadership, community structure, and a religion's role in society. Another reason is that these two areas of a religion represent the easiest aspects to study and communicate. As important and valuable as they are, however, if treated exclusively, they can be limiting and distorting. For some religions, such as Judaism, specific doctrine is less important than it is in others, such as Christianity. In many indigenous or native religious traditions, the life of the tribe is so integrated that one simply cannot separate religious considerations from every other part of the culture. Additionally, such a limited focus on doctrine and history tends to neglect the importance of religious practices and the experience of community life, which often represent the heart of a religion.

It is also the case that if one addresses another religious tradition solely in terms of doctrine and history, that religion will feel particularly foreign, or other. From such a perspective, one does not acquire a great *feel* for the religion, and appreciating it on its own terms becomes more difficult. Such a perspective also gives one a kind of permission to dismiss religious claims that simply do not resonate with one's usual way of thinking about things religious. For example, a Christian religious view typically asserts that everyone has a soul, while Buddhists reject this claim, believing instead that there is no eternal, unchanging core, or self, by which one might identify oneself, a doctrine called "no-self." A Christian might walk away from Buddhism thinking, "They don't believe in a soul, but we do." It is as though that's all one needs to consider, without seeing how no-self works in forming a kind of religious quality in pious Buddhists, perhaps one that resonates with what Jesus tried to have his disciples embrace.

There is an additional liability in considering religions within such narrow confines. That is, religions then are usually studied somewhat distinctly from each other. For example, in a world religions course, one might spend three weeks on a given religion, wrap it up with an exam, and then move on to the next religion. By the end of the semester, students often do not know what to make of the course, except that they learned an enormous amount of interesting data about various religious traditions. What do these data mean however? The question may be especially vexing if one has personal religious beliefs. Are these other religions and their claims then false? Do they represent a legitimate alternative? Given that many representatives of other religions are intelligent, moral, reflective, and spiritually mature, should one then conclude that all religious claims are equally true (or untrue) or that the truth of religious claims can never be known? What do these religions have to do with one's own religious life beyond providing alternative visions? Looked at more positively, could dialogue with other faiths help one rethink one's faith in some ways? In exploring the religious imagination of other faiths, can a person return to his or her own faith with new insights or questions? Could such experiences even help a person see one's faith more clearly? This book addresses all these questions from the viewpoint that, indeed, there is much to learn from the world's religions. The reader will see, for example, that attention to important Buddhist principles can help a Christian understand one of Jesus' parables, or how understanding Muhammad's mystical life opens new ways of understanding the Christian apostle Paul.

In this text, Christian theology and spirituality act as a counterpoint to and a comparison with the other traditions discussed. For this reason, there is no chapter on Christianity itself. The reasons for this approach are several: First is that Christianity remains the majority religion among the North American audience that will be primary readers of this text. In March 2009, a massive published study showed that 76 percent of Americans identified themselves as Christian (down from 86 percent in 1990). For this reason, Christianity is a default religion of reference in American culture. Those who belong to the religions represented in this book also will benefit from this interface with Christianity, again given its dominance in the United States. Second, such a one-to-one comparison can be particularly timely, given, for example, the scandalous way that Islam is often portrayed today, especially in contrast to the Christian West. The situation begs for direct dialogue. Finally, Christian theology has a long and rich history of interreligious discussion. Thus, this book can model for Christians and non-Christians alike how they might approach other religious traditions and then see their tradition in light of such encounters.

This book also was written to address some of the limitations in standard presentations of world religions. It will include doctrine and history when appropriate. More importantly, it intends to draw the reader into the ethos, or character, or religious imagination of a given religious tradition. It is not merely an objective description of other traditions as might appear in a book of world religions. While this book intends to be fair and accurate, it also intends to be an intentionally sympathetic engagement. Oddly, such an approach is rare. A Muslim scholar (a shaikh, no less) critiqued the chapter on Islam in manuscript form. After his review, he suggested that we write a book together on Islamic spirituality. He said that the kind of approach I brought to the chapter he read does not exist in books on Islam in English.

There is a dictum: "Spirituality unites where doctrine divides." This does not mean that people ought to ignore doctrine, and the reader will find that some claims of various traditions are questioned and even challenged here. Still, the point of the book is not merely to suggest doctrinal comparisons and contrasts, but to explore how the heart or spirit of different religious traditions can speak to the reader. Thus, this book is not a world-religions textbook that intends a wide-ranging survey of the whole of various traditions. It also does not aim at providing ethnologies of different religious cultures or detailed explanations of religious practices or holidays, arguably central to most religious traditions. Ultimately the point of this book is to provide points of contact and discussion among religions. These points are intentionally chosen, as they speak to something of the core of the spiritual imagination of each religion. When John Henry Newman was made a cardinal, his coat of arms carried the motto, *cor ad cor loquitur*, "heart speaks to heart." This is the aim.

HOW TO USE THIS BOOK

This book could be used quite successfully in a world-religions course, either augmenting a general world-religions textbook or as a grounding text as students read primary sources, such as the **Qur'an** or **Bhagavad Gita**. It could also be used in a regular theology or religious studies course, because considering theological material in light of religious plurality is becoming a popular, and even standard, vehicle for theological insight. Finally, it is envisioned as a text appropriate for spirituality courses, as it was written to address broad themes in spirituality, including prayer, religious imagination, models of holiness, stages of spiritual progression, and even descriptions of religious experience.

The chapters move from large, grounding issues to engagement with specific religious traditions, and then to final questions in interreligious dialogue. The book begins by asking what people think about religious traditions other than their own (chapter one). Then it moves to one of the most pan-religious topics— **mysticism**—and investigates whether and how religions may share some Ultimate Horizon or various experiences. The reader will also see how one's religious training can condition religious experience (chapter two). Chapter three addresses the theme of spiritual or religious mediation. Is the cosmos spiritually structured such that God uses **mediators** to affect human lives? What is the role of spiritual masters, and how do they mentor religiously serious people? In chapter four a particular religion—Judaism—is investigated with a challenging question: what does being Jewish mean? Such a question influences Jewish notions of time, space, and sacrament. The central image of Islam as surrender, or submission, is explored in chapter five. Such a concept is a daunting and glorious challenge for Muslim and non-Muslim alike.

Chapter six studies Hinduism and its wholly different notion of the soul wandering from one life to another until it becomes liberated. What is the soul and what is its association with Ultimate Reality? Chapter seven probes Buddhism and explores what happens when one accepts so much of the Hindu worldview but then dramatically denies the very soul seeking liberation. Chapter eight on Zen provides a paradoxical vision of life in which the liberation one seeks is already before one, even part of one, and only has to be realized. The question is asked whether Zen could be conceived as a way of being in the world that could combine with other religions. The reader is further stretched in chapter nine by the challenge to think religiously without an Ultimate Reality or Horizon at all. How might being religious be conceived of as profoundly skillful attention to the energies and relationships before one? Chapter ten looks at native traditions, particularly those of the Americas, and confronts assumptions about the distinction between humans and other life forms, while offering a living prophetic witness to the sacredness of the created world. Chapter eleven looks at the New Age movement. While utterly wide-ranging and varied, the movement seems to have broad similarities in its different expressions. While this chapter is the least sympathetic, it recognizes in the New Age movement modern lessons ignored at one's peril. In each of these chapters, Christianity becomes a dialogue partner, rethinking itself in light of the religious imagination each chapter provides.

Examining religious traditions leads to new questions. Are there universal lessons or insights to which most religions attest? Are holy people from different religions fundamentally alike? Is spiritual transformation more important than what one believes, and what is the relationship between the two? Can one belong to more than one religion? Addressing such questions is the aim of this text as well as a challenge for further study.

CHAPTER ONE

Christianity in a Multireligious World

A STARTING POINT

The Acts of the Apostles describes the apostle Paul spending time in Athens, distressed over the numerous idols he saw. Paul met with some philosophers who brought him to the Areopagus, a kind of public square, to have him speak to them and others about his religious beliefs. This is Paul's short speech:

> Athenians, I see how extremely religious you are in every way. For as I went through your city and looked carefully at the objects of worship, I found among them an altar with the inscription, "to an unknown god." What therefore you worship as unknown, this I proclaim to you. The God who made the world and everything in it, he who is Lord of heaven and earth, does not live in shrines made by human hands, nor is he served by human hands, as though he needed anything, since he himself gives to all mortals life and breath and all things. From one ancestor he made all nations to inhabit the whole earth, and he allotted the times of their existence and the boundaries of the places where they would live, so that they would search for God

and perhaps grope for him and find him—though indeed he is not far from each one of us. For, "In him we live and move and have our being," as even some of your own poets have said, "For we too are his offspring." Since we are God's offspring, we ought not to think that the deity is like gold, or silver, or stone, an image formed by the art and imagination of mortals. While God has overlooked the times of human ignorance, now he commands all people everywhere to repent, because he has fixed a day on which he will have the world judged in righteousness by a man whom he has appointed, and this he has given assurance to all by raising him from the dead.

—Acts 17: 22–31

There is much to consider here. As a Jew, Paul surely found idols offensive, perhaps even ridiculous. He reminds the Athenians that God transcends time, place, and anything their imaginations can produce. However, he also commends their religious spirit. In the context of both affirming and challenging their religiosity, he proclaims the true God of the heavens and Earth and Jesus Christ whom God has raised and made Lord and judge. His access point is the altar devoted to the "unknown god." Paul's message is that he can identify this unknown god, who is actually the God of the universe.

Is Paul's identification of the "unknown god" with God himself merely a rhetorical device or a clever introduction? Neither seems to be the case and for several important reasons. In his speech, Paul affirms that he thinks the Athenians are religiously minded, and some of their spiritual intuitions are excellent, particularly their worship of the unknown god. While Paul names their unknown god, he only does so partially. He identifies him as the real God of the universe but recognizes with them that God also remains unknown. That is, even as revealed, God retains his transcendence; as Paul says, he is beyond the "imagination of mortals." Paul also explains that their authentic religious sensibilities are responses to God. God creates humans, Paul says, as a single family and in a way that causes them to search for God and discover him because he is near to them. As a Jew, Paul surely would have believed that humans are made in the image and likeness of God (Genesis 1:26),

Paul preaching at Athens, 1515–1516, by Raphael (Raffaello Sanzio; 1483–1520).

IMAGE: V&A IMAGES/THE ROYAL COLLECTION, ON LOAN FROM HM THE QUEEN/ ART RESOURCE, NY

and thus, humans are spiritual beings by nature. Additionally, he states that everything human is grounded in God's presence: "In him we live and move and have our being." Indeed, Paul says, all humans are God's children. Paul is saying that God is present in their lives, that they implicitly know God, and that on some level they are already responding to God's grace. One can think of grace here as God's favor and his loving, saving presence in human life. Finally, Paul insists that humans are all part of God's plan and that he is now going to share that plan and how they might embrace it.

Paul is not inventing a new way of considering God and the graced relationship that God has with the world. Old Testament theology understands God's saving plan as universal. "All the ends of the earth shall remember and turn to the Lord," says the psalmist, "and all the families of the nations shall worship before him. For dominion belongs to the Lord, and he rules over the nations" (Psalm 22:27–28). Through the prophet Isaiah, God calls all people to his salvation: "Turn to me and be saved, all the ends of the earth! For

I am God, and there is no other. . . . To me every knee shall bow, every tongue shall swear" (Isaiah 45:22–23). Isaiah announces that God's plan is to use the faith of Israel as a vehicle for bringing salvation to the ends of Earth. Israel would be a "light to the nations" (Isaiah 42:6), guiding all peoples to God, so that "my house will be called a house of prayer for all peoples" (Isaiah 56:7; see also Isaiah 2:2–3; Micah 4:1–2; Zechariah 8:20). Paul believed that in the final period of salvation history the Holy Spirit would particularly infuse the universe with the divine presence. In fact, when the Holy Spirit begins to anoint both Jews and Gentiles, the early Church understands this as a fulfillment of prophecy for God's universal salvation (Isaiah 11:10, 43:9; Joel 2:28; Acts 2:14, 33, 15:16–17). As the prophet Zechariah proclaimed succinctly: "The Lord will become king over all the earth; on that day the Lord will be one and his name one" (Zechariah 14:9).

For Paul, as for the rest of the New Testament witnesses, Jesus Christ has become the means for God's universal salvation. In the Gospel according to John, one finds, "But to all who received him, who believed in his name, he gave power to become children of God" (John 1:12) and "For God so loved the world that he gave his only Son, so that everyone who believes in him may not perish but may have eternal life" (John 3:16). In First Timothy, one reads, "This is right and is acceptable in the sight of God our Savior, who desires everyone to be saved and to come to the knowledge of the truth. For there is one God; there is also one mediator between God and humankind, Jesus Christ, himself human, who gave himself a ransom for all" (1 Timothy 2:3–6).

Christianity teaches that God's providence has brought salvation to the entire world through his Son; that in his Incarnation, one is able to be united to God's very being, in his death, one is forgiven and ransomed from sin, and in his Resurrection, one is freed from the curse of the grave. This faith in God's plan of salvation through Jesus Christ gives Paul the impetus to share the good news with others. This is what Paul was doing at the Areopagus. However, the context for sharing this good news is telling. Paul assumes that sincerely religious people already know God and experience his presence in their lives.

THE HISTORY OF CHRISTIAN THOUGHT ABOUT NON-CHRISTIANS
The Patristic Church (Second–Fifth Centuries)

Throughout its existence, Christianity has wrestled with the issues in Paul's speech to the Athenians. On the one hand, Christianity teaches that Jesus is the absolute savior and sole mediator between God and humanity (Hebrews 5:9). "I am the way, the truth, and the life," Jesus says, "No one comes to the Father except through me" (John 14:6). On the other hand, it was often assumed, even from the beginning, that those who do not know the Gospel explicitly can still experience God in their lives. Broadly, Church fathers believed that pious, devout Jews and Gentiles who lived before Christ were saved by Christ's grace. Before the Incarnation in Jesus, the preexistent Word (*Logos*) spoke to them in the depths of their souls. Justin Martyr (100–165), for example, spoke of the seeds of the Word (*Logos spermatikos*) planted in the hearts of these pious souls. It was also believed by many that Christ's sacrifice transcends time, because it involved God's eternity. Those Christians who believed in the salvation of non-Christians who lived before Christ included many of the greatest early Church thinkers, such as Justin Martyr, Irenaeus, Origen, Clement of Alexandria, Cyprian, Gregory of Nyssa, and John Chrysostom. They presumed that God was benevolent, and in choosing Israel, God did not reject others but wanted his providence to include all nations.

Once the Church existed, its greatest challenge regarding God's universal salvific will had to do with nonbelievers. If before Christ one did not have to be part of Israel, after Christ did one have to be an explicit member of the Church? In the context of the now-present Church, optimism about the salvation of non-Christians was much more mixed. Once the Gospel had been fundamentally preached, not believing in Christ was assumed an intentional choice to reject God's explicit offer of salvation. Cyprian, who was clear that non-Christians before Christ could be saved, was equally clear that non-Christians after Christ could not be saved. Perhaps the greatest articulator of this position was Augustine (354–430). While Augustine believed in free will, he also believed in predestination; thus those who were not part of the Church were not predestined to heaven. One should remember, however, that many Church leaders believed that fundamentally the world had the Gospel and failure to convert was an intentional rejection of Christ. Even at that, many Church fathers were also ambivalent. As a group, their natural impulse was to imagine as large a net as possible, with hints of the presence of the Church outside its overt boarders.

The Medieval Church (Sixth–Fourteenth Centuries)

Despite many of the Church fathers' broad perspective toward the whole of humanity, Augustine's particular position strongly influenced the medieval western Church. Indeed several crucial teachings in the West strengthened the perspective that God's saving grace was restricted to those specifically and visibly inside the Church. In 1215, the Fourth Lateran Council declared, "There is only one universal Church of the faithful, outside which none shall be saved." In 1442, the Council of Florence issued a profession of faith that read, "All of those outside of the Catholic Church, Jews, heretics, schismatics, pagans, unless joined to the church, are damned to hell."

What does one make of such a seemingly clear and severe restriction to God's saving grace in the medieval Church? Like all doctrines in Christianity, these teachings need to be interpreted in light of their historical context, which includes the prevailing assumptions for not being in the Church. In each of the previously mentioned claims, the context was some form of schism or decided break with the Church. This constituted—in the medieval mind—a break in love, communion, and the authority that Christ invested in bishops as successors of the apostles, particularly the pope.

One could also understand the issue in terms of the metaphor of Christ's body. Since the early Church, Paul's image of the Church as the body of Christ has played an important role in Christian self-understanding. The Church is conceived as the body of Christ with Christ as its head (Romans 12:4–5; 1 Corinthians 12:12–27; Ephesians 1:22–23; Colossians 1:18). This means that Christ can never be understood as completely distinct from his body. Rather, he identifies with it in some real way (Ephesians 4:4ff). For the medieval Christian, to separate oneself from the body of Christ was tantamount to separating oneself from Christ himself. What did the Church say then about non-Christians who appear to be drawn into the same condemnations as the so-called heretics and schismatics? Like the late patristic Church, the medieval Church assumed that non-Christians chose to reject God's grace in Christ. Interestingly, the presumption of God's universal will that all be saved was never really challenged. Thomas Aquinas (1224–1274) argued that non-Christians could not be damned for what they could not avoid and that those seeking God's salvation were already responding to grace in some way and would receive that grace to be saved. Aquinas stated that there could be a kind of implicit desire for baptism if one desires God in the depths of one's heart. Centuries later, when the Church was heavily invested in missions to the newly explored Americas, this implicit baptism of desire was broadly assumed and fundamentally became the theological rule in Roman Catholicism.

The Reformation (Sixteenth Century)

During the Reformation, Protestant thought regarding non-Christians being damned corresponded to the Catholic medieval conclusions—but for very different reasons. For reformers, such as Martin Luther and John Calvin, humans had no free will regarding salvation. In Luther's mind, it was absurd to think that humans had an effect on their salvation. Salvation is a divine reality, something God alone could effect, with no cooperation on the human side. Instead, if one was predestined for salvation, God worked irresistibly in the soul, and the soul simply became Christian. While this approach may seem coercive on God's part, the experience for the soul was that it was now free and flourishing in the Holy Spirit. Calvin argued that one is saved because God predestined that individual to be so and infused his or her soul with saving grace. If one is damned, this too is predestined.

While predestination seemed unfair from a human point of view, for Calvin it all appeared fitting. Everyone is a sinner and thus deserves to be damned. Those who are damned, therefore, only end up receiving what they deserve. This highlights God's justice. Those who are saved and reconstituted in the Spirit are not any better than the damned before they received the Spirit. Thus, those saved witness God's mercy. Additionally, simply because God shows mercy to some, one should never think that God is forced to show mercy to everyone. The Catholic Church assumed God's desire was to save everyone but only if one chooses to cooperate with God's saving grace. The early reformers decidedly rejected this position as "works righteousness," or some form of self-contribution to one's salvation. On the contrary, the reformers believed that God does not desire universal salvation but only the salvation of those he chose before time even began.

THE MODERN THEOLOGY OF RELIGIONS
Introduction

Modern Christianity continues to wrestle with the issues associated with non-Christians, including what to think about other religions and how to understand the state of souls who are not Christian, particularly those who are religiously devout. For the past fifty years, theologians have been developing a discipline known as the **theology of religions**. This discipline seeks to give definition and shape to Christian reflection on the theological implications of religious diversity. It looks to scripture, doctrine, theological tradition, philosophy, and even the social sciences to discover inherent possibilities and rules that ought to guide encounters with other religions. In addition, it asks crucial questions: Does God's grace work through these religions? Are these religions vehicles of salvation? Are they in conflict with or complementary to Christianity? Compared to Christianity, are these religions as valid, less valid, invalid, or simply differently valid?

It may seem imperialistic, even obnoxious, to make such declarations about other religions, but one cannot avoid the issue. Typically, religions articulate an Ultimate Horizon of meaning and truth, one that is all embracing. Rarely would they simply claim that their adherents are comfortable considering the universe in a particular way, knowing that others feel comfortable considering it differently. Such respectful differences make sense when talking about social clubs, sports preferences, or even political systems. Religions often represent a universal, absolute vision. Christians believe that Jesus is Lord of the universe and not just Lord for those who belong to Christianity. Muslims believe that the Qur'an is the highest expression of revelation in the universe, not only for them but also as an absolute fact. Most Hindus believe that the self (**Atman**) is in some way identifiable with Ultimate Reality (**Brahman**), and that this is true whether you believe in it or not. Buddhists believe that **Nirvana** is only attainable when one renounces any sense of Atman, or self.

To have religious commitments and to believe that those commitments imply the status of others outside one's faith need not be equated with arrogance. Having universal claims is usually central to being religious. In fact, if one were talking with a Hindu who did not believe in an eternal Atman, one might very well be wasting one's time. On the one hand, no one wants an arrogant dialogue partner who considers any alternative vision of reality to be wrong or pernicious. On the other hand, no one wants a dialogue partner who is devoid of serious, universal religious commitments. This latter partner becomes minimally boring and ultimately irrelevant.

The Threefold Schema

In his groundbreaking book, *Christians and Religious Pluralism*, Alan Race categorized various Christian theologies of religions under three basic headings or fundamental positions: **exclusivism, inclusivism,** and **pluralism**. These categories have remained relatively standard. Following is the briefest of sketches:

Exclusivism is a theological position held by many Evangelical Christians that posits no grace or salvation outside of Christian confession. Unless one proclaims explicit faith in Christ, one cannot be saved. The famous dictum is *extra ecclesiam* (or *Christum*) *nulla salus* (outside the Church [or Christ], there is no salvation). The biblical evidence for such a position is daunting. Jesus says in John's Gospel: "I am the way, the truth, and the life; no one comes to the Father except through me" (John 14:6). Such exclusive language is also used by the apostles, as Peter says, "Only in him [Jesus] is there salvation; for of all the names in the world given to men, this is the only one by which we can be saved" (Acts 4:11–12). Those who are exclusivists emphasize that God's revelation acts as a judgment against any human attempt to know him without it. Given that all revelation is centered on and ultimately comes from Christ, then any truth claims not revealed by Christ are de facto erroneous. The Christian who does not start with Christ and his uniqueness has failed from the beginning.

Inclusivism is a theological position held by most mainstream Protestant, Eastern Orthodox, Roman Catholic, and Anglican Christians. This position holds that Christ is the absolute savior and that his saving grace is operative outside formal Christian confession. Inclusivism is built on three assumptions: The first is that God desires all people to be saved (1 Timothy 2:4) and, thus, makes saving a real possibility. Second, all experiences of truth, goodness, love, and so on, are experiences of God's grace working in one's heart. To respond to this inner working of God's grace by seeking the truth and embracing the good is to walk with God. In the First Letter of John, one reads, "Whoever loves a brother or sister lives in the light" (1 John 2:10) and "God is love, and those who abide in love abide in God, and God abides in them" (1 John 4:16). Third, all grace is mediated by Christ, and so to cooperate with grace is to live in and through Christ's saving presence. According to inclusivists, one is not saved because one is simply a good person who does good things. One is saved by Christ's grace. The good that one does, the love that one shares, and the truth that one pursues are all responses to Christ's saving presence. Everyone is saved in the same way—by Christ. The difference is that non-Christians only experience this grace implicitly in their lives. That is, they do not realize that it is Christ working through them. The advantage a Christian has then is that in knowing the Gospel, one has a privileged ability to cooperate with grace.

The Catholic Church has retained its historical commitment to the necessity of belonging to the Church, but the understanding of membership has changed. In the medieval Church, unless one was explicitly part of the Church, one was necessarily assumed to be separated from Christ. Today, if one is implicitly cooperating with the grace of Christ, then one is assumed to be implicitly part of the Church ("Dogmatic Constitution on the Church" [*Lumen gentium*], nos. 2, 4, 14–16; "Declaration on the Relations of the Church to Non-Christian Religions" [*Nostra aetate*], no. 2). This current position can boast of biblical support, but it is less clear. Usually inclusivists

MORE EXCLUSIVIST AND INCLUSIVIST TEXTS

For more exclusivist texts, see John 1:3, 1:17–18, 3:6, 3:18, 6:28–29, 8:24, 12:48, 14:6; 1 John 1:12–13; Acts 2:38; Romans 3:23–28; Galatians 3:22; 1 Timothy 2:4–6; 2 Timothy 1:11–12; Titus 3:7. For more inclusivist texts, see Mark 9:40; John 3:16–17, 8:12, 11:9, 12:46; 1 John 2:2, 2:5–6, 4:7–8, 4:12, 6:33; Acts 17:22; Romans 5:18; 11:32; 1 Corinthians 5:19, 15:28; Colossians 3:11; Eph 1:10; Galatians 5:22–23.

align their position with texts that point out the universal quality of Christ's salvation or that transformed lives imply God's presence. As the apostle Peter says in another speech, "Truly I understand that God shows no partiality, but in every nation anyone who fears him and does what is right is acceptable to him" (Acts 10:35).

Pluralism is a theological position professed explicitly by no formal Christian body but held by a minority of Christians in mainstream and liberal Protestant traditions as well as in Roman Catholicism. Pluralism is the most difficult position to describe because it has the greatest variety. Broadly, pluralism refuses to name Christianity as the singular normative religious revelation. Pluralism ascribes to three principles: God transcends comprehension; God is one; an absolute unity underlies all reality. It is this God, or this unity, that religions are addressing. Thus, whether one calls the Eternal Absolute the Trinity (Christianity), YHWH (Judaism), Allah (Islam), Eternal Dao (Daoism), Dharmakaya (Buddhism), Brahman (Hinduism), and so on, one is speaking about the same reality even if that reality is somewhat differently conceived. Pluralists do not suggest that these various conceptions of Ultimate Reality do not matter. The difference between a personal God in Christianity and an impersonal Dao dramatically affects one's religious life. However, these names reference the same reality; the same Ultimate Truth.

Pluralism tends to see all (or most) religions as fundamentally similar. Some pluralists argue that religions, at their core, express the same spiritual experience. Others argue that they represent different paths to the same kind of salvation project. In both approaches, pluralist scholars draw on a variety of data from very different religious traditions that show uncanny similarities in the nature of religious experience and even in how holy people are conceived.

Christian pluralists cannot boast of much biblical evidence. Perhaps they might point to texts that remind the reader that God is beyond all consideration. For example: "Then the Lord addressed Job out of the whirlwind: 'Who is this that darkens counsel by words without knowledge. . . . Where were you when I laid the foundations of the earth?'" (Job 38:1–4) or "How weighty to me are your thoughts, O God! How vast is the sum of them! I try to count them—they are more than the sand; I come to the end—I am still with you" (Psalm 139:17–18). Such texts are few and far between, however, and they are overwhelmed by counter texts. This imbalance does not daunt pluralists. They argue that the Bible is not designed to address the issue of religious plurality. Rather, the Bible's intent is to infuse a deeper faith in Christ.

To illustrate these three positions in practical terms, imagine that on a given Sunday three ministers are preaching to their respective congregations, each personally representing a different theology of religion. They might preach very similar sermons, exhorting their congregants to give their lives over to Jesus Christ. Their sole interest that day is to facilitate a deep love and reverence for Christ the Lord. Privately, the exclusivist might think, "If you don't do this, you will end up in hell." The inclusivist may think, "While it matters less if you are explicitly Christian, this is the most excellent way to encounter Christ's saving grace." At the same time, the pluralist may think, "God is, of course, beyond all religious expressions, but this is a profound one that certainly brings salvation."

A famous simile found in both Hinduism and Buddhism illustrates the point of religious pluralism: Six blind men approach an elephant. One touches its trunk and concludes that it is like a large snake; another, the tail and imagines it like a feather duster; the third, the side and describes it as a great rounded wall; another, the leg and imagines a pillar; the fifth, the ear and considers it as if a basket; and finally, the

Blind monks examining an elephant, by Hanabusa (1652–1724).

last one grasps a tusk and describes it as a plow. The elephant here represents the large and mysterious God, and each of the blind men, a different religion with its authentic, although incomplete, experience of divine revelation. While the blind men's experiences are real, and their descriptions apt, a problem arises when each man extrapolates this limited experience to the whole reality. Pluralists take a similar position, arguing that God, by definition, exceeds all comprehension and conceptualization. Concepts are limited, but God is not. Concepts are based on human experience of the world, and God is beyond the world. Pluralists argue that all religions operate as paradigms, that is, perspectives, models, or lenses in interpreting the spiritual universe. Because every paradigm is by nature limited, no religion can claim to speak for all things religious. Both the complexity of the universe and the transcendence of God demand the conclusion that all religions are in some sense relative and limited.

Truths and Problems in Each Perspective

Every theology of religions has assets and liabilities. Exclusivist Christians point to the necessity of Christian revelation in making sense of God. They also argue that central to being Christian is witness for the sake of conversion. There are, however, few bona fide exclusivists, and their position often strains credibility. For example, to take the exclusivist position at face value means that all people, even those who have had no chance to hear the Gospel, will be damned. This seems like a divine setup: to be created in order necessarily to spend eternity in hellfire.

Further, self-proclaimed exclusivists are often inconsistent in applying their own principles. For example, it is inconceivable that the death of an infant in an Evangelical Church would not occasion a Christian burial, and surely, that infant would be characterized as saved by Christ. Any theology that would claim the infant born of Christian parents is saved but the one born of Hindu parents is damned—neither child having actual Christian faith—is obviously problematic. Other Evangelicals argue that all children are saved before the age of reason, but once one has reached the age of reason then one must be Christian. Such a caveat, however, is contrary to exclusivist claims that one has to be Christian to be saved. Further, exclusivism imagines some arbitrary cutoff line for salvation and damnation. Some Evangelicals theorize that at the moment of death non-Christians are given a chance to choose Christ, if on Earth they had no legitimate opportunity. Others suppose that God will save all who would have become Christian on Earth if they had the legitimate opportunity to choose at that time—an assessment that God's omniscience guarantees. These theories reflect the problems inherent in the exclusivist position.

Many Evangelicals hesitate to make absolute claims about the salvation of non-Christians. They claim that they know Christians are saved by the grace of Christ through faith. However, they cannot claim to know God's mind about others. Perhaps all are damned; perhaps some are saved; conceivably, all are saved. This is God's domain. Their job, they say, is to proclaim the good news, nothing more or less. This was the conclusion of the evangelist Billy Graham: to speak exclusively and let God be God.

The inclusivist position appeals to most Christians because it holds a number of values or truths together. Inclusivists remain squarely in the tradition that claims that the Trinity is the full revelation of God and that Jesus Christ is the absolute, universal savior. It also recognizes that God's grace is a universal principle of love, goodness, and truth, and that non-Christians obviously seek, embrace, and cooperate with that transcendental ground. One can imagine, for example, a Christian monk absorbed in contemplation and communing with God. One can further imagine a Hindu contemplative wholly absorbed in meditation and communion with Brahman (Transcendent Absolute). Both report the same experience and both evidence the same kind of transformation. To say that one is graced, and the other is suffering delusion—simply for having a different name for God—seems ungrounded to the inclusivist. This approach does not suggest there are no differences between the two religious members. For the inclusivist, to help bring the Hindu into the fullness of the Gospel would be to support the grace already being experienced and to bring the grace to its fulfillment. The thinking is like Paul's in the Areopagus when he named what the Greeks already knew and experienced on some level.

One liability of this position is that it neglects the Christian imperative to share the Gospel. Clearly, the Bible and the consistent tradition of the Church are that spreading the faith is crucial to Christian identity and response to Christ. However, why share the Gospel when one can be saved without knowing it? One only needs to look at missionary initiatives in the past forty years. The vast majority of them are being performed by Evangelical Christians who embrace an imperative to convert others to the Christian faith. A second liability is that one tends to interpret the experience, and even the doctrines of others, through Christian lenses. Looking for Christ implicitly tends to keep one from listening to the uniqueness of another religious tradition.

Pluralists emphasize that God is beyond all concepts. While all Christian faiths concede God's transcendence, pluralists incorporate this truth with great vigor. Today's culture is increasingly characterized as **postmodern**. A postmodern perspective argues that one must take the other as truly other, as expressing a unique version of reality. Western culture has become increasingly sensitive to all conceptualizations and expressions of truth being rooted in unique places and times. No articulation of truth, therefore, is exempt from historical or philosophical critique. Society has become suspicious of a classisist notion of knowing or having privileged access to truth. What were previously understood as objective expressions of truth are now widely suspected as being assumptions of Western culture. In short, Western culture has come to a greater appreciation of the relativity of the human perspective.

One great liability in pluralism is that it does not represent the majority of Christians or the historical Christian tradition. Many have difficulty imagining how one could be a Christian, and indeed be a compelling dialogue partner with someone from another religious tradition, imagining some version of the following caveat of one's faith: "I believe that Jesus Christ is Lord (insofar as that is a useful, historically conditioned paradigm of religiosity that makes no claims on anyone else unless they too would find that it may be useful to them)."

A fourth model may be emerging: one that has been called the **mutuality model**. This form highlights the radical uniqueness of various traditions. In it, one need not seek commonalities in other religions or make proclamations about them from one's religious perspective, whether affirming or challenging. Setting aside those concerns, one is allowed to really listen to the genius of another tradition. Take, for example, **Zen Buddhism**. Instead of dismissing it as a natural religion (exclusivism) or looking for an implicit presence of the Holy Spirit (inclusivism) or stretching its description to include universal religious expression (pluralism), the Christian enters into a different way of even considering the spiritual life—allowing it to speak on its own terms. One problem with the mutuality model is that it is hard to practice, as one cannot help but bring one's religious assumptions into the encounter. A second problem lies in assessing what the encounter means. If the other is simply other, then what is the relevance of the encounter?

HOLDING A POSTMODERN CREATIVE TENSION

Is it possible to hold all these positions in a creative tension without being in self-contradiction? Instead of imagining postmodernity as hopelessly relativistic, guiding interreligious dialogue into a metaphysical no-man's land, one might see it as the best representation of reality. One might take physics as a guide. According to quantum theory, nothing exists on its own as a static, discrete reality. Rather, everything is relational and in constant process of becoming. Similarly, one might understand the truths of Christianity as dynamically interrelated with other religious expressions of truth. Consider that Newton's physics were once believed to be an absolute, universal descriptor of physical laws. Indeed, they remain absolutely true insofar as building a bridge is concerned. However, they do not answer every question; neither are they equally valid in other paradigms of physics. One does not reject Newton's laws, and one uses them as absolutes when appropriate. One does not, though, claim that alternative descriptions in other paradigms of physics are thereby necessarily false. Indeed, building a cell phone requires that some operations use Newton's laws and other operations use quantum laws. Each set of laws is employed when appropriate.

The same might be said when addressing a theology of religions. Is it possible that one could discover how to embrace responsibly the strengths and truths of a given theology of religions when useful and appropriate? Thus, in a given encounter, one may take on a posture along the lines of pluralism to highlight profoundly similar expressions of mysticism. In another forum, one may skillfully operate under the mutuality model and allow a strange and different religious expression to be just that—shockingly other. In sharing one's personal faith, one's language and posture could surely be exclusivist and experienced by others as profoundly inspiring.

Other religious traditions have their own versions of a theology of religions. Speaking very generally one could safely characterize them as follows. Islam is decidedly an inclusivist religion. The Qur'an is the ultimate revelation and other revelations are judged by it. Still, Islam believes that non-Muslims are saved just like Muslims, based on whether they have responded to God's call to submission as best they know how. Judaism allows converts, but generally does not proselytize. Judaism might be best characterized as being in the mutuality model. It delights in various expressions of unique religiosity without needing to impose its understanding on others. Buddhists typically believe that one cannot attain Nirvana unless one is a Buddhist on the Eightfold Path. However, they also believe that Nirvana is rare and that almost certainly everyone will have many more lifetimes and that a non-Buddhist religion might be very appropriate for someone in a given lifetime. This makes Buddhists strangely both pluralists and exclusivists at the same time. Hinduism would be hard to evaluate in this regard, because it varies so much. Some Hindus may believe that different gods are to be worshipped at different places and that, for example, Jesus is the god of the West and appropriate to believe in if one lives in the West. Other Hindus believe that only Brahmins who strictly practice jnana yoga will attain enlightenment.

In every chapter, this book approaches dialogue with the assumption that the other has something to teach about faith, doctrine, ways to God, and even God personally. The witness of Pope John Paul II inspired this approach, specifically the day of prayer the pope convened in 1987 with religious leaders from around the world. In a lecture on the interreligious experience of the Assisi Day of Prayer (the gathering was held in Assisi, Italy), the pope stated, "There are undeniably differences [in religions] that reflect the genius and spiritual 'riches' that God has given to the peoples" (John Paul II, "The Meaning of the Assisi Day," 562). His statement is extraordinary in that the pope is not only affirming that other religions have the presence of God, but also that some religious differences could be due to other religions having spiritual riches given by God that are unique to them. Engaging other religions can make one spiritually richer and theologically deeper than one would be without knowing about them.

Following John Paul's initiative, this text will engage in a kind of **comparative theology**, examining a number of religious expressions in their own right first and then in comparison with the Christian faith. By crossing over to the religious imagination of other traditions, one can see how they could bring new questions or insights. This kind of engagement is not merely a comparison of religions or doctrines, whereby one recognizes convergences and divergences. It is a juxtaposition to create an ongoing, reflective process of considering religious perspectives anew in the context of encountering other traditions.

HOPES AND POSTURES IN ENCOUNTERING THE OTHER

One goal in writing this book is to expose readers to aspects of profound and venerable traditions. The exposure will not only be in terms of theological claims but also will include the spiritual ethos intended by certain religious practices and the religious horizon, or vision, that a given religion intends to bring to its adherents. This book can also offer a new way of thinking religiously. There is a saying, "To learn a foreign language is to learn a different way of thinking." Learning another language can even help one understand one's own in a different light. Buddhism, for example, might challenge the non-Buddhist to rigorously consider the subjectivity of the mind or the interconnectedness of the universe. The Daoist relationship between **yin** and **yang** might teach one to better recognize when to take a posture of assertion or of receptivity and how these postures inform each other.

Encountering another faith might also provide a context for a healthy critique of one's religious sensibilities. Without stepping outside of a personal tradition in some way, one risks the danger of theological myopia and tunnel vision. Of course, such an encounter with another religion can also affirm one's religious sensibilities even more deeply. Consider the following expressions of crossing over into another worldview and returning changed:

> The great Russian author Leo Tolstoy wrestled with religious faith in his later years. At one point, he read a moving story about an Indian prince named Josaphat, who met a Christian named Barlaam. Barlaam told Josaphat the story of a man whose life was being eaten away by time. Instead of being obsessed with his incessant worries, this man decided to renounce the life he was clinging to and to embrace a whole, new life—one in which he renounces his ego and all worldly attachments. The prince was so inspired by the story that he converted to Christianity and was later declared a saint. In the medieval period, Josaphat was celebrated in both the Roman Catholic and Greek Orthodox calendars. Here, the story becomes interesting. The Latin *Josaphat* is a translation of the Greek name *Loasaf*, which itself is a translation of the

Arabic *Yudasaf,* from the Persian *Bodisaf. Bodisaf* is the Persian term for the Sanskrit *bodhisattva* (a term for the future **Buddha**). Tolstoy was inspired by a Christianized story of the Buddha, and through it found a way to become a devout Christian who particularly strove to live the spirit of Jesus' Sermon on the Mount. The story does not end here. Tolstoy's piety then inspired a number of Europeans whom the Indian spiritual leader Mohandas Gandhi met in England in the late 1890s. In crossing into their Christian faith perspective, particularly in learning to read the Bible allegorically and embracing the piety of the Sermon on the Mount, Gandhi returned to his native Hinduism with a new vigor. There, he began to read the classic on spiritual warfare, the Bhagavad Gita, in a new way. He now experienced it as a manual for social action as devotion to God and the truth. His writings and spiritual witness later inspired a young Baptist pastor named Martin Luther King Jr. While traveling in India, King met those committed to Gandhi's vision of a spiritual warrior fighting for justice in a nonviolent manner. In studying Gandhi, King came to see possibilities in his Christian faith.

—John Esposito et al., *World Religions Today,* 522–527

Interreligious encounter and the work of comparative theology succeed best when those involved embrace a kind of skillful posture. One would do well to embrace the following:

1. *Be without any ulterior or covert motives.* Do not pretend to dialogue if your real intention is to convert or prove superiority.
2. *Cultivate an essential openness.* Provide a spacious heart that listens intuitively, allows for self-reassessments, and is open to the whole process.
3. *Religious traditions are respected in their own right.* Understand them in a way those traditions would recognize and agree with.
4. *Differences are not to be avoided.* Recognize that there really are different worldviews and these make the dialogue exciting.
5. *Make no hasty determinations.* Realize that one can know and legitimately say less than one might want to.

Above all, when engaging in another religious tradition, one ought to take off one's shoes as if stepping onto holy ground. Without this foundation, one lacks the very love and respect that is, in fact, central to authentic religious life. Without this foundation, one misses the depth of insights, meaning, and spirit of those encountered. Finally, without this foundation, one forgets that God has already preceded one's arrival. At least, this is the claim of the apostle Paul in Athens.

Review Questions

1. Paul believed the Athenians were truly religious people and that they knew and were responding to God on some level. What is the evidence for this claim?
2. Christianity appears to have approached the possibility of non-Christians being saved with some inconsistency. How have the positions shifted through the centuries and can it be argued that Christianity has retained any logical continuity in this regard? If so, explain.
3. What are the theological grounds and values for the positions of exclusivism, inclusivism, and pluralism?

In-Depth Questions

1. Are you an exclusivist, inclusivist, or pluralist, and why? How would you deal with the liabilities in your given position?
2. Is the postmodern approach (one that embraces different theologies of religions at different times) intellectually coherent?
3. Do you think that fundamentally all or most religions are about the same in different ways?

Select Bibliography

Cannon, Dale. *Six Ways of Being Religious*. Belmont, CA: Wadsworth, 1996.

Esposito, John, Darrell Fasching, and Todd Lewis. *World Religions Today*, 2nd edition. New York: Oxford University Press, 2006.

Hick, John. *A Christian Theology of Religions: The Rainbow of Faiths*. Louisville, KY: Westminster John Knox, 1995.

John Paul II. "The Meaning of the Assisi Day of Prayer." *Origins* 16, no. 31 (1987): 561–563.

Knitter, Paul, ed. *The Myth of Religious Superiority*. Maryknoll, NY: Orbis, 2005.

———. *Introducing Theologies of Religions*. Maryknoll, NY: Orbis, 2002.

Lubac, Henri de. *Catholicism: Christ and the Common Destiny of Man*. L. Sheppard and E. Englund, trans. San Francisco: Ignatius, 1988. Lubac's wonderful text argues, with far-reaching theological resources, the Church's desire to include the entire human race in God's salvific plan.

Newbigin, Leslie. "The Basis, Purpose, and Manner of Inter-Faith Dialogue." *Scottish Journal of Theology* 30, no 3. (1977): 253–270. Newbigin describes the absolute need to meet the religious other in a decisively Christian manner.

Race, Alan. *Christians and Religious Pluralism: Patterns in the Christian Theology of Religions*. Maryknoll, NY: Orbis, 1983. This classic book articulates the threefold schema in theology of religions.

Smith, Wilfred Cantwell. *Toward a World Theology*. Philadelphia: Westminster Press, 1981.

Sullivan, Francis. *Salvation Outside the Church? Tracing the History of the Catholic Response*. Mahwah, NJ: Paulist, 1992. This is a resource for looking at the history of the Church's response to non-Christians. Here, Sullivan points to the most important shifts and the theological reasons behind them.

CHAPTER TWO

Mysticism

WHAT IS MYSTICISM?

Introduction

One might imagine such an exotic topic as mysticism should come at the end of this book. Mysticism is an extraordinarily complex issue, and mystical texts are among the most challenging in any religious tradition. However, there is an advantage in engaging this topic early, for it addresses foundational questions such as, Is there a core religious experience that underlies all or most religions? Do different kinds of core religious experiences point to different families of religions? Is mysticism—in whatever form or expression—the apex of a particular religion? Moreover, discussion of mysticism forms a foundation for considering other topics in this book. Finally, addressing mysticism early may help one appreciate the interrelationship among doctrine, practice, and profound experiences of the divine.

What does the term *mysticism* mean? In 1975, religious sociologist Andrew Greeley conducted a poll that asked people if they had ever had an experience they would characterize as mystical. More than 40 percent responded that they had. Two years later a Gallup poll asked, "Would you say that you have ever had a religious or mystical experience, that is, a moment of sudden religious insight or awakening?" In this poll, 31 percent responded that they had.

Both studies share the same problem: respondents were given no useful definition of *mystical*. In Greeley's survey, the term *mystical* was not defined. In the Gallup poll, mystical experience was conflated with religious experience, both defined as a "moment of sudden religious insight or awakening." This definition is broad enough to represent relatively common experiences, as indeed was the case. In follow-up questions, a number of respondents included as "mystical experiences" awakening in nature, experiencing healing, certain dreams, and even turning to God in a time of crisis.

The Christian Tradition and Mysticism

The words *mysticism* and *mystical* do not appear in the Bible. However, the related term *mysterion* does, from which we have *mystery*. The etymology of *mysterion* is "to close," particularly one's eyes or lips. Thus, it addresses something that is private, secretive, or not widely known. Jesus tells his disciples that they are given knowledge of the "mysteries of the kingdom" (Mark 4:11). Paul frequently wrote of the mysteries of God that are unknown to the unbelievers (Ephesians 3:9; Colossians 2:2; 1 Timothy 3:16).

Christians started to use the term *mystical* regularly in the patristic era. Clement of Alexandria (c. 150–215) called his allegorical interpretation of the Bible the mystical interpretation. Origen (c. 185–254), the most influential of all the early Church fathers, also understood the allegorical interpretation as mystical and included two additional expressions: the hidden presence of Christ in the sacraments, particularly the Eucharist, and profound encounters with God in the depth of the soul. For Origen, all three expressions mutually supported one another in the soul.

As the Christian tradition developed, became dominant, Origen's third use of the word, that is, mysticism understood as a profound experience of God in contemplation. Contemplation, in turn, was used to describe experiencing God so directly that one was taken beyond one's own natural human comprehension and brought into the divine mystery, which is incomprehensible to the natural working of the mind. In *The Life of Moses*, Gregory of Nyssa (335–395) described transcending natural knowledge and entering a "dark contemplation" into a "cloud of unknowing" (2.164). This was also the case with Augustine, Gregory the Great, and Bernard of Clairvaux. Bonaventure described the mystical completion of the soul as "the fire that totally inflames and carries us into God by ecstatic anointings and burning affections" (*Soul's Journey*, 7.6). Teresa of Avila defined mystical theology as "the soul being suspended in such a way that it is completely outside of itself" (*Life*, 10.1). And John of the Cross characterized the mystical as "secret wisdom infused into the soul through love" (*Spiritual Canticle*, 27.5).

Apophatic and Kataphatic

In all these examples, one finds the mystical encounter to be an experience that takes the soul beyond itself or its normal operations. Most approaches to mysticism, both historically and in the modern period, focus on the kind of contemplation that is ecstatic, that is, it takes someone outside of one's conscious framework. This way of encountering God is said to be **apophatic**. *Apophatikos* is a Greek word literally meaning "negative," and it refers to an approach to God that transcends the limits of the normal functioning mind. The apophatic approach takes on the following logic. Our minds are built to negotiate objects in the created world, but God is transcendent from creation. According to the Bible, God is "invisible" (John 6:46; 1 Timothy 1:17) and "dwells in unapproachable light" (1 Timothy 6:16), and his ways are inscrutable and incomprehensible (1 Corinthians 2:10–11; Romans 11:33). That the brain cannot comprehend God's essence is widely agreed upon in Christianity.

Recognizing that God is beyond imagination does not suggest that one can know nothing about God. Christianity holds that God has revealed himself in Christ who is "the image of the invisible God" (Colossians 1:15), and the Word of God who embodies the divine nature (John 1:2). Further, God has sent the Holy Spirit to dwell within believers (Romans 8:9, 16). Indeed, Christians generally recognize the whole of the Bible as representing God's revelation about his will and way to salvation. Christians see Jesus' self-offering on the cross as the supreme evidence of God's love for humanity; the cross even paradoxically represents God's glory

(John 8:28; 17:1; Philemon 2:5–11). Christians further learn about discipleship in the Gospel, from serving those most in need (Matthew 25:31–46) to receiving justification in the posture of faith and total trust in God (Romans 3:24–28). Knowing God in ways that are conceptually mediated or worked through one's psyche is often referred to as **kataphatic**. *Kataphatikos* is a Greek word literally meaning "affirmative." Kataphatic spirituality approaches God through what one can know.

Modern Approaches to Christian Mysticism

The Roman Catholic and Eastern Orthodox traditions continue to support the possibilities of mysticism. In 1926, the Catholic Church proclaimed John of the Cross a **doctor of the Church**, and in 1970, Catherine of Siena (1347–1380) and Teresa of Avila (1515–1582) were also made doctors of the Church. This designation means that their profound theological insights are considered perennially important. What is interesting is that these insights are thought to be important precisely because they are mystical.

Prior to the past thirty years, Protestant Christianity was, by and large, suspicious of mysticism. Some of the hesitation to embrace it has to do with the very apophatic quality that distinguishes much of it. Mystical knowledge seems divorced from the specific content of the Gospel. Others have charged mysticism with being too aligned with Neoplatonic philosophy, which blurs the differences between God and the soul. Most major Protestant figures of the mid-twentieth century, such as Karl Barth, Emil Brunner, and Rudolf Bultmann, believed that mysticism represented a deviation from the true Gospel.

Today, many Protestants are quite open to mysticism. One reason is that the ecumenical movement has taken down some barriers between Catholics and Protestants. Another is the field of spirituality has become a widely respected discipline in theology. This field has made classic mystical texts and commentaries available to both academia and the public. Finally, lay contemplative practices, such as centering prayer, have become popular among both Catholics and Protestants, and these practices are aligned to the contemplative, mystical tradition.

MYSTICISM AS APOPHATIC

As previously stated, some Protestant critics have charged mysticism with bypassing the specific content of the Gospel and even blurring distinctions between God and the soul. In some respects, the Bible expresses a kind of interpenetration of the divine life in the soul and a fusion of the divine identity with the identity of one who lives in God's **grace**. While God is understood as radically Other, Israel was taught that it could participate in God's transcendence: "You shall be holy, for I the Lord your God am holy" (Leviticus 19:2). Devout Jews participate in God's holiness by keeping his covenant (Leviticus 11:44, 20:26; Psalm 119). This impulse to identify with and participate in God's life intensifies in the New Testament. By faith, believers are born anew in God (John 1:12–13) and anticipate becoming as he is (1 John 3:2, 4:17). Peter describes God's grace as that which allows believers to "become participants in the divine nature" (2 Peter 1:4). The apostle Paul also sees the Christian life as taking on the very holiness of God (2 Corinthians 3:17–18, 5:20–21). Paul even imagined that at the end of time human existence would be totally suffused with the divine life. Those saved would be utterly saturated with Christ— "the fullness of him who fills all in all" (Ephesians 1:23)—drawing all into the glory of the Father "so that God may be all in all" (1 Corinthians 15:28). Imagining an eternity as a sharing in the divine nature is broadly embraced by Christians and is the formal teaching of the Catholic Church (Vatican II: "Dogmatic Constitution of the Church," [*Lumen gentium*], no. 16; "Pastoral Constitution on the Church in the Modern World" [*Gaudium et spes*], no. 18; "Dogmatic Constitution on Divine Revelation" [*Dei verbum*], no. 2; and "Decree on the Church's Missionary Activity" [*Ad gentes divinitus*], no. 3).

Criteria for Apophatic Mystical Experiences

Christian Soundings

Origen (185–254): "His perfect bride will also follow Him there; cleaving entirely to Him and united with Him, she will climb up there for she has been made one spirit with Him" (*Commentary on the Song of Songs*).

Cyril of Jerusalem (d. 386): "[B]y contemplating the glory of the Lord, as in a mirror, you may be transformed from glory to glory in Christ Jesus our Lord" (*Mystagogia*, 4).

Bernard of Clairvaux (1090–1153): "In the kiss of his mouth we receive a full infusion of joys, a revelation of secrets, a wonderful and inseparable mingling of the light from above and the mind on which it is shed, which, when it is joined with God is one spirit with him" (*Sermon 2, Song of Songs*).

Jan van Ruysbroeck (1293–1381): "The loving contemplative in the ground where he now rests, sees and feels nothing but an incomprehensible Light; and through that simple nudity which enfolds all things, he finds himself and feels himself to be that same Light by which he sees and nothing else. I must be completely He, and He I: so that this He and this I become and are one" (cited in Evelyn Underhill, *Mysticism*, 420).

John of the Cross (1542–1591): "God makes the soul die to all that he is not . . . so it becomes divine, united with the divine; informs the will with love of God so it is no longer less than divine and loves in no other way than divinely" (*Dark Night*, II.13.11).

Thomas Merton (1915–1968): "What happens is that the separate identity that is *you* apparently disappears and nothing seems to be left but a pure freedom indistinguishable from the infinite Freedom, love identified with Love. . . . He is the *I* who acts there. He is the one Who loves and knows and rejoices" (*New Seeds of Contemplation*, 283, 287).

Non-Christian Soundings

Plotinus (204–270; Greek philosopher): "Many times it has happened: lifted out of the body into myself; becoming external to all other things and self-encentered; beholding a marvelous beauty . . . acquiring identity with the divine" (*Enneads*, IV.8.i).

Philo of Alexandria (20 BCE–50 CE; Jewish): "There is a mind more perfect and more purified, which has been initiated into the great mysteries, a mind that discovers the First Cause not from created things . . . but transcends creation and obtains a clear impression of the Uncreated . . ." (*Legem allegoriarum*, 3.100).

Babylonian Talmud (fifth century; Jewish): "As a river empties into the ocean, empty yourself into [Divine] Reality. When you are emptied into Reality, you are filled with compassion, desiring only justice. When you desire only justice, the will of Reality becomes your will" (cited in Andrew Harvey, *Essential Mystics*, 101).

Abraham Abulafia (1240–1291; Jewish): "[They] will be united with it after many hard, strong and mighty exercises, until the particular and personal prophetic [faculty] will become universal, permanent and everlasting similar to the essence of its cause, and he and He will become one entity" (cited in Moshe Idel and Bernard McGinn, *Mystical Union in Judaism, Christianity, and Islam*, 30).

Nahman of Braslav (1772–1810; Jewish): "When a person merits to be integrated in Eiyn Sof [God], his Torah and prayer are those of God Himself" (Ibid, 45).

Adin Steinsaltz (b. 1937; Jewish): "At the highest level of holiness are those persons who have achieved a state in which their whole personalities and all of their actions are inseparably joined to the divine holiness. Of these persons it is said that they have become a 'chariot' for the *Shekhinah* [Divine Manifestation] . . . and they constitute a part of the throne of glory itself. . . ." (*The Thirteen Petalled Rose*, 62).

Abu Yazid al-Bistami (c. 801–874; Islamic): "I looked upon my Lord with the eye of eternity, after that he turned me away from all that was not he, and had illumined me with his light; and he showed me marvels from his secret being, and he showed me his *He-ness*. And through his *He-ness* I looked on my *I-ness*, and it vanished away, my light in his light, my honor in his honor, my power in his power. . . . And he transmuted me from my *I-ness* into his *He-ness*, and caused me to cease from my selfhood in his *He-ness*" (cited in R. C. Zaehner, *Hindu and Muslim Mysticism*, 198–199).

Ibn Arabi (1165–1204; Islamic): "If that God who is One and All-Conquering reveals Himself to one. . . . Then, everything is in **annihilation** except His face. . . . While this is so, God grants him an existence from His own existence and paints him with the Divine Color" (cited in Harvey, *Essential Mystics*, 147–148).

Jalal ad-Din Rumi (1207–1273; Islamic): "The prayer of the holy one is different from other prayers. He has so completely dissolved his ego—nothinged himself—that what he says is like God talking to God. . . . His spirit grows wings, and lifts. His ego falls like a battered wall. He unites with God, alive, but emptied of identity" (*Rumi*, 163, trans. slightly adjusted).

Prashna Upanishad IV.11 (Hindu): "[T]he spirit of man finds peace in the Spirit Supreme and Eternal. . . . He knows the All and becomes the All."

Svetasvatara Upanishad I.11 (Hindu): "When a man knows God, he is free. . . . When in inner union he is beyond the world of the body, then the third world, the world of the Spirit, is found, where the power of the All is, and man has all: for he is one with the ONE."

Chandogya Upanishad VI.12.3 (Hindu): "Believe me, my son, an invisible and subtle essence is the Spirit of the Whole universe. This is reality. That is Atman. THOU ART THAT."

Sri Aurobino (1872–1950; Hindu): "You must grow in the divine consciousness till there is no difference between your will and hers. . . . The last stage of this perfection will come when you are completely identified with the Divine Mother" (cited in Harvey, *Essential Mystics*, 59–61).

What does one make of the texts cited here? Given that they represent vastly different times, cultures, and religions, it is shocking how alike they really are. In each case, the conventional sense of oneself is transcended as one enters into communion with the Divine or Absolute. One then relocates oneself into the Divine, both identifying with it and, in some way, being in relationship with it. While these texts were specifically chosen to exemplify such a convergence of experience, they also fairly represent both authors and their respective traditions. Moreover, distinguishing some of John of the Cross's poems from those of Rumi or some texts from the Upanishads would be difficult. This is not a new insight. Many early Christians, for example, saw in platonic philosophers, from Plato to Plotinus, a profoundly similar spiritual core. As Clement reflects,

"What, after all, is Plato but Moses in Greek?" (*Strom.*, 1.21), or Augustine: "There are none nearer to us than the Platonists" (*City of God*, 8.5).

Characteristics of Mystical Witness

Is there, then, a universal, perennial religious experience as addressed in chapter one? These particular kinds of experience referenced have quite common, even universal, characteristics. They are: (1) direct, (2) beyond comprehension, (3) ineffable, (4) noetically profound, (5) really-real reality, (6) disorienting/reorienting, (7) indubitable, and (8) irresistible.

What do these characteristics mean? Mystical experiences are said to be direct, that is, they are unmediated and "objective." This is to say that they do not work through the standard conscious categories of the mind, but are claimed to be a kind of absolute union with God. Such experiences then are beyond comprehension because they go beyond the way the mind conceives of reality. The psyche, or soul, does not understand them in a conventional way. Because of humans' inability to understand them, they are ineffable and cannot be spoken about directly. Thus, mystics often use analogies and metaphors to describe the indescribable. Such ineffability does not at all suggest that the mystic knows nothing about them. Rather, these experiences are known on a deeper level than any other kind of knowledge. So deep is this experience of ultimacy that mystics believe that they have encountered Ultimate Reality or really-real reality.

Broadly speaking, the mystical witness is that, while the world is indeed real as is our experience of it, it is nothing compared to absolute reality. The great Christian writer C. S. Lewis called the created world "the shadowlands" in comparison to the divine realm. To enter the core of ultimacy is to become disoriented, to lose one's normal sense of self and place. Mystics might even use the word *annihilation* to describe this experience, that is, their conventional sense of self completely disappears as they dwell in God. To see God as the core of all reality is to reorient all things in light of this truth, including oneself. The experience, because it is so profound, so real, simply cannot be doubted. Finally, it is widely reported in mystical literature that the experience simply happens to one, and that, because one is drawn into it by absolute truth, it is not something that one would or even could resist.

Criticisms

The previous representation of mysticism has been challenged. Some prominent scholars, such as R. C. Zaehner and Steven Katz, have argued that there is no such thing as an apophatic, unmediated, "objective" experience. Every experience, they say, is mediated in some way through one's consciousness. If one did not have an experience through the psyche, how would one even know that a mystical experience had occurred? The citations listed in the section "Criteria for Apophatic Mystical Experiences" suggest distinctions that appear to reflect the training and expectations of the mystic. And this points out, these critics say, the "subjective" quality of the experience. The Christian and Islamic texts are relational, while Plotinus and the **Upanishads** are not—as one would expect from these different traditions.

Some scholars argue that one needs to distinguish the *essence* of a mystical experience from the *theology* that the mystic uses to describe it. The essence, they argue, is universal, while the concepts that the mystic uses to articulate the experience (even to oneself) would reflect the mystic's religious tradition. These critics, however, question such a claim as presumptuous. How can an outsider really delve underneath the theology to some pure experience? What if this "universal essence" interpretation conflicts with what the mystic says? Can one imagine that one knows more about a given mystic's core experience than the mystic does? These critics also believe that the articulated meaning of the experience should not be divorced from the description of the experience. That is, the experience and its interpretation are inseparable parts of a single whole.

Interestingly, some adherents of the position of universal mystical experience argue that if one were to concede that all mystical experiences are mediated and conditioned by the mystic's faith, such a concession might actually support the claim that there is a *fundamental* universal mystical experience. The differences in description are really so small, and the background of the various mystics is so great, the mystical experience itself must be essentially universal, these adherents say.

MYSTICISM AS KATAPHATIC
Considerations
What and How to Study

Many scholars of mysticism focus on these fundamentally direct experiences of the Divine, perhaps for several reasons. First, a direct experience of God seems plausible as the most pure and profound expression of mysticism. Some mystics even regard experiences other than direct union to be lesser experiences. These lesser experiences also are more likely to be part of a stage of mystical progress. For example, Teresa of Avila believed that some of her most exotic experiences, such as levitating in prayer, were because her soul was not yet mature enough for full union with God. Once she reached a stage of union in which she regularly encountered God directly, these other experiences subsided. Second, one finds that there are uncanny convergences in descriptions of such unitive encounters. In contrast, religious experiences other than these seem to be far more particular to the specific mystic and religious tradition. As a result, they are more difficult to compare. There may be a third reason, which is that other forms of extraordinary religious experience are simply too difficult to categorize. Straying from the narrow focus of direct encounters with the Divine forces one to decide what other experiences count as mystical and by what criteria.

John of the Cross, Teresa of Avila, and Catherine of Siena were made doctors of the Church because of their mysticism. None of Catherine's mystical doctrines, however, came from radical unitive experiences. Rather, she had visions, heard voices (locutions), and received mystical insights given to her in prayer. All these experiences are understood to be mediated through her mental faculties (kataphatic). Instead of some ineffable, transrational absorption, God worked through her mind's ability to use images and insights. Should one accept her experiences as mystical because they came from

The Ecstasy of Saint Catherine of Siena, by Agostino Carracci (1557–1602).

God? What then about charismatic prayer meetings in which some regularly claim to receive prophetic messages from God? Are these mystical experiences of the same order?

One could push the issue further. Julian of Norwich is considered a great medieval mystic. During a grave illness, she had a series of what she called "showings." Sometimes, she reported that God the Father spoke to her; at other times, Jesus. On three occasions, she saw Mary, the Blessed Mother. In other occasions, she seemed to have religious insights that were infused into her consciousness; she was sure they came from God directly but without any specific encounter with God. Should we only include showings from God and not Mary? Should we include God and Mary but not the spiritual intuitions? Julian experienced them all with the same kind of surety, and all became integral to her mystical landscape. What ought one to think of saints who report spiritual flights into hell and purgatory? Are these mystical though there is no encounter with God or God's representative?

Criteria

Perhaps restricting mysticism to certain categories, whether they are only mystical union or only mediated encounters with the divine, is unnecessary and even arbitrary. Many holy people have had a variety of profound, extraordinary experiences, and these do not easily lend themselves to clear distinctions between mystical and nonmystical. Even while respecting the complexity of the issue, one could still posit a general framework. One could distinguish two kinds of related mystical experiences: The first represents those apophatic experiences that point to a fundamentally unmediated union with God. The second is a dramatic experience of the supernatural order that is kataphatic. Just as apophatic, unitive experiences have regular characteristics, so can kataphatic. They are (1) nonnormal states of consciousness, (2) immediately transformative, (3) deeply penetrating, (4) irresistible, (5) seared into memory, and (6) fundamentally indubitable. A brief consideration of each follows:

The first characteristic suggests that a mystical experience is not simply a regular religious experience, even if it differs in intensity. For the experience to be mystical, it must differ from how the vast majority of people experience spiritual reality. The rest of the characteristics are helpful because they are widely reported by mystics, and they give one confidence that a mystical experience has actually taken place, rather than a psychologically self-induced phenomenon.

Imagine that Jane has a mystical experience. If Jane receives a locution (hears a voice) from God telling her that she has been forgiven, she would immediately and unquestionably experience herself to be so. This experience penetrates the soul deeply. Jane is transformed; her soul is in some way fundamentally remolded. Like apophatic experiences, this kind of experience is also irresistible. Jane is swept into it. It is nothing that she creates; neither can she ignore it. This experience is so dramatic for Jane that she will remember it in detail long after the experience. Finally, Jane has no doubt that this was a gift from God.

An additional consideration, which also applies to apophatic experiences, is that such encounters are deeply humbling. One is overwhelmed by the undeserving graciousness of God. Apophatic experiences are rarely discussed or shared, given their profundity and that they are beyond conceptualization. The same is not true with kataphatic experiences, which can also more easily be counterfeited in one's psyche. A good measure for determining a mystical experience is whether it inflates the ego or humbles the soul.

Contrast Alice with Jane. Perhaps Alice has a vivid imagination. In the context of a highly emotional state, she believes that she hears God speak to her. Is this a bona fide mystical experience or a counterfeit? Say that while Alice is emotionally energized by the experience she seems very loving or spiritual; but when the emotional intensity leaves, so does her loving disposition or she simply seems to be the same Alice. Of course, one would not expect Alice to become an instant saint, but one should expect some kind of change. Alice may also describe the experience differently in different contexts. Perhaps the communication from God supported an interest of hers, and now she has divine approval to pursue the very thing she already wanted. That this experience was authentically mystical might be doubtful. Of course, it is possible that even though Alice is a bit immature, that she received the message she wanted to hear and was emotionally primed for such an experience, it still could have been a bona fide mystical experience. There is still reason to doubt it, though.

Three Principles

At this moment, it might be helpful to offer three principles regarding mystical experiences: First, anyone can have a mystical experience, apophatic or kataphatic. However, to be considered a mystic, one would need to have enough of these experiences that their content or transforming dynamic is a permanent part of one's spiritual consciousness. Second, mystical experiences are typically part of the landscape for those who are far along in their spiritual progress, and even here, they are not typical. Additionally, apophatic mysticism is most rare and usually represents the deepest of mystical engagement.

For a religious believer to have a profound mystical experience early in the believer's journey is a wonderful gift. For such experiences to happen often at this earlier stage is highly suspicious. The third is an ancient teaching about religious experience. It is so common that many theologians know it as a Latin axiom: *Quidquid recipitur per modum recipientis recipitur* (Whatever is received is received according to the mode of the receiver). This axiom tells that God speaks to one or moves one according to one's consciousness and that this is indeed the only way the experience can be appropriated.

Religious experience, particularly kataphatic mystical experience, comes in the context of the paradigm of the mystic. A paradigm is a way of seeing and engaging reality. It is a lens one uses to filter and interpret experience. According to the principle of *quidquid recipitur*, God speaks to, or moves, the soul in the way that is comprehensible, or makes sense, to the soul. Religious experience that the soul cannot integrate or make sense of would be pointless. This principle is extraordinarily important in interpreting religious experience, mystical or otherwise, because it illuminates that historical, cultural, theological, and personal factors actually condition and are part of the religious experience. This principle does not suggest that believers manufacture the religious experience. It does mean, however, that the experience must be understood in its context.

Christian Witness: Francis of Assisi (1181–1226)

Consider the following experience of Francis of Assisi. Francis was spending a forty-day retreat on Mount Alverna to celebrate the feast of Michael the Archangel. This is the account of his receiving the stigmata, the wounds of Christ in his hands, feet, and side.

> While he was praying on the mountainside, Francis saw a Seraph [**angel**] with six fiery wings coming down from the highest point in the heavens. The vision descended swiftly and came to rest in the air near him. Then he saw the image of a man crucified in the midst of the wings, with his hands and feet stretched out and nailed to a cross. Two of the wings were raised above his head and two were stretched out in

flight, while the remaining two shielded his body. Francis was dumbfounded at the sight and his heart was flooded with a mixture of joy and sorrow. He was overjoyed at the way Christ regarded him so graciously under the appearance of a Seraph, but the fact that he was nailed to a cross pierced his soul with a sword of compassionate sorrow. He was lost in wonder at the sight of this mysterious vision; he knew that the agony of Christ's passion was not in keeping with the state of a seraphic spirit which is immortal. Eventually he realized by divine inspiration that God has shown him this vision in his providence, in order to let him see that, as Christ's lover, he would resemble the fervor of his spirit. As the vision disappeared, it left his heart ablaze with eagerness and impressed upon his body a miraculous likeness. There and then the marks of nails began to appear in his hands and feet. . . . His right side seemed as if it has been pierced with a lance and was marked with a livid scar which often bled, so that his habit and trousers were stained.

— *St. Francis of Assisi*, 730–731

St. Francis of Assisi Receiving the Stigmata, ca. 1607–1633. Engraving by Jean Leclerc.

Not considering this profound experience a mystical one would be difficult. It has all the signs—particularly that it had a dramatic, transformative, and lasting effect. Francis lived with the wounds of Christ for the rest of his short life. One amazing thing about the stigmata is that

STIGMATA

Stigmata (Greek for "marks") are wounds that imitate the wounds of Christ supernaturally infused on a Christian's body, usually the hands, feet, and side. Francis of Assisi (d. 1226) has the earliest documented case, when he received and sustained stigmata the last years of his life. Stigmata have been attributed to several hundred persons after Francis, though not all of these have been authenticated.

they never heal. For Francis and other stigmatics, such as Catherine of Siena or Padre Pio, these wounds bled daily for years, but they never showed infection, neither did the flesh around them deteriorate.

Skeptics have interpreted the stigmata as psychologically self-induced. These saints, they argue, so identified with the crucified Christ and so wanted to share in Christ's passion that their minds literally created the wounds in a period of interior intensity. This position is problematic, for it implies that these saints would then have to retain that psychosomatic intensity perpetually for the rest of their lives or else the wounds would heal like any other wounds. Such an interpretation also goes against what the saints who experienced them reported. That is, they did not describe being in an intensely concentrated mode of interior angst about Christ's passion. Rather, the experience happened to them from the outside, and they were themselves wondering what was going on. They report being surprised at what happened.

While the charge that Francis's stigmata were psychosomatically produced seems far-fetched, receiving them does not mean they happened outside of the context of Francis's subjective mind and the cultural condition in which he lived. Why, we might ask, is there no miracle of the stigmata before the twelfth century? Why to Francis? Consider the great shifts in spirituality between the patristic period and the High Middle Ages. The early Church was highly influenced by platonic philosophy. While the Church fathers considered nature, particularly their bodies, to be good and something that was redeemed by Christ, they also believed that the body was a modest mediator of the divine. They were more likely to seek God in the depths of their souls in a contemplative manner. Certainly, many Church fathers recommended disciplines such as fasting, but the purpose was usually expressed as freeing the soul from its attachments to physical pleasures so that it could engage in contemplation. In this period, one did not find a great deal of focus on literally imitating Christ as crucified.

The spirituality of the High Middle Ages, in contrast, focused piety on Christ crucified. Medievals identified the suffering of the world with Christ's suffering on the cross, and they wanted to participate in that redemptive suffering for the good of the Church. Thus, while medievals might have agreed that fasting is a good means of freeing the soul from gluttony, they also would have considered fasting a way for their bodies to become sacraments of their souls' hunger and thirst for holiness. They wanted to *embody* Christ's passion.

Francis embraced such a spiritual culture. He saw the poverty and passion of Christ as the premier expression of God's love and compassion. So he became radically poor himself, even compromising his health. Identification with the suffering Christ, living out the humility and poverty of Christ, serving lepers and the poorest of the poor, whom he identified with Christ, were integral to his spirituality and that of the times. In this context, Francis, who also had a particular devotion to Michael the Archangel, made a long retreat centered on Michael's feast day. In his vision, he saw a seraph, which the prophet Isaiah identified as a six-winged angel that dwelt closest to the throne of God. Thus, in the context of the feast of an angel, he met an angel. The inner figure of the angel is Christ crucified. Francis had a spiritually infused insight that to become Christ's lover (another medieval theme), he must resemble Christ perfectly. In addition, the wounds, which symbolize Christ's suffering, also symbolize his compassion for the suffering world. Francis realized that they must be for him as well. When he perceived that he had these same wounds, he was filled with great joy and gratitude. He had become fully *christified*.

Non-Christian Witness: Sri Ramakrishna Paramahamsa (1836–1886)

Mystical experience is by no means exclusive to Christianity. One of the greatest Hindu saints and mystics since the Enlightenment, Ramakrishna, reports having such an experience while serving as priest at a temple dedicated to the Divine Mother goddess Kali. Ramakrishna had come from a highly pious Hindu home in which his father was particularly devout and had experienced divine visions. In fact, before Ramakrishna's birth, his father had received a vision that told him his wife would bear a son who would be an expression of the god Vishnu. Before the experience that follows, Ramakrishna was a spiritually intense priest who had already had a history of ecstatic spiritual experiences. He loved Kali and felt profound longing to know her directly. His longing was so great that he felt he would be better off killing himself than languishing without seeing Kali. This is what happened next:

> When I jumped up like a madman and seized [a sword], suddenly the blessed Mother revealed herself. The buildings with their different parts, the temple, and everything vanished from my sight, leaving no trace whatsoever, and in their stead I saw a limitless, infinite, effulgent Ocean of Consciousness. As far as the eye could see, the shining billows were madly rushing at me from all sides with a terrific noise, to swallow me up. I was caught in the rush and collapsed, unconscious . . . within me there was a steady flow of undiluted bliss, altogether new, and I felt the presence of the Divine Mother.
>
> —Mahendranath Gupta,
> *Gospel of Sri Ramakrishna*, 15

What is fascinating about this experience is that Kali was not experienced in a vision or voice of a specific person, but as an "Ocean of Consciousness" and "undiluted bliss." Later in Ramakrishna's life, he did experience Kali more personally, and she even spoke to him. However, he did not experience her in that manner here. How did he know it was Kali? Examining the religious context of the event provides an explanation. Most Hindus believe that there is an absolute

reality called Brahman, and that the deepest self (Atman) is aligned
to or even identical with Brahman. (Refer back to apophatic mysticism.) Brahman, however, is recognized in two forms: **Nirguna-
Brahman** and **Saguna-Brahman**. Nirguna-Brahman is Brahman
understood without qualities or distinctions. It is pure, undifferentiated Being-Bliss-Consciousness (*sat-chit-ananda*). Another way
to experience Brahman is with qualities, Saguna-Brahman. In this
mode, Brahman is experienced as benign, loving, merciful, or even
as that which participates in the world. For some Hindu mystics,
such as **Shankara**, Saguna-Brahman is a less than pure appropriation
of actual Brahman, and worshipping the gods ultimately limits one
from realizing Nirguna-Brahman.

Ramakrishna accepted the distinction between Nirguna- and
Saguna-Brahman, but his religious experience did not suggest that
Saguna-Brahman was a lesser or diluted expression of ultimacy. He
came to this realization by his experience of Kali. He adored Kali, he
worshipped her, and he longed to know her personally. He did not
believe that Kali was simply an exceptional symbolic expression of
spiritual excellence or something to transcend when he was mature
enough. For Ramakrishna, Kali represented the primordial divine
energy (*shakti*). Further, he saw her as supremely loving and that one
who entered her love perfectly would attain Brahman. Kali is no mere
vehicle. Ramakrishna taught that she can no more be distinguished
from Brahman than the power of burning can from fire. Thus, his
mystical encounter is seen as both the Being-Bliss-Consciousness of
Nirguna-Brahman and a personal experience of divine grace. While
he had no sight of Kali, he had no doubt that his vision could only
be of her.

As Ramakrishna matured in his mystical life, he continued to hold
the traditional distinction between Nirguna- and Saguna-Brahman.
He also believed, however, that they could not be separated. That
is, Ultimacy is both personal and nonpersonal at the same time. The
goal of the spiritual life is to experience both as true in a spiritual
paradox. Kali became the key to his "both-and" mysticism.

CONCLUSIONS

What can one make of mysticism? In the beginning of this chapter, some questions were addressed that might make later chapters in this book more profitable. Does a core religious experience underlie all religions? On the one hand, in order to insist such a core exists, one would have to force fit some religious traditions. This position also carries the great burden of proof as to why some versions of a unitive experience are impersonal while others are lovingly relational. Positing a core universal religious experience cannot avoid a kind of circularity of argument whereby one tends to dismiss or demote mystical experiences that are unique to a given religious tradition.

On the other hand, scholars who maintain a belief in universal mystical experiences argue (along with many mystics themselves!) that the highest expression of mysticism would obviously be a unitive experience. The more profoundly one encounters God, the more one is taken outside any conceptual framework. They also point to extraordinary mystical similarities among religions that are otherwise quite diverse.

The challenge, posed earlier, that all mystical experiences (apophatic or kataphatic) have a subjective element and reflect what the mystic is trained to experience—and expects to experience—is probably quite sound. If this is the case, then that so many experiences are similar is particularly striking. Those that are kataphatic are less similar than the apophatic and are far more likely to reflect the specifics of the mystic's religion. However, the characteristics that define a mystical experience are quite stable within the broad range of mystical accounts.

The final question raised in the beginning of the chapter is perhaps the most challenging: is mysticism, in whatever form or expression, the height of a particular religion? Certainly Buddhists and Hindus would say yes, because Nirvana or the self's unity with Brahman represent the fullness of the spiritual path. The Christian tradition, however, would say no. While many saints were mystics, not all were. Broadly speaking, Christianity recognizes its exemplars as marked not by extraordinary supernatural experiences but by having an extraordinary love for God and the world.

Review Questions

1. Until recently, Protestants have been suspicious and even disdainful of mysticism. Why is that, and what has changed in the last several decades?
2. What specifically distinguishes apophatic from kataphatic mysticism?
3. R. C. Zaehner, Steven Katz, and others argue that the claim for a universal mystical experience is overplayed, and that there is no such thing as an objective or immediate experience of God. What are the principles and data that they rely on to make these arguments?
4. The two famous mystical experiences of Francis of Assisi and Ramakrishna were kataphatic. How does the principle of *quidquid recipitur* work in both the kinds of experience they had and the interpretation of that experience?

In-Depth Questions

1. Many believe that mysticism, particularly apophatic, tends to blur the distinction between God and humanity. Does such a belief seem surprising? Blasphemous? Inspiring? What evidence would you draw on that would support your response to this claim?
2. Many expressions of mysticism seem to be pointing to the same experience. It can even be difficult to distinguish between some of the writings of Christian, Muslim, Hindu, and Greek philosophical mystics. Do you find this data compelling? What are the implications for believing in Christianity if all these religions report the same experience?
3. The highest expressions of mystical experiences in Hinduism and Buddhism represent the apex of that religion, but they would not for Christians. Yet, what could be better than directly encountering God? What is the relationship between experiencing God and becoming holy?

Select Bibliography

Bernard of Clairvaux. *Bernard of Clairvaux: Selected Works.* G. S. Evans, trans. Mahwah, NJ: Paulist Press, 1987.

Butler, Dom Cuthbert. *Western Mysticism: The Teachings of Saints Augustine, Gregory, and Bernard on Contemplation and the Contemplative Life.* New York: E. P. Dutton, 1923.

Dan, Joseph, ed. *The Early Kabbalah.* Ronald Kiener, trans. Mahwah, NJ: Paulist Press, 1986.

Egan, Harvey. "Affirmative Way." In *The New Dictionary of Catholic Spirituality.* Michael Downey, ed. Collegeville, MN: Michael Glazier, 1993: 14–17.

———. "Negative Way." In *The New Dictionary of Catholic Spirituality.* Michael Downey, ed. Collegeville, MN: Michael Glazier, 1993: 700–704.

———. *Christian Mysticism: The Future of a Tradition.* New York: Pueblo, 1984.

Francis of Assisi. *St. Francis of Assisi: Writings and Early Biographies: English Omnibus of the Sources for the Life of St. Francis.* Marion Habig, ed. Chicago: Franciscan Herald Press, 1983.

Greeley, Andrew. "Is America a Nation of Mystics?" *New York Times Magazine,* January 26, 1975.

———. "Mysticism Goes Mainstream." *American Health* 6, no. 1 (1987): 47–49.

Gupta, Mahendranath. *The Gospel of Ramakrishna.* Vol. 1. Swami Nikhilananda, trans. Mylapore: Sri Ramakrishna Math, 1952.

Harvey, Andrew, ed. *The Essential Mystics: The Soul's Journey into Truth.* Edison, NJ: Castle Books, 1998.

Howard, Evan. *The Brazos Introduction to Christian Spirituality.* Grand Rapids, MI: Brazos Press, 2008. This is a wonderful synopsis of a variety of expressions of Christian spirituality. It is particularly helpful by being so broadly ecumenical.

Idel, Moshe, and Bernard McGinn, eds. *Mystical Union in Judaism, Christianity, and Islam: An Ecumenical Dialogue.* New York: Continuum, 1996.

John of the Cross. *The Collected Works of John of the Cross,* revised. Kieran Kavanaugh and Otilio Rodriguez, trans. Washington, DC: ICS Publications, 1991.

Katz, Steven, ed. *Mysticism and Religious Traditions.* New York: Oxford University Press, 1983.

———. *Mysticism and Philosophical Analysis.* New York: Oxford University Press, 1978. In this classic compendium, first-rate scholars address various aspects of mysticism, particularly on whether it is a universal phenomenon.

Matt, Daniel Channan, trans. and ed. *Zohar: The Book of Enlightenment.* Mahwah, NJ: Paulist Press, 1983.

McGinn, Bernard. *The Foundations of Mysticism* New York: Crossroad, 1992. The first of a four-volume series on Christian mysticism in the West, it is seminal in understanding the Greek tradition that grounded much of later mysticism in Christianity.

Merton, Thomas. *New Seeds of Contemplation.* New York: New Directions, 1961. This is an extraordinarily thoughtful, highly accessible collection of opinions about the spiritual life by the most celebrated spiritual author of the twentieth century.

Origen. *Origen: An Exhortation to Martyrdom, Prayer, and Selected Works.* Rowan Green, trans. Mahwah, NJ: Paulist Press, 1979.

Philo of Alexandria. *Philo of Alexandria: The Contemplative Life, the Giants, and Selections.* David Winston, trans. Mahwah, NJ: Paulist Press, 1981.

Plotinus. *The Enneads.* Stephen MacKenna, trans. New York: Penguin, 1991.

Rumi, Jalal al-Din. *The Essential Rumi.* Coleman Banks, trans. New York: HarperSanFrancisco, 1995.

Michael Sells, trans. and ed. *Early Islamic Mysticism: Sufi, Qur'an, Mi'raj, Poetic, and Theological Writings.* Mahwah, NJ: Paulist Press, 1996.

Semaan, Kahil. "Islamic Mysticism in Modern Arabic Poetry and Drama." *International Journal of Middle East Studies* 10, no. 4 (1979): 517–531.

Steinsaltz, Adin. *The Thirteen Petalled Rose: A Discourse on the Essence of Jewish Existence and Belief,* 2nd ed. Yehuda Hanegbi, trans. New York: Basic Books, 2006.

Underhill, Evelyn. *Mysticism.* Mineola, NY: Dover, 2002 (reproduction of 12th ed., 1930). This was the first, great treatise on mysticism, particularly Christian, for a popular audience, although its assumption that all religious traditions operate in the same way has been widely challenged.

Upanishads. Juan Mascaro, trans. New York: Penguin, 1965.

Woods, James, ed. *Understanding Mysticism.* Garden City, NY: Image Books, 1980.

Zaehner, R. C. *Hindu and Muslim Mysticism.* Oxford: Oneworld, 1960.

CHAPTER THREE

Masters and Mediators

THE ROLE OF A MEDIATOR

The Necessity of Mediators

Two seemingly contradictory principles were discussed in chapter two: first, that God is wholly Other and transcendent from all created things; second, that the soul can unite with God utterly. How then does one cross the chasm between creature and Creator for such intimacy? How does this uncreated absolute spirit become experienced in this world? Responding to these questions plays a large part in the very fabric of most religions.

Ancient Israel took God's transcendence and the need to mediate the divine very seriously. The **Torah**—which can mean teaching, way, or law—was a crucial mediator, because its precepts allowed Israel to embody holiness (Leviticus 19:2; Psalms 119). Priests also had a crucial mediatory role. Not only did they instruct the people in the Torah, they also offered sacrifices.

Sacrifices were made for a variety of reasons. One was to offer first fruits, whereby one would offer to God a tithe of the harvest

(Deuteronomy 14:22–29). Another was to expiate sins (Leviticus 6:24–30). A common sacrifice was a peace offering (Leviticus 3:1–17), and this one in particular demonstrates how the gulf between humans and God is bridged.

For a peace offering, one brought an unblemished sacrificial animal to a priest, who ritually blessed it, thus marking it for a holy purpose. The animal was then sacrificed to God on an altar, which itself was considered holy. Presuming God accepted the sacrifice, the animal was then understood as having entered God's realm and taken on something of God's holiness. The priest and the person offering the sacrifice ate the sacrificed (and cooked) animal, now also considered holy, and in doing so, communed with the holiness of God. Priests were Israel's institutional mediators and provided entrance into the sphere of the divine.

Israel had an additional mediator: the prophet. A prophet was one who, inspired and led by God, interpreted the signs of the time in light of covenant faith and spoke to the people on behalf of God. Three descriptions of a prophet pointed to the prophet's role and the gifts the prophet brought to the community. A prophet was a visionary (*hozeh*), a seer (*roeh*), and a proclaimer (*nabi*). Israel recognized in prophets holy people in its midst who were particularly set apart to discover divine mysteries and express God's will.

Christianity and Mediation

Christianity claims that Jesus Christ, as both divine and human, is an absolute mediator. Christ mediated the new covenant (Hebrews 12:24) and claimed to be the "way, truth, and the life" and the only access to the Father (John 14:6). Christ is the fullness of divine revelation (John 1:14, 18; 2 Corinthians 3:16-18) and to see him is to see the Father (John 10:30, 14:9). Given these claims, what is fascinating then is that Christianity broadly recognizes *other* expressions of spiritual mediation. Roman Catholics, Anglicans, and Eastern Orthodox, for example, seek the intercession of saints.

For centuries, many Protestant Christians have questioned the appropriateness of such intercessors. Why, they ask, seek the mediation of a saint when one could go directly to Jesus, the

WORSHIP AND VENERATION

Church fathers used the terms *adoration* and *veneration* interchangeably. From the early Middle Ages on, however, Catholics and Orthodox more precisely have distinguished *worship* (Greek: *latreia*; Latin: *adoratio*) of God from *veneration* (Greek: *douleia*; Latin: *veneratio*) for angels and saints. Mary, because of her supreme place among the saints, is commended to receive *hyper-douleia*.

absolute mediator? They also question the kind of devotion offered to saints, particularly Mary, and whether such devotion borders on idolatry, as if Mary is quasi-divine. While the Catholic and Orthodox Churches have been clear distinguishing between worship that belongs to God and veneration that ought to be offered to the blessed, these lines have seemed blurred in some devotions of the past.

Even if Roman Catholic and Eastern Orthodox Christians keep these distinctions straight, as is largely the case, does the supposed mediatory role of the saints compromise or distract one from the role of Christ? Christians broadly and regularly intercede for each other. Paul often interceded for others in prayer (Acts 26:29, 28:8; 2 Corinthians 13:7, 9; Colossians 1:3, 4.3; 2 Thessalonians 1:11). He also sought the intercession of others for himself (1 Thessalonians 5:25; 2 Thessalonians 3:1). James too recommended intercessory prayer (James 5:16). Thus, Christians have, from the beginning, appealed to each other to mediate or facilitate God's grace. Most Christians also believe that angels are agents of God's blessings. The logic of all these mediations is really the same. There are spiritual beings that exist as part of the body of Christ (*mysticum corpus Christi*). Until the last day, these members of the body are said to be active in worship and service of God. This is the case for one's Christian neighbors, who can mediate God's love as well as intercede on one's behalf. It

GRACE

The term *grace* encompasses much and is used variously. Above all, grace represents God's very gift of himself to humanity. Specifically, grace represents God's favor, love, forgiveness, and sanctification. God's grace unites the individual to God and enables one to become holy, as God is holy. Grace can be understood generally as God's presence in one's life, and specifically as God's particular blessings.

is even more the case, some argue, for those members in the body of Christ, such as saints and angels, who have a particular intimacy with and access to God.

MEDIATION AND COSMOLOGY

The role of mediators in a given religion has a great deal to do with that religion's **cosmology**, that is, how the spiritual structure of the universe is imagined. For example, in many native or oral traditions, the universe is understood to be three-tiered: heaven, Earth, and the underworld. The **shaman** learns to enter a hole in the fabric of the universe. He or she may enter into a heavenly realm to seek out friendly and powerful spiritual beings that are able to bring to the tribe a blessing it particularly needs, such as rain. Shamans may also have to go into the underworld to discover which demons are harassing members of the tribe and how to counter them. To these tribes, the shaman is an indispensable mediator between them and a spiritual realm that the people do not have access to, but which affects their lives dramatically.

While the following is an overgeneralization, consider these various cosmologies:

Religious Cosmologies	
Jewish	God, **sefirot**, seraphim, angels, humans
Christian	God, celestial powers/angels, saints, humans on Earth, fallen angels
Muslim	God, angels, spirits (*jinn*), humans on Earth, **Satan**
Haitian Voodoo	God, powerful spirits (*lwa*), humans on Earth, spirits of the dead, animals
Shinto	Creator Couple, gods (*kami*), ancestors (potential *kami*), humans on Earth
North Asian Yakut	God, gods, supernal beings, humans on Earth, animals, plants, master of the dead, human souls in the realm of the dead, demons
Hindu	Brahman, creator gods (*brahmas*), high gods (e.g., Shiva), gods (*devas*), humans on Earth, dangerous beings, animals, beings in hell states

Discussed next are two relatively complex cosmologies and how within them one could both experience mediations of God's blessings and proceed to intimacy with God.

Jewish Kabbalah Cosmology

Kabbalah (literally, "receiving") is often regarded as the quintessential expression of Jewish mysticism. As a tradition, Kabbalah has developed into a description of how the spiritual universe works. It describes the nature of God's manifestation, the spiritual structure of creation, and even how the soul works. Kabbalistic theology is critical in understanding modern Judaism, because it represents many spiritual assumptions that have clearly become central in the spiritual imagination of many mainstream Jews.

According to Kabbalistic cosmology, God is *Eyn-Sof* (Hebrew for *endless*), and cannot be understood or approached directly. However, God created the universe, including the structure of the human soul, according to a pattern called the *sefirot* (Hebrew for *numbers*).

This pattern is understood to be the countenance of God. Thus, the structure of both the universe and the soul is the very face of God. The cosmic pattern emanated from God in the following order: The first emanation is *Kether* (crown), which contains the entire universe. From *Kether* comes the mother *Binah* (understanding), who forms and gives birth to the masculine *Hokmah* (wisdom). All the following emanations proceed from here and are grounded in these three master *sefirot*. Proceeding from *Hokmah* is the feminine *Gevurah* (power), which represents judgment and rigor. From *Gevurah* emanates the masculine *Hesed* (love), which is produced by the union of wisdom and understanding and is the life-giving power of the universe and the soul. The next level is *Tifereth* (beauty), which represents compassion and harmony. *Tifereth* precedes the feminine *Hod* (majesty) and represents a form of prophecy that recognizes the majesty of God as well as the majesty of the universe. Related to *Hod* is *Nesah* (endurance), a masculine presence that supports mercy. From *Nesah* comes the masculine *Yesod* (foundation), the grounding of the *sefirot* and which represents creative energy. The lowest emanation is the feminine *Malkuth* (presence). *Malkuth* represents the people of Israel as well as the recognized presence of God among them.

Cosmic Emanations from God

Kether (Crown)

Binah (Understanding)   **Hokmah** (Wisdom)

Gevurah (Power)   **Hesed** (Love)

Tifereth (Beauty)

Hod (Majesty)   **Nesah** (Endurance)

Yesod (Foundation)

Malkuth (Presence)

Collectively, the *sefirot* represent God manifest and the structure of all things. Their order is critical in that the spiritual aspirant who wants to achieve union with God will take on a spiritual master, such as a Hasidic **rebbe**, and cultivate spiritual practices that provide a spiritual mastery at a given level or quality. Thus, one begins by deeply practicing the Jewish faith in order to come to a certain intimacy with God and an awareness of one's spiritual dignity. This is the cultivation of *Malkuth* (presence). Grounded in *Malkuth*, one receives practices from a spiritual master that ground and give energy to ascend the *sefirot*. When the master believes one is ready, one then focuses on the spiritual reality at the next level, which itself provides the condition for one to approach the next. Mystical knowledge of God is said to come when one has reached *Hokmah*. One's spiritual awareness becomes utterly apophatic in *Binah*. To have attained *Kether* is to see God radically.

Interestingly, most of the *sefirot* qualities are counter to normal sexual stereotypes. For example, love is masculine and is the condition for and subordinate to power, which is feminine. The aspirant, whether female or male, would have to enter his or her shadow interior. A male aspirant would have to become more integrated with his *anima*, or feminine side, and recognize it as a source of power, while a female aspirant would be challenged to claim her power but also see how to love through her *animus*, or masculine part, of her psyche. The *sefirot* pattern is not only the path of ascent to God, but also it mediates God insofar as the spiritual aspirant is ready to encounter God. By embracing spiritual practices that correspond to one's ascent, one experiences God according to that category. To achieve the level of *Tifereth* is to know profoundly the beauty of God and to recognize the presence of divine beauty in the world. The compassion one becomes infused with by cultivating the spirit of *Tifereth* directly corresponds to recognizing the world as filled with the dignity and beauty of the divine.

Christian Cosmology

The cosmology of Kabbalah strikes most Christians as quite exotic and complex, especially when contrasted with Christianity's angels, which for most Christians have little to do with their spiritual imagination. The Bible, however, has a rich tradition of angels being quite active as God's emissaries. The word *angel* (Greek: *angelos*; Hebrew: *mal'ak*) literally means, "messenger," though angels functioned more broadly, including as intercessors (Revelation 5:11;

SATAN

Fallen angels only appear late in the Old Testament. *Satan* in Hebrew means "accuser" or "adversary" (Greek: *diabolos*) and appears as a tempter or tormentor in Job, 1 Chronicles 21:1, and Zechariah 3:1–2. Wisdom 2:24, a very late Old Testament text, identifies Satan as he who caused death to enter the world. Later important but noncanonical Jewish writings, such as *Enoch, Jubilees,* and the *Testament of the Twelve Patriarchs,* portray Satan as the archangel Lucifer who led a rebellion against God. The New Testament accepts and expands on these teachings. Satan, or the devil, tempts Jesus (Matthew 4:1–11; Luke 4:1–13), and Jesus describes Satan as the father of lies, who sinned from the beginning (1 John 3:8, 8:44). Jesus also regularly expels demons from the possessed, and the kingdom of God is understood as the decisive victory over evil (Luke 10:18). Further references allude to angels who sinned and are now consigned to the underworld (2 Peter 2:4; Jude 1:6).

8:3–4), ministers (Hebrews 1:13–14), guides (Acts 8:26), and even liberators (Acts 12:6–11).

The authors of the New Testament also believed in other celestial powers. Paul mentions five that later came to be interpreted as separate classes of angels: Rulers, Authorities, Powers, Lordships, and Thrones (Colossians 1:16, 2:10, 2:15; Ephesians 1:21, 3:10, 6:12). By the Middle Ages, Christians believed that the spiritual universe was layered by a hierarchy of angelic orders that mediated God's grace and supported one on the path. Not all of the lists were identical, but the following is a fair representation:

Seraphim circle immediately around God, united in love.

Cherubim circle around God and enjoy immediate vision.

Thrones sit in the divine presence without immediate vision.

Principalities preside over the remaining orders.

Powers express the divine principles of power, courage, and perseverance.

Virtues express the divine principle of strength.

Archangels provide divine enlightenment.

Angels provide comfort and revelation.

The twelfth-century theologian Alan of Lille described the graces that each of the angelic orders mediates. Seraphim draw humans to love God and mediate God's love to humans. Cherubim bring knowledge of God. Thrones mediate the graces of equanimity and spiritual discernment. Principalities support spiritual practice, especially in terms of wise leadership. Powers teach piety and help guard human souls from evil forces. Virtues mediate miracles in the world. Archangels reveal celestial mysteries, while angels provide true teachings about God. Angels also support humans in need.

Like the *sefirot* pattern, this structure not only expresses how God mediates his grace to the human race, but also shows how the spiritual journey ought to be imagined. For example, because angels give comfort to humans in need, Christians who want to emulate angels offer compassionate support to those most in need. This beginning level of the hierarchy precedes and grounds announcing the Gospel, which is aligned to archangels, because if one does not care for another's physical needs, then one's preaching lacks both authenticity and credibility. By embracing a life that lives the Gospel in word and deed, one comes to experience the grace of spiritual strength (virtues). A long-practiced faith then gives one the spiritual vigor and the ability to act courageously and practice perseverance on the path in the midst of its inevitable challenges (powers). Only with tested faith does one's whole life come under a unified, integrated order (principalities). Such a tried-and-tested faith provides the possibility for contemplative intimacy with God (thrones). This intimacy can become so profound that one can even have an immediate knowledge of the godhead, called an intellectual vision (cherubim). Cultivating a life of contemplation provides the condition to receive the grace of full union with God, living the divine life in God (seraphim). Thus, each higher level of the hierarchy depends on the practiced cultivation of what precedes it, and together this hierarchy describes the conditions for deepening spiritual practice.

Surely, few Christians follow this line of spiritual development, and indeed, most have never heard of an angelic hierarchy, despite references to it in some classic Church hymns. This section is simply calling to consciousness that the Christian tradition resonates with Kabbalah in that imbedded in it are assumptions about how the spiritual universe is structured, and how that structure speaks to spiritual growth. Chapter seven will address the tradition of spiritual paths, particularly that of St. Teresa of Avila, which many still take seriously today.

SPIRITUAL GUIDES AS MEDIATORS
The Christian Spiritual Master

Christianity has known two principal kinds of human mediators: the bishop (or pastor) and the spiritual master (or director). They parallel the ancient Jewish mediation of priests and prophets in many ways. In ancient Israel, both priest and prophet mediated divine guidance and grace, but the priest held an official or institutional role. The institution could support prophets, but they were unique because they had received particular gifts and insights from God, not because they had an official function in the formal religious life of the people. Additionally, these gifts were more likely to be used to challenge the status of the institution rather than to support it.

From the beginning, one crucial criterion that Christians used to choose their bishop was spiritual depth. Bishops were understood to be mediators in many ways. One was that they led the Church as shepherds. In this sense, they mediated something of Christ's shepherding as well as that of the apostles. St. Paul insists that bishops must be beyond reproach in every way and living an orderly life, "for if someone does not know how to manage his own household, how can he take care of God's church?" (1 Timothy 3:5). In preaching, teaching, and organizing pastoral care, bishops were broadly experienced as mediating Christ's care of souls and of the Church. As presidents of the community, they were also presiders in Church rituals, particularly baptism and Eucharist. Thus, they increasingly took on something of the priestly role found in the Old Testament.

As Christianity developed in the patristic period, however, the role of spiritual master became distinct from that of the bishop. Bishops tended to come from the governing class of the empire, a class identified by birth, culture, and even autocratic temperament. A bishop represented a *vir venerabilis* (revered man) and was often contrasted with the *vir religiosus* and *femina religiosa* (holy man and woman). These unique people tended to live a radical lifestyle of prayer and asceticism. Many of them lived in the desert and formed the earliest expression of monasticism. To junior monks and nuns as well as many ordinary Christians, they were spiritual fathers and mothers (**abbas** and **ammas**).

Spiritual masters, because of their profound engagement with the interior life, were understood to be mediators in several ways. People would seek them and ask them to pray to God on their behalf, as many do with saints. Some were also known to have the gift of healing. More importantly, they were known to be able to discern God's will for others. Their abilities included identifying spirits, which the Bible recognizes as very important. "Beloved, do not believe every spirit, but test the spirits to see whether they are from God . . ." (1 John 4:1). One had to distinguish between an angel and supernatural evil "disguising himself as an angel of light" (2 Corinthians 11:14). Indeed, Paul numbered discernment of spirits to be among the gifts of the Holy Spirit (1 Corinthians 12:10).

The most important way that spiritual masters acted as mediators was as spiritual directors. Given their deep insight into the spiritual journey, their ability to read souls, and their intimacy with the Holy Spirit, they were considered fully equipped to guide others. In collections of the sayings of these desert masters, the passages frequently begin with a junior monk approaching a master, "*Abba (Amma)*, give me a word that I may be saved." The elder would read the aspirant's soul, which could take many hours or even days. The master would then offer a scriptural verse or spiritual teaching to meditate on or a spiritual practice to perform. Masters had an uncanny ability to know just what a given disciple would need to progress at that moment. Because of their knowledge, experience, and ability to guide, these masters garnered extraordinary authority and trust.

One reason that spiritual masters were successful is that the spiritual path was considered relatively predictable. Christians had a one-size-fits-all mentality. All a master had to do was to discern what stage of spiritual development the aspirant had attained and counsel accordingly. Spiritual masters also realized that paths were not utterly linear for everyone. Still, these differences represented variations of the same grand scheme of spiritual development. John Climacus listed twenty-six stages to union with God, Evagrius Ponticus held that there were five major stages, the medieval master Richard of St. Victor taught a twelve-step progression, and Teresa of Avila named seven stages. Nevertheless, all follow a consistent pattern: the awakening of the soul and a determination to pursue holiness, a purgation of sin and the embrace of a spiritually disciplined life, a development of prayer and deepening interiority, an illumination whereby one becomes a contemplative; a crisis of faith or dark night, and finally a resolution in full intimacy with God. Christians who were not monastics could embrace spiritual practices and monastic wisdom insofar as their state in life allowed, or be content at being a "standard" Christian in the world.

In the modern period, there are at least two interrelated changes in the assumptions about the nature of the spiritual journey. These reflect a change in understanding of a spiritual master. First, Christianity has come to recognize the Holy Spirit as self-empowering. The absolute authority of a spiritual director is questioned more and more. In his *Spiritual Exercises*, Ignatius of Loyola instructs the director to support the aspirant's personal discovery of God's will. Thus, there is no "master" who is presumed to know where God is taking the soul. Rather, a director facilitates the aspirant's listening to the movements of the Holy Spirit within. Second, the concept of a singular Christian spirituality is widely challenged. One's spiritual path should align to one's unique personality, relationships, and state in life. As Francis de Sales once wrote,

> Devotion must be exercised in different ways by the gentleman, the worker, the servant, the prince, the widow, the young girl, and the married woman. Not only is this true, but the practice of devotion must also be adapted to the strength, activities, and duties of each particular person. I ask you . . . is it fitting for a bishop to want to live a solitary life like a Carthusian? Or a married man to want to

own no more property than a Capuchin, for a skilled work-
man to spend the whole day in church like a religious, for
the religious to be constantly subject to every sort of call
in his neighbor's service, as a bishop is? . . . Still this is a
common fault. . . . When it goes contrary to a man's law-
ful vocation, it is undoubtedly false.

— Francis de Sales, *Introduction to the
Devout Life*, 43–44

Today, spiritual directors who represent a contemplative, monastic
spiritual tradition are likely to be more directive than those in other
spiritual traditions, as this spirituality delineates a moderately stable
spiritual progression. Most spiritual directors follow the Ignatian
principle of supporting aspirants' discernment of the unique movements of the Holy Spirit in their hearts.

Hindu Guru

In Hinduism, in order to engage profoundly in the spiritual life, it is
assumed that one needs a spiritual guide. The great Hindu theologian
Ramanuja (1017–1137 CE) underscores the importance of the **guru**
with a parable of a boy prince who is lost in a forest throughout his
entire childhood. When the prince comes of age, a fully trustworthy
person discovers him, reveals his true royal heritage, and helps him
through the labyrinthine forest so that he may return to the palace
and his rightful heritage. The trustworthy person is a guru who
reveals to the spiritually ready aspirant his or her real divine identity
and guides one to experience this truth.

Given the guru's importance, one has to make sure that the
guru is up to the task of guidance, because the number of self-
proclaimed holy people in India is dizzying. One classic text, the
Sribhasya, describes a good guru as one entirely free of egoism,
always desirous of the welfare of others, and never swayed by love
of fame or profit. Just as one needs an excellent guru, one also needs
an excellent disciple. Ramanuja taught that if a guru accepts an
aspirant, it is assumed that the aspirant is capable of enlightenment,
that is, already has spiritual depth, is committed to moral purity, is
invested in spiritual growth, and, above all, is willing to fully trust
the guru.

YOGA

The word **yoga** means "union," as this practice joins a religious aspirant to a particular path or spiritual focus (*marga*). *Jnana* (knowledge) yoga cultivates progressive insight into the ultimate nature of reality. *Karma* (action) yoga cultivates selfless service for others. **Bhakti** (devotion) yoga develops profound emotional bonds to a manifestation of the divine. *Raja* (royal) yoga cultivates deep levels of meditation and concentration. *Kundalini* (who lies coiled) yoga nurtures opening up centers of spiritual energy in the body (opening a coiled serpent), culminating in great spiritual insight and bliss.

This final quality of the disciple—trust in the guru—is crucial. For example, in some forms of bhakti yoga, the guru is the personal representative of God, and possibly even an incarnation of God. One saying goes that, "The guru must always be worshipped; the guru is exalted because the guru is one with the mantra. Hari [God] is pleased if the guru is pleased. Millions of acts of worship are otherwise rejected. If Hari is angry, the guru is our defense; but from the guru's wrath there is no protection" (Klaus Kostermaier, *A Survey of Hinduism*, 237). In jnana yoga, gurus are not incarnations, but they do have transcendental knowledge that they transmit to aspirants.

What does the guru do? First and foremost, a guru initiates the aspirant into a discipline, a *sadhana*. Within the framework of this spiritual practice and lifestyle, the guru communicates spiritual knowledge and becomes a vehicle for spiritual transformation. The following are a few striking examples from famous masters and disciples:

- Seemingly out of the blue, Ramakrishna places his foot on Vivekananda's chest and immediately plunges his disciple into a deep state of spiritual realization.

- One day Yukteswar simply announces to his disciple Yogananda, "Your heart's desire shall be fulfilled." Then he lightly strikes Yogananda on the chest, sending him into a direct experience of the bliss of Brahman.

- Mahara-ji (Neebkatori baba) walks up to his disciple Ram Dass and taps him three times on the forehead, causing him to go instantly into ecstasy.

Apart from triggering and constantly reinvigorating the spiritual process in a disciple, the guru also serves as a guide, primarily by being a living example of holiness. The guru exemplifies the kind of life the disciple needs to embrace and the kind of person the disciple needs to become. In doing so, gurus try to create masters of their disciples. That is, they try to facilitate their aspirants' transformation so that the guru would become obsolete. It is a relationship designed ultimately for spiritual self-authorization in the disciple.

There is something powerful in a guru–disciple relationship. One is not on one's own but guided in worn and sure paths. As risky as it may seem to give so much influence and power to a guru, it is often argued that it is riskier still to go it alone. A similar assessment was made regarding the Christian desert masters. Self-delusion or simple ignorance makes running one's own spiritual life dangerous. It is far better to place oneself in the hands of an experienced guide, the tradition maintains.

Given how important gurus are and the authority they have over their disciples, the danger of developing a personality cult is ever-present. A healthy disciple recognizes that guru devotion has a use but is not an end in itself. Adoration for an unintegrated, unholy guru is a setup for grave spiritual harm.

Buddhist Tibetan Lama

As important as a guru is for the Hindu devotee, the **lama** might be even more so for the religiously serious Tibetan (Vajrayana) Buddhist. If a guru can be a kind of incarnation of God in bhakti yoga or a mediator of transcendent truth in jnana yoga or a catalyst for enlightenment in raja yoga, a lama might be all of them at the same time.

IMAGE: © CYRIL HOU/SHUTTERSTOCK

His Holiness the Dalai Lama.

To understand a lama's role, one needs to appreciate **Mahayana Buddhist** cosmology. In Mahayana Buddhism, one finds the three-Buddha-body teaching (*trikaya*: doctrine): ultimate reality (*dharmakaya*), divine manifestation (*nirmanakaya*), and the bodies of supernatural buddhas (*samghogakaya*). **Tibetan Buddhism** adds more, such as heavenly bodhisattvas, who act like deities and interact with humans as needed. The Dalai Lama, for example, is an expression of the bodhisattva Avalokishvara. Because Tibetan cosmology involves the interpenetration of these three Buddha bodies, the aspirant who wants to proceed the farthest needs the lama to act as initiator, mentor, and at times incarnation of the Buddha bodies for the disciple.

Like the guru, the qualified lama represents a traditional enlightenment strategy, is highly spiritually developed, and has no ego interests in his ministry. Karma Chagme Rinpoche, who is said to embody three bodhisattvas, offers signs of a good lama: learned, wise, free of greed, awakened, compassionate, long-suffering, light-hearted, energetic, practical advisor, liberated, articulate, and discerning of spiritual progress (*A Spacious Freedom*, 18).

The lama's mediatory work depends on the kind of spiritual discipline being engaged. In Unexcelled Yoga, the disciple sees the lama as a living embodiment of the Buddha, **Dharma**, and Sangha, the three refuges. The lama leads the aspirant into visualizations of being enlightened and seeing the world as enlightened. Thus, one is taught to imagine the true underlying nature of the universe and to develop an archetypal model for one's actual transformation. In other exercises, disciples attempt to adopt the lama's vision of them, because the lama sees their **Buddha-nature**. This enlightened vision is communicated through rituals of progressive initiation. In the Three-Body Mentor Yoga, the lama embodies, through a series of complex meditations, the Emanation-Body Buddha, then the Beatific-Body Buddha, and finally the Truth-Body Buddha. The lama becomes everything transcendent. In one tantric tradition, the lama is also revered as the historical Buddha, Siddhartha Gautama. When the aspirant is ready, the lama, as the Buddha, gives permission to summon a deity whom the lama chooses. The lama then initiates the disciple into the ministry, function, and life of the deity and ritually helps the aspirant identify personally with this personal god. Finally, in guru yoga, one takes refuge in the lama, who represents all the Buddha's, bodhisattvas, gods, and goddesses combined. The aspirant invites the lama to abide in his or her heart and bestow success.

Lama and disciple have a deep communion between them. The lama imparts not only knowledge but also part of the lama's very being. There is a kind of melding of hearts and minds, and this intimacy is crucial for deep spiritual advancement.

Many of the elements of the guru seen in Hinduism are also seen in the lama of the Tibetan tradition. Lamas take on the burden of guiding disciples into the cosmic realization of their own spiritual truth. Lamas also mediate cosmic blessings. To accomplish both, the disciple has to be totally devoted to the lama and believe that the lama embodies such spiritual power. As in Hinduism, it is crucial for the lama to have personally achieved profound spiritual realization. If the mentor lacks this realization, no reverence or devotion is going to get the aspirant very far. Disciples must have spiritual depth and intensity too. Finally, as shown in most strains of Hinduism, the mentor ought to become redundant. The lama, as the personification of a bodhisattva, tries to empower the disciple to become a bodhisattva.

Jewish Hasidic Rebbe

Hasidic Judaism may bring some to a more familiar Western religious world, but this kind of Judaism nonetheless feels for many quite exotic. Very briefly, **Hasidism** began in eastern Europe as a reaction to a highly scholastic, abstract, and dry approach to Jewish thinking, and even to Jewish life. Under the eighteenth-century-mystic Israel ben Eliezer, known as Baal Shem Tov (1700–1760), devout spiritual practice was integrated with ecstatic religiosity. *Hasidut* means "piety."

The Lubavitcher rebbe, Rabbi Menachem Schneerson (1902–1994) (center), leader of the Lubavitch sect of Hasidic Judaism for decades, reads the Torah with a fellow Lubavitcher scholar and a young boy. They are at the Lubavitch world headquarters in Crown Heights, Brooklyn, New York. In the Hasidic movement, the rebbe, or master, guides his followers by virtue of his spiritual power and holiness.

Therefore, the Hasidim are the pious ones, and the rebbe was the pious among the pious. The traditional model of the **rabbi** is that of the Talmudic scholar. Studying the interpretations and applications of the Torah is a potent forum to encounter the divine and the spirit of Judaism. The Hasidic movement replaces the rabbi-scholar with the rebbe, the master, who now guides his followers by virtue of his spiritual power and holiness. This rebbe is understood as a *tzadik*, a holy man who could mediate intimacy with God. The rebbe has gravitas both in terms of his role in the community and in terms of profound spiritual depth.

For Hasidic Jews, the rebbe is the instrument chosen by God to make the divine will known and implemented; the rebbe is the supreme authority in the community. Accounts of the power of rebbes are legion. Some were clairvoyant; others could see past or future. Most importantly, they had power in heaven. There is a famous and humorous story about Rebbe Israel Maggid of Kozhenitz: His prayers were always obeyed by heaven, except for one night. Israel Maggid was shocked, and he demanded an explanation from heaven. When he received it, he understood and forgave God. It turns out that another rebbe, Naphtali of Ropshitz, was working that night. He went to the rescue of a wedding party that, due to a family tragedy, was sad. Naphtali entered the gathering, charmed and amused them, and led them in songs of love. By Naphtali's own charismatic presence, he healed the entire wedding party. Like the wedding guests, the angels in heaven were completely under his spell. Thus, the angels were not paying attention to other rebbes' prayers at the time.

It would be easy to imagine a rebbe simply standing over and above his people. Interestingly, Hasidic theology understands a rebbe's spiritual profundity as a representation of the holy dignity of each of his followers and of the community itself. There is in Hasidism, as well as Judaism at large, a great respect for the unique religiosity of every individual Jew. There is an often-quoted saying by Rebbe Zusya: "In the world to come, I will not be asked, 'Why were you not Moses?' I shall be asked, 'Why were you not Zusya?'" (Martin Buber, *The Way of Man*, 17).

The confidence that a rebbe must have in his role should be coupled with deep humility. A master once said, "If the Messiah should come today and say to me, 'You are better than the others,' then I would say to him, 'You are not the Messiah.'" While modern rebbes are not popularly believed to have the powers of Baal Shem Tov, Israel Maggid of Kozhenitz, or Naphtali of Ropshitz, there remains an extraordinary solicitude to the rebbe as the capable and necessary mediator of the divine life for souls and for the community.

LESSONS

Themes

One may have difficulty imagining how such various and exotic religious expressions can teach anything about Christian spiritual masters. Nevertheless, they contain important and relevant lessons, particularly because these extraordinary examples of mediators of God's grace endorse claims or religious perspectives that are very much like those seen in Christianity's tradition of masters and bishops. In fact, compared to the expectations of spiritual leadership shown in the previous three traditions, Christian claims are rather modest.

One theme that comes out clearly is the insistence on the authentic holiness of the mediator. Mediators do not merely announce the sacred but communicate it with their very person, and doing so requires profound communion with God. One cannot be simply a very good person; one has to have extraordinary spiritual depth. This leads to an additional insight or theme: spiritual mediation is fraught with potential for harm. In all three examples in this chapter, the mediator has a great deal of power, and the disciple or community invests much authority in the master. An immature, egocentric, or incompetent spiritual guide could wreak havoc.

Another theme is that mediators have a function, or role, that points beyond themselves. Disciples need to be truly devoted to and invest authority in the master. They do this, however, not as an end in itself, but in order to engage a spiritual transformation that goes well beyond the master.

Finally, mediation is for empowerment. While the rebbe does not intend to become redundant like the guru or lama, even the rebbe facilitates the individual and community's unique identities. In world religions, one can safely embrace the axiom that the more one matures in the spiritual life, the more one becomes one's own master.

Insights

Considering these themes in the Christian religious milieu can give several direct insights about Christian spiritual mediators. First, to choose truly holy people is crucial. This is particularly true with spiritual directors, but also with pastors, bishops, and indeed anyone empowered to influence spiritual lives.

Mediators are successful when intimate with those who follow them, individually and as communities. One sees such need reflected in the desert master tradition in which an *abba* might require many hours or even days to look into the soul of an aspirant. To be out of touch with the lives of those whom leaders intend to guide is to guarantee poor leadership.

Perhaps one can best appropriate these spiritual insights by seeking personal guides and directors who are both intensely holy and competent in facilitating spiritual development. Spiritual paths vary, and spiritual masters or wisdom figures will be most appropriate when their piety and expertise match with what one needs at the time. In India, a disciple usually follows several masters throughout his or her life. Under the tutelage of a given master, one learns a spiritual practice and way of being holy. When the time comes to learn another practice, one simply leaves and takes on another master. Perhaps Christian spiritual direction can follow this pattern. John of the Cross once described the variety of spiritual directors that one might need as corresponding to the making of a statue. Some are excellent in training the soul in broad woodwork, others in detail, still others in sanding and varnishing. One should see the appropriate master at the point at which one is in the pattern.

Bishops or pastors, obviously, are a different kind of mediator than a spiritual master. As shown earlier, from the patristic Church on, the bishop (*vir venerabilis*) and spiritual master (*vir religiosus, femina religiosa*) were considered differently. However, these institutional leaders can indeed mediate God's presence to the community. It is broadly agreed that they do this most obviously when their love of God radiates to the people of God. God then becomes credible for Christians. As we shall see throughout this text, love dominates the Christian path (Romans 13:8; John 13:34–35, 15:10; 1 Corinthians 13:3; 1 John 4:11–12; Galatians 5:6).

CONCLUSIONS

Religions the world over recognize the spiritual possibilities and even necessity of spiritual mediation. This chapter has reviewed snapshots of several venerable traditions. The Christian tradition points to Christ as the absolute mediator between God and humanity. Additionally, by virtue of Christ, one is filled with the Holy Spirit, who transforms and guides one (Galatians 5:22–26). Nonetheless, Christianity has also always embraced a world of spiritual mediation. It is not that Christianity thinks that Christ is not enough. Rather, the tradition claims that Christ himself uses these means for the sacramental encounter of his saving grace. Such sacramental expressions include encountering his love though the mediations of angels and intercessions of saints and experiencing his care through the love and prayers of family, friends, and neighbors. Mediators and masters can dramatically facilitate Christians' realization of their dignity as sons and daughters of God, co-heirs with Christ (Romans 8:17; Galatians 4:7). The challenge is to use such mediation wisely.

Review Questions

1. Christians believe Christ is the absolute mediator between God and humanity. Why would one need other mediators as well?
2. Compare two cosmologies, the Jewish Kabbalah and the Christian tradition of classes of angels. How do they represent both a description of God's emanating grace to us and reciprocally our path to union with God?
3. What are the most important qualities a spiritual guide ought to have?
4. Why is being a Christian spiritual master or director more complicated in the modern period than it was in the patristic Church?

In-Depth Questions

1. Are there people in your life, now or in the past, who act as spiritual guides or mentors? Is your religious community leader (e.g., pastor) a spiritual guide or a spiritual master?
2. Are bishops or pastors actual mediators of God's grace? Explain. Also, how might their "official" roles actually limit their capacity to be so? Do other religious leaders, such as rabbis in Judaism or Imams in Islam, mediate God's grace in the same way? Are they limited in this capacity as well? Compare them in this regard with Christian leaders.

3. Spiritual masters necessarily acquire a good deal of authority. The danger is that the master might not be competent or may even abuse that authority. Given this twofold danger, should one ever surrender one's autonomy to a master? Are there more and less skillful ways of surrendering authority over one's life?
4. Do you think you can become holy without a spiritual guide?
5. One way many college students jump-start their spiritual lives is through campus-sponsored retreats. Would you ever consider participating in such a retreat? Why or why not?

Select Bibliography

Athanasius. *Athanasius: The Life of Antony and the Letter to Marcellinus.* Robert Gregg, trans. Mahwah, NJ: Paulist Press, 1980.

Bokser, Ben Zion, and Baruch M. Bokser. "Introduction." In *The Talmud: Selected Writings.* Ben Zion Bokser, trans. Mahwah, NJ: Paulist, 1989.

Brown, Peter. *Authority and the Sacred: Aspects of the Christianization of the Roman World.* Cambridge, MA: Cambridge University Press, 1995. In this small volume, Brown distinguishes the patristic Church's experience between the bishop and the spiritual master.

———. "The Rise and Function of the Holy Man in Late Antiquity." *Journal of Roman Studies* 61 (1971): 80–101.

Buber, Martin. *The Way of Man according to the Teaching of the Hasidim.* Secaucus, NJ: Carol Publishing Group, 1995.

———. *Hasidism and Modern Man.* Maurice Friedman, ed. and trans. Amherst, NY: Humanity Books, 1958. This is a classic and highly influential text on the spirit of Hasidism.

Burton-Christie, Douglas. *The Word in the Desert: Scripture and the Quest for Holiness in Early Christian Monasticism.* New York: Oxford University Press, 1993. This is a widely revered modern study of the character of early desert monasticism.

Chagme, Karma Rimpoche. *A Spacious Path to Freedom: Practical Instructions on the Union of Mahamudra and Atiyoga.* B. Alan Wallace, trans. Ithaca, NY: Snow Lion Publications, 1988.

Chase, Steven. *Angelic Spirituality: Medieval Perspectives on the Ways of Angels.* Mahwah, NJ: Paulist Press, 2002.

Dan, Joseph, ed. *The Early Kabbalah.* Ronald Kiener, trans. Mahwah, NJ: Paulist Press, 1986.

Green, Arthur, ed. *Jewish Spirituality*. Vol. II. New York: Crossroad, 1997. An excellent chapter is included on Hasidic Judaism.

Harmless, William. *Desert Christians: An Introduction to the Literature of Early Monasticism*. Oxford: Oxford University Press, 2004.

Jung, C. G. *Memories, Dreams, Reflections*. A. Jaffe, ed., and Richard and Clara Winston, trans. New York: Vintage, 1989.

Klostermaier, Klaus. *A Survey of Hinduism*, 2nd edition. Albany, NY: State University of New York, 1994. This text details the history and variety of many different aspects of Hinduism. It is considered a highly reliable, critical text.

Lyman, Rebecca. *Early Christian Traditions*. Cambridge, MA: Cowely Publications, 1999.

Ram Dass. *Be Here Now*. New York: Crown Publishing Group, 1971.

Sales, Francis de. *Introduction to the Devout Life*, revised. John Ryan, ed. and trans. New York: Image Books, 1989.

Sholem, Gershon. *Major Trends in Jewish Mysticism*. New York: Schocken Books, 1961. Fifty years since it was first published, Sholem's classic study on Jewish mysticism is still considered one of the best modern treatments.

Telushkin, J. *Jewish Literacy*. New York: Image Books, 1982.

Thurman, Robert, ed. and trans. *Essential Tibetan Buddhism*. New York: HarperSanFrancisco, 1995.

———. *The Tibetan Book of the Dead*. New York: Bantam, 1994.

Wiesel, Elie. *Four Hasidic Masters and Their Struggle against Melancholy*. Notre Dame: University of Notre Dame, 1978.

Yogananda, Parmanhansa. *The Autobiography of a Yogi*. Los Angeles: Self-Realization Fellowship Press, 1998.

Yoshinori, Takeuchi, ed. *Buddhist Spirituality*. Vol I. New York: Crossroad, 1995.

CHAPTER FOUR

The Jewish Vision

ENTERING THE JEWISH IMAGINATION
Shammai and Hillel

There is a story from the **Talmud** of a gentile and two famous rabbis. The young potential convert to Judaism approached Rabbi Shammai and told him that he would embrace Judaism if Shammai could teach him the Torah while the young man stood on one foot and listened. Shammai had little patience for such a frivolous request. He must have thought, "The depth and breadth of the Torah or even its essence, you think you will discover in mere moments?" Shammai happened to have a measuring stick in his hand and hit this seemingly ridiculous young man with it. The young gentile then went to Rabbi Hillel with the same challenge. Hillel thought for a moment and said, "What is hateful to you, do not do to your fellow man. This is the entire Torah; the rest is commentary. Now go and learn it." Shortly thereafter, the man converted to Judaism (see *Shabbat* 31a).

One can resonate with the pithy response of Hillel. He speaks to a universal sense of compassion and empathy that appealed to the young man. However, is this the essence of Judaism?

THE GOLDEN RULE

Some have argued that the Golden Rule appears in every religion and thus must represent some kind of religious core. Consider the following:

- *Christianity:* As you wish that others would to you, do so to them (Luke 6:31).
- *Islam:* No man is a true believer unless he desires for his brother that which he desires for himself (*Al-Nawani's Forty Hadiths*, 13).
- *Confucianism:* Do not do to others what you would not like yourself (*Analects*, XII.2).
- *Daoism:* The good person will regard the gains of others as if they were his own, and their losses in the same way (*Tai Sang* 3).
- *Zoroastrianism:* One's nature is only good when one shall not do to another whatever is not good for one's own self (*Dadiustan I, dinik,* 94:5).
- *Hinduism:* One should never do that to another which one regards as injurious to one's own self (*Anusharna Parva* 113.7).
- *Buddhism:* Hurt not others in ways that you yourself would find hurtful (*Udana* 5.1).

Attempts to Define Judaism

What is Judaism? Some claim that Judaism is primarily a people united by a history and ethnic heritage. It could be argued that Judaism is grounded in the Ten Commandments, the core of the Law of Moses (Exodus 20:1–17; Deuteronomy 5:6–21). The first five of these are said to deal with one's relationship to God and the last five with human relationships; in this sense, Judaism could be understood as that which embraces the laws of God. Another focus of Judaism is faith. According to Rabbi Simlai, an influential voice in the Talmud, all 613 commandments contained in the Torah are summed up by the prophet Habakkuk's words: "The righteous live by faith" (Habakkuk 2:4).

Moses Maimonides, a twelfth-century Jewish philosopher, cited thirteen tenets that a Jew must embrace in order to be considered authentically Jewish. They are the following:

1. God exists.
2. God is singular.
3. God is absolute spirit.
4. God is eternal.
5. God alone should be worshipped.
6. God has used prophets to make his revelation known.
7. Moses is the greatest prophet.
8. All of the Torah comes from God and was given to Moses.
9. The Torah cannot be changed or superseded.
10. God knows the actions of human beings.
11. God rewards those who keep the Torah and punishes those who do not.
12. There will come a Jewish Messiah.
13. There will be a resurrection from the dead.

By the sixteenth century, Maimonides' list was published as a set of dogmatic principles, each of which was preceded by the affirmation, "I believe with absolute faith that. . . ." For medieval and early modern Jews, this set of principles worked like a catechism or creed and eventually found its way into Jewish prayer books. It is the basis for the popular "Yigdal" hymn, which is sung in many synagogues today. Here one sees Judaism principally understood as a religion of beliefs. Obviously, Maimonides believed in the ethical demands of his faith and saw them as essential. For Maimonides, to neglect Torah makes one a bad Jew; to reject one of these tenets makes one a non-Jew.

None of these approaches actually hits the mark, however. Many Jews understand the Ten Commandments as natural law that all people should embrace. Faith is a constant with most religions; thus, Judaism would not be distinguished from the others. In terms of Maimonides' tenets, many devout Jews do not accept every one of them. Many Jews, in fact, maintain that being Jewish has little to do with doctrines. For most, orthopraxy (right behavior) is far more important than orthodoxy (right doctrine).

Shammai and Hillel Revisited

Without question, Rabbi Hillel is supposed to be the hero of the conversion story. He addresses Judaism's core as compassion. This may be Judaism's greatest theme, and certainly a central theme in the Hebrew Bible, in which the cry of the oppressed or those in need (Hebrew: *tsa'aq*) particularly moves God. The most important prophetic challenge to the people of Israel was in the form of social justice, especially regarding those who are the most powerless, most in need. The prophetic worldview was one in which true fasting was acting justly (Isaiah 58:1–9), reversing oppression was the only way to make the Temple holy (Jeremiah 7:3–11), and sacrifices to God without care for those in need had become blasphemous (Amos 5:6–165). Hillel's response correlates well with Rabbi Yohanan's response to the destruction of the Temple:

> Once, as Rabbi Yohanan ben Zakkai was coming forth from Jerusalem, Rabbi Joshua followed him and beheld the Temple in ruins. "Woe unto us," Rabbi Joshua cried, "that this, the place where the iniquities of Israel were atoned for, is laid waste!" "My son," Rabbi Yohanan said to him, "be not grieved. We have another atonement as effective as this. And what is it? It is acts of loving-kindness, as it is said, 'For I desire mercy and not sacrifice.'"
>
> —Hosea 6:6; cited by Arthur Green,
> *Jewish Spirituality I*, 194

Could it be that Rabbi Shammai's response to the young gentile was also excellent? Judaism has a deep and rich religious culture. It provides an imaginative world with multiple layers of revelation, mystical cosmologies, and divine sparks among worshippers. Judaism teaches identifying with all peoples and their plights even as it intentionally advances its own unique identity. From Shammai's point of view, how could such a dazzling kaleidoscope of spiritual wealth be reduced to a lesson brief enough for one to hear while standing on one leg, much less by a pithy single line that any secular humanist might be most comfortable hearing?

Hillel might challenge questioners not to underestimate the complexity or depth of his seemingly simple response. To focus on compassion is to take on a posture that grounds much of the complexity in Judaism. According to an important Jewish tradition, God invites humans to join him in healing and recreating the world. Jews can only embrace this invitation if they recognize that all of humanity is in exile together. Torah allows them to be light to the world (Isaiah 42:6, 60:3) and guides them to walk compassionately with a compassionate God. Thus, compassion is the door to Torah.

Hillel might also argue that the second part of his statement to the young man cannot be ignored: "The rest is commentary. Now go and learn it." This statement is more potent than it may appear. The commentary, particularly Talmud, teaches one how to think like a Jew. *Torah* is a complex Hebrew word. It could be translated as *law*, *way*, or *teaching*. One might best consider it as *revelation*. To study Torah is to investigate how God reveals himself to his chosen people. Torah represents God's laws and their interpretations (*halakah*), as well as narratives and explanations on Jewish life (*aggadah*). Study is crucial for Jews, because in study, one comes closest to God, who

IMAGE: © ANNIE GRIFFITHS BELT/CORBIS

Talmud scholars discuss in a Yeshivah in Jerusalem. For Jews, study is critical in bringing one close to God.

reveals himself through Torah. For Hillel to say that "the rest was commentary" is not to suggest that the rest is a mere addendum. Studying the commentary represents immersing oneself in the Jewish vision. "Now go and learn it," he commands.

Both Shammai and Hillel respond well to the potential convert. From Shammai, the young man receives a sharp rebuke that points to Judaism's vast complexity. There is no axiom that will contain this complexity, and no shortcut in understanding it. From Hillel, he receives an invitation and a challenge. The invitation tells him of core interrelatedness in compassion. The challenge is to take that core and discover over a lifetime its meaning in the Jewish vision of the universe.

One valuable approach to the Jewish vision is to consider it from two different perspectives: time and space. Jews have a way of considering time that may inspire and challenge gentiles. Jews also are heavily invested in the concrete world, or that of *space*, and have a profound mission. Study of Torah assumes a middle position that unites time and space in important ways.

JEWISH VISION OF TIME
Sabbath

According to Genesis 1:1–2:4, God created the universe in a week's time. On the first day, he created light; on the second, a dome that represented the sky; on the third, dry land and vegetation; on the fourth, the sun and moon; on the fifth, water creatures; and on the sixth, animals for Earth, with humanity as the capstone being created in God's own image and likeness. The seventh day was then a day of rest. Certainly, this narrative is intended to parallel the human experience of a seven-day week. One should not, however, imagine that **Sabbath** refers to merely resting from a long workweek.

According to Jewish theology, the Sabbath is something that God actually created; specifically, he created *menuha*, which is usually translated as "rest." More profoundly, it refers to tranquility, peace, and repose. In the biblical mind, *menuha* is the same as happiness, harmony, and even stillness. Consider that God reckoned the first six days of creation as good. The Sabbath, however, was blessed and deemed holy (Genesis 2:3).

One sees in the Sabbath, which begins on Friday at sundown and ends on Saturday at sundown, an attempt by Jews to unite time with eternity. One of the great Jewish theologians of the modern era, Abraham Joshua Heschel, describes Sabbath as a taste of eternity, a day of being instead of doing. He argues that unless one learns how to cultivate a contemplative soul and relish the Sabbath while still in the world and is initiated into a contemplative mental posture, one will be unable to enjoy eternity in the world to come. In this sense, the Sabbath is training for, and a foretaste of, eternal life.

Throughout the history of Jewish theology, the Sabbath has been personified and given names such as *bride*, or *queen*. There is even a popular Sabbath hymn, *"Lecha Dodi Likrat Kallah"* ("Come, My Beloved, to Meet the [Sabbath] Bride"). The language of the Talmud is to sanctify the Sabbath. The Hebrew word is *le-kadesh*, which is also the term the Talmud uses to describe consecrating a woman into marriage. Symbolically, the destiny of Israel is to be the groom of this sacred day, and in cleaving to the Sabbath, one cleaves to God. The Sabbath is even understood as providing a greater grace to the world. According to the Talmud, on the eve of the Sabbath, the Lord gives humanity *neshamah yeterah*, "additional spirit," or "increased soul," and, at its conclusion, takes it away. Thus, Jews are particularly challenged to take advantage of this day. The Sabbath morning liturgy includes the following:

> To God who rested from all action on the seven day and ascended upon His throne of Glory; He vested the day of rest with beauty; He called the Sabbath a delight. This is the song and the praise of the seventh day, on which God rested from His work. The seventh day itself is uttering praise. A song of the Sabbath day: "It is good to give thanks unto the Lord!" Therefore, all the creatures of God bless Him.
>
> —Abraham Joshua Heschel, *The Sabbath*, 24

The first six days of the week represent creation, that is, activity designed to be creative or to exercise some kind of control over the environment. Sabbath is a time to step back from this kind of engagement with the world. Gentiles typically think of Jewish law as forbidding work on the Sabbath, but Sabbath distinctions are subtler.

For example, many Orthodox Jews would not think of turning on an electric light during Sabbath, but would certainly perform household duties of family care. Attending to children's needs would obviously take more effort than flipping on a light switch, itself hardly a work. However, what the Torah prohibits is *melachah*, or what one does six days a week; that is, how in some way one dominates the environment. One creates, as God did, for six days. Such work is itself potentially very holy and important. However, its perspective and grounding comes from *menuha*—rest and repose.

A typical Sabbath might look like this: By afternoon, observant Jews begin to return home for Sabbath preparations. The family bathes and dresses well, and the best dishes and tableware are set for a festive meal. The Sabbath begins at sunset as Jewish days run from sunset to sunset. Several minutes before sunset, the female head of the house lights two Sabbath candles and recites a blessing. These represent the two commandments to remember (Exodus 20:8) and observe (Deuteronomy 5:12) the Sabbath. The family then goes to synagogue for a brief service, after which they come home to a festive dinner. The male head of the house recites a blessing (*Kiddush*) over the wine, sanctifying the Sabbath, and a prayer over the bread—traditionally two loaves of sweet bread called *challah*. The meal is long and leisurely and ends with a grace that may even include singing. After dinner, the family talks, reads, studies Torah, and so on. The morning service usually begins at 9:00 a.m. and continues until around noon. Afterward, the family enjoys another leisurely, festive meal that usually has been prepared in advance and is reheated. The afternoon is spent studying, taking walks, or perhaps napping. Sabbath ends at nightfall, when three stars are visible. At the conclusion, the family performs a concluding ritual called a *Havdalah* (separation). Blessings recited include one that formally recognizes the distinction between the Sabbath just celebrated and the rest of the week.

Festivals

The Jewish sense of time is also expressed in its specific holy days or yearly festivals. Many of the Jewish festivals emerged when most Jews lived in an agricultural society as celebrations of central activities such as sowing and harvesting. Eventually, these festivals took on religious meanings. The Jewish New Year, Rosh Hashanah, celebrates the creation of the world. Every day during the preceding month, a ram's horn (shofar) is blown to remind the people that they stand before God. The single most sacred day of the year follows ten days after Rosh Hashanah: the Day of Atonement, Yom Kippur. This is a day of strict fasting and prayer, when Jews repent of their sins, seek divine forgiveness, and renew themselves by solemn intention to live holier lives. The Feast of Booths, Sukkot, reminds Jews of their days wandering in the desert before entering the holy land. Hanukkah, the eight-day winter celebration, commemorates the rededication of the temple during the Maccabean period. Purim recalls the time when Esther, the Jewish queen of Persia, saved her people from genocide at the hands of Haman, the corrupt minister of the Persian king. Passover, or Pesach, recalls the Jewish exodus from slavery in Egypt and symbolizes liberation.

In each of these commemorations, one should not imagine that devout Jews merely look back at something that God or their ancestors did and celebrate it as part of their history. The purpose of these celebrations and the meanings they confer are much deeper: Rosh Hashanah, while happy and festive, brings people to recognize themselves as creatures before their creator. In Sukkot, many Jews stay outside over the entire night in order to experience their sense of dependence on God. They sleep in a semi-open hut, without the comforts and security of normal life. While these celebrations are festive and ground Jewish identity in its sacred history, they are also meant to be personally transformative by collapsing time between past, present, and future. Passover is the clearest example of this kind of temporal fusion.

Passover begins with the Seder supper, at which Jews eat a number of highly symbolic foods such as unleavened bread (*matzot*), which takes them back to the Exodus event; bitter herbs (*maror*), which remind them of bitter slavery; chopped nuts and fruits (*charoset*), symbolizing the mortar they were compelled to make by their Egyptian taskmasters; and a bone (*z'roa*), which is left on the plate as a symbol of God's mighty hand. By chewing the bitter herbs, for example, one's palate sympathetically recognizes the bitterness being recalled. It becomes one instance of a symbolic anamnesis of the original event. *Anamnesis* is a technical term in sacred ritual. It literally means, "remembering." However, at a Seder, the term does not mean "recalling something"; rather it "re-members," that is, it connects one's membership or identity with the past. Anamnesis in ritual is for the purpose of mimesis, which is to embody the original event and make its meaning part of oneself. The experience of Passover is to reenter symbolically into the original event in order to experience the saving power of God. At one point in the Seder ritual, a participant says the following:

> It therefore becomes the sacred obligation of every parent to be a teacher—to teach his children the meaning of freedom, so that it will be learned anew. As it is written: "On that day shalt thou teach my son, saying, 'It is because of this [pointing to the symbols on the table] that God delivered me from Egypt.'" Because of *pesach*, *matzot*, and *maror* did redemption come to us. Not only our fathers alone did God redeem from Egypt! We too were redeemed; we too were with them in spirit. Each of us, living today, is a beneficiary of the struggle and salvation of ages gone by. [The leader responds:] In every generation, it is the duty of each of us to imagine that it is we—we ourselves—who are saved from the bondage of Egypt. For it is written: "And thou shalt tell my son on that day; it is because of what the Lord did for me when I came forth from Egypt." Not only our forefathers did the Only One, Blessed be he, redeem. He liberated us along with them. . . . Passover becomes real only when it is personal; freedom becomes real only when we identify ourselves with it and strive to spread its fruit to all people, everywhere.
>
> —Alfred Kolatch, *The Family Seder*, 53–54

In these and many other words, those who celebrate the Passover identify with their ancestors who experienced God's saving power. In doing so, they too experience God's liberating blessings. The Seder supper concludes by making this point vivid. All the participants proclaim: "May this festival of freedom infuse us with a new appreciation for all the blessings of mind and spirit which Thou has bestowed on us" (ibid., 97).

Even as the past and present unite during the Seder supper, so too does the future. At every Seder table, an additional place is set for Elijah. In 2 Kings 2:11–12, Elijah does not die but is taken in a chariot to heaven. The prophet Malachi predicted that he would return during the final days of complete universal restoration and deliverance (Malachi 4:5). Toward the end of the Seder, Elijah's cup is filled, and the door of the house is opened to welcome him. After the door is opened, all participants recite an expression of divine wrath on those who oppress others and then say: "Thy kingdom will yet shine. Elijah the prophet . . . may he soon come, soon in our day, with the Messiah—son of David" (Kolatch, 77). Making room for Elijah, and opening the door for his entrance, ritually opens the hearts of those gathered to God's plans. It directs the participants to see where divine history is going and how they might avail themselves to it and participate in its arrival.

Christian Reflection

Sabbath and Time

Christians too are called to embrace Sabbath piety and celebrate a day consecrated to the Lord. Christians have always been less strict than Jews. Jesus said, "the Sabbath was made for man and not man for the Sabbath" (Mark 2:27). Sunday was also a workday for Christians in the first several centuries. This is not to suggest, however, that for Christians the Sabbath or Lord's Day should not be particularly devout. The *Catechism of the Catholic Church* reflects what most Christians believe: "Because it is the 'first day,' the day of Christ's resurrection recalls the first creation. Because it is the 'eighth day' following the Sabbath, it symbolizes the new creation ushered in by Christ's resurrection. For Christians it has become the first of all days, the first of all feasts, the Lord's Day" (*CCC*, no. 2174).

Most Christian communities insist on the importance of attending Church services. Catholics are specifically charged with participating in the **Eucharist** (Mass). The *Catechism* reads, "On Sundays . . . the faithful are to refrain from engaging in work or activities that hinder the worship owed to God, the joy proper to the Lord's Day, the performance of works of mercy, and the appropriate relaxation of mind and body" (*CCC*, no. 2185). Most Christian communities also teach that it is a day of rest. Fewer and fewer Christians, however, observe Sunday as such. Only about a third of Christians who belong to a Church community attend services, and even among those who do worship regularly, many feel no hesitation to shop, work on their yard, or even engage in their regular employment. Of course, it is easy to romanticize Judaism as if all observant Jews embraced the Sabbath as groom to bride. Still, the Jewish witness is profound and well exceeds Christian practice.

The Christian tradition is replete with witnessing to the virtues of contemplation and simply resting in the Lord. Traditionally, this insight is reflected by comparing Martha to Mary in the Gospel according to Luke. While Martha was preparing to feed Jesus and his disciples, her sister Mary simply sat at his feet, absorbed by his words. When Martha complained to Jesus, he told her, "Martha, Martha, you are worried and distracted about many things; there is need of only one thing. Mary has chosen the better part" (Luke 10:38–42).

Contemplation need not be restricted to a monastic absorbed in prayer, for it expresses a posture of quiet receptivity, a way of allowing the mystery of life and the sacred to reveal itself. One might also say that westerners are afraid of leisure. Most people love time off. However, not much observation is required to see that they go from one set of stimuli to another, from one distraction to the next. In *Leisure, the Basis of Culture*, philosopher Joseph Pieper recognized in the 1940s that western culture had already lost its sense of leisure. He argued that from leisure one gains perspective and creativity. Without cultivating the art of leisure, he predicted many decades ago, the West would become a prisoner of technology, of mindless expansion of dehumanizing work, and of an ironic boredom in the midst of many entertainment venues.

Festivals and Time

As stated previously, extraordinary interplay exists with past, present, and future time in the celebration of Passover—particularly in the Seder meal. Rituals do this; they make a representation of the original sacred event and allow worshippers to enter the depth of that event. Through sacred symbols, those who live today enter into the spiritual dynamic that they are celebrating. In this sense, symbols no longer merely point to a sacred reality. They become, instead, the means to engage that same reality now. Rituals become instantiations or embodiments of that original saving event. Past and present blur when one encounters the eternal life of God and his saving grace.

The great Christian celebration of Eucharist is the classic example. As Jesus' earthly ministry comes to a close, he draws his disciples together. The Synoptic Gospels (Matthew, Mark, and Luke) state that the most sacred Seder meal becomes Jesus' forum. In the context of celebrating the Passover and encountering the liberating grace of God, Jesus announces the long-awaited new and eternal covenant. However, this new covenant is not simply about being saved from oppression, as profound as that is. It is about being freed from what ultimately binds the human condition: sin and death. Thus, Jesus takes bread and breaks it, identifying his body with the broken loaf. He takes wine and identifies this with his blood. In doing so, he is also anticipating his sacrifice on the cross the very next day. He becomes both the priest offering the sacrifice and the sacrificial victim offered to God (Hebrews 9:11–14). As sacrifice, he ratifies the new covenant and acts as a perfect atonement offering to God. He overcomes sin and death and ushers in the victorious kingdom. Finally, he tells his disciples to eat the bread and drink from the cup—his body and blood. In so doing, they are communing with Christ and participating with the sacrifice he will offer. That is, in uniting with Christ, his disciples are implicated in his offering as they must follow his way and offer themselves (Matthew 10:38; 16:25; Mark 8:34; Luke 17:33; John 12:25).

What about the Eucharist today? As stated previously, there are numerous themes and various layers of meaning. This is particularly the case for Eastern Orthodox and Roman Catholics. For them and other Christians, such layering includes the Last Supper, the Crucifixion, the Resurrection, the nature of the Christian life, communion with Christ, and the future fulfillment of that life in heaven. Because the Eucharist celebrates the salvation of God in Christ, it involves all these layers, and they mutually implicate each other. Christians gather, like Christ and his disciples at the Last Supper, to celebrate and encounter the saving power of God. They enter into the very

A minister elevates the Communion host. For Christians, the Eucharist celebrates the salvation of God in Christ.

dynamics of the Crucifixion when Christ offered himself for all people. Like the Seder meal and many sacred rites, it is an anamnesis, a re-membering that intends to be a mimesis, an embodiment of the original event. Thus, Catholics call part of the central dynamics of the Eucharist the "sacrifice of the Mass." This celebration of the Eucharist is not to suggest re-sacrificing Jesus every Sunday, as he died once and for all (Hebrews 7:27). Rather, the Eucharist enters into and embodies the reality of that original sacrifice and, thus, mediates its saving grace.

In the Eucharist, Christians celebrate the wedding feast of the kingdom of God. The celebration is a foretaste of heavenly union with God, as well as a real uniting here and now. Christians rejoice and ritually experience the saving power of God in Jesus Christ. They also enter into the dynamics of the cross, the sacrifice that brings salvation to the world. The new and eternal covenant of love is founded on the death of Christ and to take communion is both to commune with Christ and to accept the conditions of his covenant in order to make a complete offering of self to the Father as Jesus did. This is what it means for Christians to participate in the Eucharist.

TORAH STUDY: AN INTERSECTION BETWEEN TIME AND SPACE

Torah as Divine Wisdom

The Sabbath grounds Jewish spirituality with a sense of time, a way of being present. As shall be shown, sacred deeds (***mitzvoth***) express the way for Jews to negotiate space or the world. Study of Torah represents the intersection between the two. For Jews, studying Torah is the most important religious exercise. When the Romans destroyed the physical temple in 70 CE, Judaism still affirmed that the sacred could be experienced in the spiritual temple of Torah. Torah represents the primary symbol of Judaism. It is the revelation of God and is the tangible expression of the love and intimacy shared between God and the Jewish people. Torah has even been anthropomorphized:

> Human beings are so confused in their minds! They do not see the way of truth in Torah. Torah calls out to them every day, in love, but they do not want to turn their heads. . . . She reveals herself to no one but her lover. Torah knows that he who is wise of heart hovers about her

TORAH

The word *Torah* can be translated to mean "law." It represents God's specific ordinances, traditionally 613, and also can be understood collectively as the first five books of the Old Testament. In this latter sense, the entire Hebrew Bible, or Old Testament, is understood by Jews as the *Tenakh*, which is an acronym for *Torah* (Law), *Nevi'im* (Prophets), and *Khetuvim* (Writings). *Torah* can also refer to the "oral law," which includes authoritative reflections and interpretations of Jewish life and law in the Mishnah and Talmud. Finally, *Torah* can mean "way," or "teaching," and is understood to refer to the sum total of the Jewish spiritual character.

gate every day. What does she do? She reveals her face to
him from the palace and beckons him with a hint, then
swiftly withdraws to her hiding place. No one who is
there knows or reflects; he alone does, and his heart and
his soul and everything within him flows out to her. That
is why Torah reveals and conceals herself.

—Moses de Léon, *Zohar*, 123–124

This quote shows resonance between Torah and biblical Wisdom, which acts as an expression and mediation of God (Proverbs
1:20–33, 8:22–18). In these biblical texts, wisdom is also personified
as a woman who invites the wise to dine with her and to learn her
secrets. The challenge is that one has to love her and seek her for her
own sake. A pious Jew follows Torah because it is Torah.

Torah as the Structure of the Compassionate Universe

Torah, and submission to it, also has cosmological significance.
Torah, among many of its meanings, refers to God's law, and
according to tradition, there are 613 laws in the first five books of
the Hebrew Bible, a collection that Jews also refer to as the Torah.
They did not come up with this number by counting distinct commands throughout the Torah. Rather, the number has a symbolic
function. Rabbi Hammuna, third-century CE, argued that the
613 represented the numerology associated with the word *Torah*:
tav = 400, *vav* = 6, *resh* = 200, and *hay* = 5, producing 611. The
remaining two laws are represented by monotheistic statements: "I
am the Lord, your God" and "You shall have no other gods before
me." Rabbi Simlai, a contemporary of Hammuna, arrived at 613 by
adding together the number of days in a solar year (365) and the
number of parts of the human body, which were believed to be 248.
These numbers aligned with the 365 prohibitions in the Torah, and
the 248 positive commandments.

For Jews, to investigate the Torah is to enter into the divine
mystery. The biblical texts and subsequent commentary are understood to be many layered. There is no sense that the text is static and
has only one meaning or even several meanings. Its possibilities for

deeper engagement are inexhaustible. To interpret the text, to work the text, is to encounter deeper levels of revelation as God reveals himself more profoundly to the soul.

The Jewish tradition is famous for arguments between its members over the meaning of a biblical or commentarial text. To an outsider, these arguments appear to be confrontational, even raucous. Dialogue partners push themselves and each other toward deeper insight. If one partner becomes stuck or appears to have lost the argument, the other typically takes the opposing side, entering into the other frame of reference to see how the position might more deeply proceed. The process is called *l'shaym shamayim*, argument for the sake of heaven.

God expects and in fact desires such arguments about the Torah, and they have even cosmic significance. The Zohar, one of the greatest books of Torah commentary and Jewish mysticism, describes supernatural spirits who daily stand in the presence of God. On the Sabbath, they leave heaven and enter Earth to learn more about the Torah from those studying it. At the end of the Sabbath, they return to heaven, and God asks them what new insights they learned about Torah. It is considered a spiritual scandal if they remain silent and have nothing additional to relate.

Christian Reflection

From the patristic period to today, Christianity has emphasized the importance of doctrine. Whether Christ's divine nature is the same as the Father's (*homoousia*), or virtually the same (*homoiousia*), or whether both Jesus' divine and human natures has a will—answers to these questions distinguish authentic from heretical Christianity. In contrast, Jews accept an enormous latitude of beliefs. One Jew could believe in reincarnation; another, in resurrection from the dead; and still another, in no afterlife at all. All three Jews could be friends and respected members of the same synagogue.

For Christians, many core beliefs are nonnegotiable. For Jews, little is nonnegotiable. What is ironic is that most Christians have little knowledge of their faith and even less of the Bible. Indeed, many Christians are, by Christianity's own assessment, heretics. Some see Jesus as vaguely or only seemingly human, but really God (Docetism).

Others imagine Jesus as like God but less than God (Arianism). Still others believe that the divine and human natures fused into a hybrid person (Monophysitism), and so on. How many Christians really have all these dogmas right? According to the latest sociological data, adolescent and young-adult Christians are woefully ignorant of even the basics of their faith. Among them, Roman Catholics are the least knowledgeable, while Evangelicals are the most.

Torah study assumes that there are layers and layers of revelation in the text. Jews are not afraid of engaging deeper and harder questions so that they can evermore penetrate that revelation. They are not looking for only one answer. Instead, study is a form of religious exercise and experience. For Jews, pursuing the questions themselves brings them closer to God, while being satisfied with a definitive answer can create a self-satisfied trap, a static religious life. Jewish witness to Christians is that finding a definitive answer is less important than encountering God in pursuit of wisdom. Saint Jerome echoed this belief in his dictum: "Ignorance of the Bible is ignorance of Christ."

JEWISH VISION OF SPACE
Torah in Action

Judaism has little dogma and certainly no agreed upon catalogue of beliefs. Rather it is organized around *mitzvot,* or sacred deeds. *Mitzvot* involves following laws, such as observing the Sabbath in specific ways, tithing, and so on. It is also an expression that describes a holy action. As shown in chapter three, the Kabbalistic tradition imagines the world being created through the *sefirot* pattern. This pattern emerged from God and was the manifestation of him. Once this pattern emerged, it could never be completely distinct from the divine identity. While God is *Eyn-Sof* (Absolute Transcendence), the *sefirot* became an extension of God and is the pattern of the spiritual substructure of creation. According to the influential Lurianic tradition, God self-contracted (*zimzum*) in order to make space for creation. In contracting, God's light remained as his immanent, underlying presence in creation. This light then filled the *sefirot* vessels. The first three of the ten *sefirot* were able to retain the divine light. However, the next six *sefirot* burst (*shevirat ha-kelim*). The final *sefirah*, representing both Earth and the Jewish people, was cracked but did not break. Most of the divine sparks of this supernal light returned to the Godhead, but some were trapped in the fragments of the burst vessels. The order of creation and the possibility for life and love come from these divine sparks. That the world is also disordered, especially morally, reflects the breakup of the *sefirot* pattern in the created universe. Repair (*tiqqun*) is the challenge of devout humans, Jews and non-Jews alike.

When humanity sins, these divine sparks become increasingly stuck in the world and can even be used as spiritual energy for evil, as evil is a disorder of good. When humans act with compassion and love, they repair the broken vessels and contribute to the spiritual order in the universe. For many Jews, the task of humanity, until the coming of the Messiah, is to raise the divine sparks and restore them to their appropriate place in the divine realm. This process will come to its final conclusion in the Messianic Age.

What is most fascinating about this cosmic theory is that once God created anything outside of himself, God became vulnerable to that reality. The *sefirot* structure is not the same as God himself (*Eyn-Sof*), but God cannot be separated from this order either and, thus, is affected by it. In some way, God became attached to his manifestation and, in this sense, was wounded in creation. Thus, the process of repair is a way to love and heal God (or at least God's countenance). If asked, most rabbis—even those who are sympathetic to Kabbalah—would not fully embrace the idea that performing *mitzvot* heals a bleeding God. Still, many do describe the universe as filled with divine sparks, that humans participate in their return, and that God is, indeed, affected by human deeds.

Regardless of whether a given Jew embraces this exotic theory, it is widely believed in Judaism that the world is wounded and broken and that it is up to humanity, and particularly to Jews, to heal and repair it. Such healing and repairing comes through acts of justice and compassion. Rabbi Akiva, in response to the question on how to be holy, said that holiness is the imitation of God, who clothed the naked (Genesis 3:21), visited the sick (Genesis 18:1ff), comforted mourners (Genesis 25:11), and buried the dead (Deuteronomy 34:5–6). Do these, he commanded. Rabbi Simlai found an interesting way to consolidate the 613 laws according to the principles of justice and compassion. The following comes from the Talmud:

> David came and reduced them [the commandments] to eleven principles, which are listed in Psalm 15: "Lord, who shall sojourn in Your tabernacle? Who shall dwell on Your holy mountain? He who walks with integrity, and pursues righteousness, and speaks the truth in his heart, who does not slander with his tongue, who commits no evil against a fellow-human, who does not bring shame to a neighbor, who despises a vile person, but honors those who revere the Lord. If he takes an oath to his own heart, he does not change it; he takes no interest on a loan, and does not take a bribe against the innocent." Isaiah came and reduced them to six, as it is stated: "God's providential love will be extended to one who walks in the path of righteousness, and speaks uprightly, who despises profit gained by oppression, and spurns bribes, who avoids hearing violence, and shuns looking at evil" [Isaiah 33:15]. Micah reduced them to three: "What does the Lord require of you, but to do justly, to love mercy, and to walk humbly with your God" [Micah 6:8]. Isaiah subsequently reduced them to two: "Thus says the Lord, keep justice and do righteousness." (Isaiah 56:1)
>
> —cited in Baruch Bokser,
> *The Talmud*, 28

Hillel's famous response to the young man who wished to know the meaning of the Torah was quite apt. For Jews, the commandments of God, and indeed the way of God, are centered on justice and compassion. This is not particularly Jewish. Most religions recognize these qualities as fundamental. What is Jewish is how the qualities are lived in the Jewish spiritual horizon. All humans are called to heal and repair the world, Jews believe. All have a common origin and destiny. Judaism, by her laws and practices, makes her distinct from others. Such a distinction is to witness Torah to the world as a "light to the nations" (Isaiah 42:6). Many rabbis have explained that the sacrifices at the temple during the Feast of Tabernacles included seventy offerings to invoke God's grace for each of the seventy nations.

They also foresaw an era of universal peace. From the liturgy of the New Year (Rosh Hashanah), it is envisioned that the "kingdom of wickedness" will pass, and the entire human race will join to form "one fellowship to do the divine will with a perfect heart."

Christian Reflection

In terms of the focus on justice and compassion, a great resonance is sounded between Christians and Jews. One can easily imagine Jesus approving of Rabbi Hillel's golden rule, or imitation of God, as attending to the needy and, indeed, Rabbi Simlai's consolidation of the law to justice and righteousness. Jesus' version is his vision of the last judgment, which describes Jesus returning with all the angels, sitting on the throne of glory, and separating the righteous from the unrighteous. Those on Jesus' right are welcomed into his kingdom, because when he was hungry they fed him; thirsty, they gave him drink; a stranger, they welcomed him; naked, they clothed him; sick, they cared for him; and in prison, they visited him. They will ask when they did this, and his reply will be that whenever they did this for those least, they did it for him. Likewise, those on his left will be the ones who did not feed him when hungry, and so on. For ignoring "the least of these," they ignored him (Matthew 25:31–46).

Two things are particularly interesting in this vision: First, Jesus mentions nothing about having correct doctrine in order to become one of the righteous. Second, Jesus identifies with those in need. The text does not suggest that he will reckon service to others *as if* it were service to him. Rather, it was direct service to him. Like Jewish *mitzvot* piety, the spirituality of Christ is one of mercy, compassion, and justice. These themes dominate his description of what it means to be a Christian (Matthew 5:6–7, 9:13, 23:23; Mark 6:34; Luke 10:37). Paul likewise challenges Christians to embody the compassion of Christ (Philippians 1:8; Colossians 3:12).

If Jewish sensibilities can challenge Christianity, it is to remind Christians of what they theologically already claim, that justice can never be merely private acts of mercy. Often American Christians are among the most vocal supporters of policies that advance American political or economic interests at the expense of others. For example, 80 percent of white Evangelical Protestants supported the war in

Iraq even though broadly Protestant theology forbids preemptive war. Most Catholics—between 50 and 65 percent, depending on the poll—support the death penalty, even though Catholic moral teaching forbids it. The problem detailed above is one of privatized religion, in which the common good or justice initiatives are not attended to. According to Catholic teaching, service to the common good prolongs the work of God the Creator and contributes to the fulfillment of the divine plan. While humans are cautioned not to seek a utopia here on Earth, a commitment to justice foreshadows, anticipates, and in a mysterious way, participates in the final kingdom (*Church in the Modern World*, nos. 34, 38). This is widely affirmed by other Christian communities.

Christians do not imagine divine sparks trapped in creation or a bleeding God who in some way needs humans to repair the super-natural *sefirot* substructure of the universe. However, along with Jews, Christians do recognize that the world is quite broken. Further, Jews and Christians alike recognize that their spiritual response ought to be grounded in justice, compassion, and love.

Review Questions

1. Both Rabbis Shammai and Hillel answered the young potential convert well even though one hit him and the other inspired him to convert. What insights did they provide regarding Jewish identity and essence?

2. What are the various points of alignment between the Sabbath and heaven?

3. Jewish ritual intends to unite past, present, and future—particularly during Passover. How is the Seder supper structured to do this?

4. *Torah* is a complex term in Judaism. What are its various meanings and how do devout Jews express Torah faithfulness?

In-Depth Questions

1. What if Christians were to embrace the Lord's Day with the same intentionality as one finds in the Jewish tradition? Would they be happier? Holier? Would their lives be more purposeful and have greater clarity and direction?
2. Because Christians believe that the Bible is inspired by God for spiritual development (2 Timothy 3:16) and reveals the Word through whom the universe was made and who enlightens believers (John 1:1–5), why do the vast majority of Christians fail to read it, study it, and pray with it regularly?
3. Many Jews believe that they affect God in some way by their works of justice and compassion. Do you believe that this is the case? What are the implications (metaphysical and otherwise) for such a position?

Select Bibliography

Barton, Stephen, ed. *Holiness: Past and Present*. London: T & T Clark, 2003. This text offers a variety of biblical themes regarding holiness. It also provides traditions of holiness representing various Christian traditions.

Bokser, Baruch, trans. and ed. *The Talmud*. Mahwah, NJ: Paulist Press, 1989.

Catechism of the Catholic Church. New York: Doubleday, 2003.

Green, Arthur, ed. *Jewish Spirituality*. Vol. 2. New York: Crossroad, 1987.

———. *Jewish Spirituality*. Vol. 1. New York: Crossroad, 1986.

Heschel, Abraham Joshua. *The Sabbath*. New York: Farrar, Straus, and Giroux, 1951. This text is a classic in understanding the theological and mystical tradition regarding the Sabbath.

Holtz, Barry, ed. *Back to the Sources: Reading the Classic Jewish Text*. New York: Simon & Schuster, 1984. An excellent study of central, important traditions in Judaism, it is one of the finest single books on the Jewish religious character.

Kolatch, Alfred, ed. *The Family Seder: A Traditional Passover for the Modern Home*. New York: Jonathan David Publishers, 1967.

Kushner, Lawrence. *Honey from the Rock: An Introduction to Jewish Mysticism*, 2nd ed. Woodstock, VT: Jewish Lights, 2000. Kushner shows how modern Jews have appropriated Kabbalah, Hasidism, and Talmudic spiritual traditions.

———. *God Was in This Place & I, I Did Not Know*. Woodstock, VT: Jewish Lights, 1994.

Leon, Moses de. *Zohar: The Book of Enlightenment*. Daniel Chanan Matt, trans. Mahwah, NJ: Paulist Press, 1983.

Montefiore, C. G., and H. Loewe, eds. *A Rabbinic Anthology*. New York: Schocken Books, 1974.

Pieper, Joseph. *Leisure, the Basis of Culture*. Gerald Malsbary, trans. South Bend, IN: St. Augustine's Press, 1998.

CHAPTER FIVE

Islam

The Surrendering Soul

WHAT MAKES A MUSLIM?

> In the name of God the Compassionate, the Merciful
> Praise be to God, Lord of the Universe,
> The Compassionate, the Merciful,
> Sovereign of the Day of Judgment!
> You alone we worship, and to You alone we turn for help.
> Guide us to the straight path,
> The path of those whom you have favored,
> Not of those who have incurred Your wrath,
> Nor of those who have gone astray.
>
> —Qur'an, Sura 1

The above text is the first chapter of the Qur'an and is known as the *Al-Fatihah* (The Opening). It begins every one of the five formal prayer periods during each day. The Opening is a grounding text for the soul of devout Muslims. Who is God? God is the Compassionate, the Merciful, the Sovereign. What does a Muslim seek from God? A Muslim seeks the grace to follow the straight path, the one God has already lain out. The word *Islam* means "surrender" or "submission" to God. This surrender is the principal act of faith. Interestingly, the opposite of faith is not doubt in Islam. Rather the term is *jahil*, which represents someone arrogant and quick-tempered. This is someone who has surrendered not to God but to one's passions, to one's ego. Islam provides a structure, a straight path, to ground one's soul in this life, and to assure one's destiny in the next. The straight path has **five pillars**:

1. Confession of faith (*Shahadah*)
2. Prayer (*Salat*)
3. Charity (*Zakat*)
4. Ramadan (*Sawm*)
5. Pilgrimage (*Hajj*)

This straight path includes basic theological tenets and moral standards. Theological tenets involve belief in such things as God's absolute will, the Day of Judgment, the Qur'an, and the Prophet. Moral precepts include abstaining from such things as pork, alcohol, and gambling. The pillars are understood as multilayered.

Confession of faith: The first pillar is simply the overt declaration that "there is no God but God and Muhammad is his Prophet." Muslims would call this the "witness with words." More important is the "witness with the body," that is, with one's acts of justice and generosity. Finally, there is the "witness of the heart," which represents true transformation. One does not simply act justly, but one's heart has become compassionate.

Prayer: Prayer, likewise, is multilayered. On the surface, it is a gathering to praise God five times a day. As shown in the following, its depth moves the devout Muslim to know something about experiencing Muhammad's original revelation and ascent to heaven.

Charity: The third pillar represents a yearly alms-tax of 2.5 percent of one's wealth. Interestingly, the Arabic term is *zakat*, which literally means "purification." *Zakat* is only superficially satisfied when one honestly assesses one's worth and gives the tax for the support of those in need. *Zakat* also requires generosity with one's time in volunteerism, support of one's family members in need, and helping those who have great want. One does not fulfill *zakat* until one's heart is purified from greed.

Ramadan: During this month Muhammad first received revelations, and during the same month many years later, he made his historic flight or migration (*hijrah*) from Mecca to Yathrib (Medina). Muslims celebrate Ramadan with rigid fasting, even from water, during the daylight hours. To just observe this pillar is daunting enough, but to really embrace Ramadan is to recognize the opportunity to identify with Muhammad's plight on behalf of God's mission. Ramadan represents a kind of monthlong retreat to promote greater devotion. It is a pillar that bonds Muslims as they collectively strive in this discipline.

Pilgrimage: Finally, all healthy Muslims who can afford to are expected to make a *hajj* to Mecca. In the *hajj*, all trappings of social status are stripped away. The pilgrim relies on nothing but faith, one's submission. The experience marks the Muslim for life, and for many, the *hajj* is the highlight of their life.

Muslims get ready to pray at Haram Mosque, Saudi Arabia, facing the Kaaba during hajj season in late 2007. Non-Muslims are not allowed to enter Haram Mosque or Mecca.

Religions have principles or root metaphors that ground their spiritual energy and religious imagination. The very name of a Muslim's religion says a great deal: *Islam*. To submit is to recognize that God places demands on one. More profoundly, one surrenders one's life and destiny into God's hands. This also is the witness of Muhammad.

MUHAMMAD AND THE HUMAN CONDITION
Muhammad (570–632 CE)

Muhammad, whose given name can be translated as "the highly praised one," is so important to Islam that he is often said to be a living Qur'an, the witness whose words and behavior reveal God's will. His actions and teachings, called *sunnah* ("trodden path" or "example"), are extraordinarily influential. Muslims take Muhammad's examples, or the principles that underlie them, and apply them analogically in the present. These very examples have become precedents that ground Islamic law (*shari'a*).

Much of what is known about Muhammad comes from the Qur'an. Some knowledge additionally comes from biographies written much later and based on oral tradition. The biography by Muhammad Ibn Ishaq (d. 768) is most generally accepted. While some of Ishaq's claims seem stretched—he asserts that Muhammad satisfied nine wives in one night!—the vast majority of the biography is accepted as a general outline by scholars and historians. Muhammad seemed to do everything well. As a warrior, he was brave, just, and never the aggressor. As a prophet, he was bold, fearless, and long-suffering in the midst of many years of rejection and persecution. As a statesman, he succeeded in uniting contentious factions into a cohesive, well-functioning city of Yathrib, later known as Medina al-Nabi (City of the Prophet). Muhammad also dramatically transformed the morally corrupt city of Mecca into a center of pilgrimage for the worship and service of the one God. Finally, as an administrator, he showed himself a tireless servant who lived modestly and made himself available to those who sought his service.

Above all, Muhammad was a man of prayer. His life of prayer is perhaps his greatest witness to his vocation; surely, it provided the

ISLAM AND WAR

To imagine that Islam is a warring religion is simply false, both theologically and historically. This is not, however, to suggest that it has nothing to do with war or violence. Muhammad led battles, and early Islam spread through the help of military conquest. Further, there are passages in the Qur'an that support fighting against one's enemies, emphasizing also that such a fight must be defensive: "Defend yourself against your enemies, but do not attack them first: God hates the aggressor" (Qur'an 2:190). Following Muhammad's example, Islam embraces a just war policy virtually identical to that of the Christian tradition. In Islam, violence is only acceptable when (1) the cause is just, (2) it protects public order, (3) it is proportionate to the injustice it addresses, (4) it is the last resort, (5) it is likely to succeed, (6) it would result in lasting peace, (7) it would never directly intend killing noncombatants, and (8) it would never include treachery or dishonor, e.g., agreeing to a treaty while intending to break it.

context for his reception of the Qur'an. Muhammad spent his childhood minding his uncle's flocks. This gave him a great deal of time to be alone and thoughtful. As a child, he had a reputation for being devout. When Muhammad reached adulthood, a widow named Khadijah employed him as leader of her caravan business. Later, Muhammad married Khadijah. The life of trade and travel gave him the opportunity to meet religiously serious Jews and Christians, particularly monks who led lives of contemplation. When Muhammad was home, he spent many nights alone in solitary prayer, particularly on the top of Jable Nur (Mountain of Light), a few miles north of Mecca.

In 610, on the Night of Power and Excellence, Muhammad was in a cave on Jable Nur when an angel, whom he realized was Gabriel, commanded "*Iqra!*" which is, literally, *recite*. Muhammad did not know what to recite. Gabriel then said, "Proclaim in the name of your Lord who created! Created man from a clot of blood. Proclaim: Your Lord is Most Generous, Who teaches by the pen; teaches man what he knew not" (Qur'an 96:1–3). Muhammad received messages from Gabriel for the next twenty-three years. At times, receiving these messages was agonizing. Muhammad was often seized with violent shuddering, and his experiences frequently left him covered with sweat and exhausted. Often they came when he least expected it, and sometimes the messages contradicted his personal judgments. Another striking thing about these experiences is that Muhammad could remember them infallibly for the rest of his life. In chapter two, mystical experiences are described as non-normal states of consciousness, deeply humbling, seared into memory, and irresistible. Muhammad's experiences shared these characteristics. Muslims accept the divine source of the revelations to Muhammad without question, and the vast majority believe that Muhammad received these without any internal filter. That is, the messages had nothing to do with Muhammad's subjectivity or personal consciousness. He simply received and conveyed the content of an eternal Qur'an.

In Muhammad's most famous mystical experience, he was taken body and soul from Mecca to the temple mount of Jerusalem. The event is called *Laylat al-mi'raj*, or the Night of Ascension. From the temple mount, he entered a kind of access realm into the spirit world. He first witnessed hell and the suffering of its inhabitants. Then, with the help of Gabriel, he ascended toward the Divine Presence. Along the way, he met previous apostles and prophets and even saw paradise. In seeking and finding the face of the Lord, Muhammad expresses humanity's highest possibilities, which are to see and know God. Doing so is what makes humans superior even over the angels. In fact, although Gabriel helped Muhammad approach the divine throne, the angel had to withdraw before seeing the throne itself, the splendor of which would have been too much for him. Al-Suyuti's famous account of Muhammad's encounter with God shows one traditional telling:

> Now when I was brought on my Night Journey to the place of the Throne and drew near to it, a green *rafraf* [brocade] was let down to me, a thing too beautiful for me to describe to you, whereat Gabriel advanced and seated me on it. Then

he had to withdraw from me, placing his hands over his eyes, fearing lest his sight be destroyed by the scintillating light of the Throne. . . . By Allah's leave, as a sign of His mercy toward me and the perfection of His favor to me, that *rafraf* floated me into the presence of the Lord of the Throne, a thing too stupendous for the tongue to tell of or imagination to picture. My sight was so dazzled by it that I feared blindness. Therefore, I shut my eyes, which was by Allah's good favor. When I thus veiled my sight, Allah shifted my sight to my heart, so with my heart I began to look at what I had been looking at with my eyes. It was a light so bright in its scintillation that I despair of ever describing to you what I saw of His majesty. Then I besought my Lord to complete His favor by granting me the boon of having a steadfast vision of Him with my heart. This my Lord did, giving me a favor, so I gazed at Him with my heart till it was steady and I had a steady vision of Him. There he was, when the veil had been lifted from Him, seated on His Throne, in His dignity, His might, His glory, His exaltedness, but beyond that is not permitted me to describe Him to you. . . .

— cited in Seyyed Hossein Nasr,
Islamic Spirituality I, 78–80

This account is but one of Muhammad's *al-mi'raj*, and it is understood that such anthropomorphisms as God being "seated on His Throne" is but imagery for an experience that is beyond words or concepts. The account continues with a much longer dialogue about how God has favored Muhammad as he favored Abraham, Moses, and other prophets.

Dyed in the Dye of Allah

While God placed Muhammad in an exalted position, Islam understands Muhammad as an exemplar of the entire human race. He was charged to submit, and he submitted, just as all humans ought to. He was placed before the divine throne just as all humans are in daily prayer and hope for eternity. Something in human dignity is spiritually charged and reflects divinity itself. A traditional Islamic saying goes, "We are dyed in the dye of Allah." Such a rich metaphor imagines that a human's truest self is immersed in divine truth. While angels are made of pure spirit and have daunting power and knowledge compared to that of humans, Islam holds that humans are superior. There is something utterly transcendent in us that other creatures, even angels, do not have. God declares, "We have created humanity of the best stature" (Qur'an 95:4). The Muslim tradition states that after God created Adam, he said, "Now remember My favors to you, for I have made you the masterpiece of My creation, fashioned you a man according to My will, breathed into you of My spirit, made My angels do obeisance to you and carry you on their shoulders, made you a preacher to them, loosened your tongue to all languages. . . . All this I have done for you as glory and honor . . ." (cited in Arthur Jeffery, *A Reader on Islam*, 187).

The Christian tradition generally holds that Satan was a great archangel who refused to bow to God. He and his followers were then banished from heaven and became positively antagonistic to God. Islam also imagines a heavenly revolt. In this case Satan—the Qur'an also calls him Iblis—did not refuse to bow down to God but did so most readily. However, after God created Adam and Eve, he told Satan to bow down to them. The idea of prostrating himself before mere humans was inconceivable to Satan, who in Islam is not an angel but a spiritual being created out of fire. Satan refused and was then banished.

Actually, Islam holds that before any creation happened, angelic or otherwise, a part of every human soul dwelt in a divine assembly. God rhetorically asked these souls, "Am I not your Lord?" All most clearly and happily conceded he is. Thus, from the beginning of time, all souls knew God as absolute truth, even before humans were fully created as "dyed in the dye of Allah." Given this history, everyone is expected to have the capacity to know and follow God in one's now fully human life. If there is a kind of **original sin** in Islam, it is that humans have forgotten what they knew prehistorically. Islam calls humans to remember what they already know deep down.

The usual Arabic word for what is right is *al-ma'ruf* (known) and for what is wrong is *al-munkar* (unknown). One passage in the Qur'an reads, "You are indeed the best community that has ever been brought forth for the good of humanity; you enjoy doing what is right [*al-ma'ruf*—known] and you forbid doing what is wrong [*al-munkar*—unknown]" (3:110). One can also see this perspective in the word for *unbelief* (*kuffar*), which has the etymology of "covering over something." Not to believe the truth is to cover over it. For if the truth were not covered, it would naturally reveal itself; it would be easy to recognize.

Christian Reflection
Christian Anthropology

Christians, like Muslims, also believe that there is something extraordinary about being human, even more so than being angelic. Humans, not angels, are created in the image and likeness of God (Genesis 1:26). The Letter to the Hebrews makes this clear as well. Not only is Christ superior to the angels (Hebrews 1:4ff), so also are humans (Hebrews 2:5–8).

Christians do not believe in the preexistence of souls, but they do accept that the soul recognizes God's voice as the truth. Catholicism, for example, teaches, "Deep within his conscience man discovers a law which he has not laid upon himself but which he must obey. . . . For man has in his heart a law inscribed by God. His dignity lies in observing this law, and by it, he will be judged. His conscience is man's most secret core, and his sanctuary. There he is alone with God, whose voice echoes in his depths" (*Church in the Modern World*, no. 16).

Unlike Muslims, Christians believe in original sin, which posits that something is profoundly, structurally disordered about the soul due to Adam and Eve's first sin. Yet, what would happen if a Christian listened to the Islamic insistence that the primary reason one sins is that one forgets who is Lord? In his *Confessions*, Augustine addresses the issue of memory. One might paraphrase Augustine this way: If you do not know something but are looking to discover it, how will you know it when you find it? If you know something already, why are you looking for it? With regard to God, Augustine realized that he already knew God because God was present to his soul from the beginning. "I have found you not outside my memory, but in my memory" (10.24); "Where did I find you to be able to learn of you were you not already in my memory before I learned of you?" (10.26).

Augustine anticipates Islam's great insight, which is that deep down God has already drawn humanity to himself. The deeper one enters into one's consciousness, the closer one comes to recognizing a presence that is already abiding and a voice that has already spoken. Christianity insists, with the doctrine of original sin, that there is something truly disordered about the human soul. The apostle Paul calls himself a "slave to the law of sin" (Romans 7:25) and, thus, in need of Christ. For Christians, sin is no mere forgetting. On the other hand, Islam invites Christians to attend to their deepest self, their deepest truth. "Am I not your Lord?" God asks. Islamic wisdom says one need only remember this.

Mystical Authority

In chapter two, one read that deep, long-term spiritual development creates the conditions for the possibility of a mystical life. The principle of *quidquid recipitur per modem recipientis recipitur* (whatever is received is received according to the mode of the receiver) was also discussed. Religious experience comes through the preparation, posture, and religious sensibilities of the person experiencing God. One can imagine Muhammad sitting on Jable Nur in vigil through many long nights. He was contemplative, night after night, year after year, sitting before God in loving receptivity. One can also easily imagine that throughout this time he faced Jerusalem, all the while longing, waiting, and quietly adoring God. It is due to such a soul's preparation that God draws one to himself via Jerusalem. Many of the images found in Muhammad's experience align classical, mystical literature from the Bible and other spiritual texts. The prophet Ezekiel is taken into a heavenly abode, dazzling and awesome, and encounters the glory of the Lord (Ezekiel 1:4–28). Isaiah too is taken before the divine presence and appears to have been allowed to see not only God's glory, but also God himself on his throne (Isaiah 6:1–13). In First Enoch, an important mystical and apocalyptic text of Jesus' day, one finds Enoch's experience dramatically like Muhammad's:

> And I observed and saw inside a lofty throne . . . and from beneath the throne were issuing streams of flaming fire. It was difficult to look at it. And the Great Glory was sitting upon it. . . . None of the angels was able to come in and

see the face of the Excellent and Glorious One; and no one
of the flesh can see him. . . . I was prostrate on my face
covered and trembling. And the Lord called me with his
own mouth and said to me, "Come near to me, Enoch . . ."
and he lifted me up and brought me near to the gate, but I
continued to look down with my face.

—1 Enoch 14:8–25

Mystical experiences were as formative for Paul as mystical experiences were for Muhammad. Paul speaks in the third person, though
it is obvious that he refers to himself:

I will go on to visions and revelations of the Lord. I know a
person in Christ who fourteen years ago was caught up to
the third heaven—whether in the body or out of the body I
do not know; God knows. And I know that such a person—
whether in the body or out of the body I do not know; God
knows—was caught up into Paradise and heard things that
are not to be told, that no mortal is permitted to repeat.

—2 Corinthians 12:1–4

Direct, mystical knowledge of God seems crucial to Paul's sense of
divine authorization, and he refers to this mystical experience to
defend that authority. Consider, "the gospel that was proclaimed
by me is not of human origin . . . I received it through a revelation of Jesus Christ" (Galatians 1:11–12) and "Am I not an apostle?
Have I not seen Jesus our Lord?" (1 Corinthians 9:1). In two other
places, Paul describes direct encounters with the risen Christ (2
Corinthians 12:1–10; Acts 22:17–21). These encounters give him
a divinely conferred authority. The dynamic reflects the Jewish
mystical milieu from which Paul writes: the ascent into heaven and
the vision of the Glory of God (which Paul identifies with Christ)
involves a transformation of the visionary into this glory. Paul, in
fact, regularly speaks of Christians coming to know Christ as sharing in his glory (Romans 5:2; 1 Corinthians 2:7; Colossians 1:27;
3:4; 1 Thessalonians 2:11–12).

Both Paul and Muhammad speak of similar experiences and
similar results. Being zealous, faithful men, they find themselves surprisingly taken up into profound mystical realms where they are also

transformed and authorized. The witness of Islam and the witness of the Gospel in this respect are the same: the more profoundly one encounters God, the more extraordinary one becomes. Paul claims this throughout his letters: "[W]e shall bear the image of the man of heaven," (1 Corinthians 15:49) and become "the righteousness of God" (2 Corinthians 5:21), coheirs, true children of God, sharing Christ's very glory (Romans 8:14–17), sharing in the "fullness of him" (Colossians 2:9–10).

THE QUR'AN
God's Ultimate Revelation

The Qur'an, which means "recitation" or "proclamation," is the collection of revelations that Muhammad received for twenty-three years from the Archangel Gabriel. It is considered God's speech to humanity. Thus, Islamic reverence for the Qur'an cannot be overstated. When Muhammad's opponents challenged him in Mecca, he was asked to prove his divinely authorized mission with signs and wonders. His response was that the only miracle he was given was the Qur'an. Muhammad was known to be unlettered, which probably meant that he had only rudimentary reading and writing skills. Given this, Muslims point out that he simply could not have produced the Qur'an. It would be analogous to someone barely literate creating a Shakespearean play. The miracle of the Qur'an is said to be *balaghah*, which literally translates as *eloquence*, though it means much more—something like "intoxicating profundity." The recitation of the Qur'an is said to even cause spiritual rapture in a person who knows no Arabic.

Arabic is delightful to listen to even though it has possibilities lost in Western languages. Many words are multilayered and have double meanings, and many phrases are poetic in their own right. This alone would be reason enough for Muslims to blanch at translations that inevitably flatten and even distort the original text. Another much more profound reason why Muslims avoid translations is their belief the Arabic text came directly from God. One could ask, What does it mean to say that a verbal revelation came directly from God? Is it God's speech? Did it preexist in the mind of God from eternity?

Most Muslims do believe that the Qur'an is the written expression of a perfect spiritual revelation that existed eternally in the mind of God. The Qur'an is not like other books or religious expressions that are produced from, or influenced by, time, place, or culture. There are three widely used Islamic names for the Qur'an. The Qur'an is known as *al-furqan*: "Discernment," enabling one to distinguish truth from falsehood, good from evil; *al-huda*: "Guide," containing the knowledge Muslims need to stay on the straight path; and *umm al-kitab*: "Mother of Books," because it is a prototype of all books, the archetype of all things, and the root of all knowledge. Memorizing the Qur'an is one of the most meritorious of all religious activities for a Muslim. In the very act of repeating these eternal words, one assimilates and internalizes their spiritual truth. The text becomes part of one's being and the filter through which one sees the world.

Christian Reflection

Knowing how to assess Islamic claims of the Qur'an is difficult. Is the Qur'an for Muslims, then, the same as the Bible is for Christians? Yes, but only in some ways. Christians embrace the Bible as revelatory. Many memorize meaningful passages and pray using the text. In this way, Christians are like Muslims, seeking divine wisdom and even mediation of the divine presence through the text.

On the other hand, a more interesting parallel could be made between the Qur'an and Jesus. Both are understood as the absolute Word of God. The vast majority of Christians would not dare to ascribe Muslim attributes of the Qur'an—that it is an eternal absolute revelation, unaffected by its culture—to the Bible. They are more likely to ascribe these to Jesus, eternal Son of the Father. Obviously, Muslims do not worship the Qur'an as Christians worship Christ, as the second person of the Trinity. However, there is much to the parallel, as Scripture describes Christ as "the reflection of God's glory and the exact imprint of God's very being" (Hebrews 1:1–3); "He is the image of the invisible God" (Colossians 1:15).

For most Christians, the Bible is the word of God because it authentically witnesses to the Word of God, who is Jesus Christ, the fullness of God's revelation. The Bible is not an eternal revelation, and God did not write it. Luke, who did not know Jesus personally, tells us that the sources of his narrative come from trusted eyewitnesses and preachers (Luke 1:2). The distance between the claims Christians make about Christ and those they make about the Bible allow them room to assess the Bible with modern tools of interpretation. Though Christians widely affirm that the saving truths in Scripture are eternal, these truths are expressed in a complex, historically conditioned manner (affected by, for example, gender assumptions or social conventions). While the Bible is critically examined as both revelatory and culturally affected in Christianity, Islam believes that the Qur'an is an eternal, perfect word from God that was in no way affected by the culture from which it was revealed. Therefore, nothing in the Qur'an can be critiqued or scrutinized on any level.

Something about the Islamic posture distinguishes Muslims from Christians. For many Muslims, Islam's religious practices and beliefs are set in stone. Like the Qur'an itself, the faith is, in important ways, already believed to be perfect. Christians do not hold the same of the Bible or their religious practices. The ancient Christian dictum is *ecclesia reformata et semper reformanda* (the Church is reformed and always reforming). The fundamental energy in Islam is not directed toward reconsidering its faith in light of modern questions, issues, or ways of knowing. Rather it is a spiritual culture of surrender. Fundamentally, a devout Muslim knows what God demands. These demands are not questioned—they are surrendered to.

SALAT: BEFORE THE THRONE OF GOD
Praying through the Day

Salat, prayer, is one of the five pillars of Islam, and certainly it is considered by Muslims to be the most essential, profound, and transformative. Muslims pray five times a day: at dawn, noon, midafternoon, sunset, and night. The prayer in each of these periods is essentially the same, only varying in number of units of prayer; each unit is known as a *rak'ah*. Prayer is rigorously mandatory for all Muslims. If, for example, one slept late and did not perform the prayer at sunrise, one still owed this prayer to God and had to make it up through the day. However, this missed opportunity is considered unfortunate, because part of the logic of prayer is that it consecrates one throughout the day. The point is not merely owing God a number of prayer units but creating the spiritual condition of being before God always. That is, one ought to have a consciousness devoted to and in communion with the Divine perpetually through the day.

A unit or *rak'ah* of prayer is essentially invariant. Morning prayer requires two units; noon and midafternoon, four units; evening, three units; and night prayer requires four units. Morning prayer of two units would look like the following:

The Preparation of Ablution

One prepares for prayer by purifying oneself ritually, by washing parts of one's body. One washes one's hands three times, rinses one's mouth, sniffs water into one's nostrils, then washes one's face three times, one's arms to the elbow, one's ears, the nape of one's neck, and one's feet three times.

Standing, facing Mecca, and placing one's hands around one's ears:

God is Greater.

Standing, one proclaims the first chapter of the Qur'an known as the *Al-Fatihah*:

In the name of God the Compassionate, the Merciful
Praise be to God, Lord of the Universe,
The Compassionate, the Merciful,
Sovereign of the Day of Judgment!
You alone we worship, and to You alone we turn for help.
Guide us to the straight path,
The path of those whom you have favored,
Not of those who have incurred Your wrath,
Nor of those who have gone astray.
Amen.

Standing, one recites at least three verses from the Qur'an: [ending with]

God is greater.

Bending and placing one's hands to one's knees:

Glorify my Magnificent Lord.
Glorify my Magnificent Lord.
Glorify my Magnificent Lord.

Standing Straight:

God is Greater.
God listens to him who praises God.
Our Lord, praise be for You only.

Kneeling prostrate with head and hands on the ground:

Glorify my Highest Lord.
Glorify my Highest Lord.
Glorify my Highest Lord.
God is greater.

Sitting on one's knees:

God is greater.

Kneeling prostrate with head and hands on the ground:

Glorify my Lord the Highest.
Glorify my Lord the Highest.
Glorify my Lord the Highest.

Standing, one repeats the above exactly for the second *rak'ah* (unit).

Prayer ends with the believer sitting on one's knees:

All Greeting to Allah and prayers and good will.
[line omitted by Shi'ites]
Peace be on you Prophet as well as mercy and blessing of Allah be on you.
May peace be upon us and on the devout worshiper of Allah.
I testify that there is no God but Allah and
I testify that Muhammad is His slave and messenger.
O God, send Your mercy on Muhammad and his posterity
As you sent Your mercy on Abraham and his posterity.

O God, send Your blessings on Muhammad and his posterity
As You have blessed Abraham and his posterity.
You are the Most Praised, the Most Glorious.

Moving one's head to the right and addressing all in this direction:

The peace and mercy of Allah be on you.

Moving one's head to the left and addressing all in this direction:

The peace and mercy of Allah be on you.

Making Sense of Salat

A famous Qur'anic passage states, "Woe to those who pray, but are heedless in their prayer" (107:7). While prayer is obligatory and invariable, it should not be approached legalistically or performed perfunctorily. There must be a unity between one's outer actions and inner disposition. The ablution, or washing ritual, is a good example. On the surface, a Muslim approaches prayer realizing that intentionally coming before God requires a kind of preparation. The washing is a sign of respect in this case. However, far more is going on. The inward disposition of the soul ideally seeks to make this preparation a profound prayer in itself. In washing the hands, one seeks forgiveness of sins. In washing the mouth and nostrils, one is freeing that space to taste and smell the scent of paradise that comes by being close to God. Washing the face seeks to symbolize removing the darkness that stains one's soul; and the arms, that one acts with righteousness. Finally, washing the right foot designates being set on the straight path of God, while washing the left seeks the protection from evil. One saying (*hadith*) of Muhammad is, "He who makes ablution afresh revives and refreshes his faith."

The same dynamic can be said for the rest of the prayer. The opening of all prayer is the first chapter of the Qur'an, the *Surat al-fatihah*. In many ways, it constitutes the core of the whole of the Qur'anic revelation. In the *hadith qudsi*, the Prophet narrates what God says when a person recites the *Surat al-fatihah*. Following is a dialogue that suggests what may go on in a Muslim's heart:

Muslim: In the name of God the Compassionate, the Merciful.

God: *My Servant mentions Me.*

> **Muslim:** Praise be to God, Lord of the Universe,
> **God:** *My servant lends Me grace.*
> **Muslim:** The Compassionate, the Merciful,
> **God:** *My servant praises Me.*
> **Muslim:** Sovereign of the Day of Judgment!
> **God:** *My servant glorifies Me and submits himself to me.*
> **Muslim:** You alone we worship, and to You alone we turn for help.
> **God:** *This is shared between Me and My servant, and My servant will receive what he asks.*
> **Muslim:** Guide us to the straight path,
> The path of those whom you have favored,
> Not of those who have incurred Your wrath,
> Nor of those who have gone astray.
> **God:** *All that comes back to My servant, and My servant will receive that for which he asks.*

The *Surat al-fatihah*, then, is no mere recitation of the first chapter of the Qur'an, though such would still be profound for a Muslim. It is also a forum for intimacy with God. In the first half, one finds the believer's invocation of God's attributes. This pleases God. It appears as a request that God awaken to attend to the words of the believer. The second half has the believer pleading with God for the grace to be led rightly in life. God's response is that the servant will receive what is asked, which is nothing other than to follow God. One sees that the prayer guarantees an authentic believer will indeed be kept close to God and guided rightly by God.

After the Qur'anic recitation, the supplicant bends and puts hands on knees, proclaiming three times in the imperative: "Glorify my Magnificent Lord." The believer not only glorifies God but also commands the world to do the same. When straightened again: "God listens to one who praises God." This announcement is to the supplicant and those nearby, including angels and jinn (genies). It is intended to be the voice of God working through the believer. The believer then articulates the response of those who hear the word of God: "Our Lord, praise be for You only." The substance of the bowing before God is obvious in that it represents a very physical symbol of humility and submission. Finally, the believer sits in a posture of a humble servant and bears witness to the centrality of the Prophet Muhammad and unity of humanity. Thus, prayers and blessings are sent upon the Prophet and upon all those from the East to the West.

Following Muhammad, Preparing for Eternity

Much in the units of daily prayer involves recitation of the Qur'an. Of course, because the Qur'an is believed to be the eternal, immutable word of God, its recitation is a great blessing. Recitation, then, makes every believer a kind of Muhammad, a prophet, in that each experiences the original revelations given to Muhammad. In this sense, believers find that they are participating in this initial revelation.

In standing and kneeling before God, they also imitate and re-experience Muhammad's al-mi'raj, sitting before the Throne of God. Muhammad referred to the daily prayers as the mi'raj of the faithful. Standing before the Divine Presence is considered the ultimate boon for many Muslims. The Qur'an is filled with many images of paradise, including verdant gardens and even beautiful women at the waiting. Few Muslims take these images literally. However, most do imagine some kind of spiritualized analogue. Some Muslims even believe that there are levels of heaven and that these joys and pleasures, even spiritually understood, represent the lower levels. Many hope to be in the presence of God eternally. For them, the expression *ila rabbiha naziratun*, which means, "gazing upon their Lord," represents the highest reward.

Prayer is a practice on Earth to behold the Face of God and to anticipate and experience a foretaste, no matter how indirect it now is, of the utter bliss that comes from the full beatific vision of God. Prayer prepares the believer for such an experience, and it provides something of the experience now. On the Day of Judgment, some souls will be allowed to behold God's face. Muhammad proclaimed that these blessed will see the Lord as one sees the full moon on a cloudless night. Prayer is a *mi'raj*, "an ascension," to the Throne of God. Thus prayer is an experience of, and a preparation for, the full meeting between believer and God, face to face.

Christian Reflection

Muslim daily prayer shows such aims as worship, praise, petition, and gratitude. Muslims also know that they are free to pray in different ways in addition to the structure of the *salat* routine that is performed five times daily. If there is a general ethos in *salat*, it is that one places oneself before God in awe and reverence throughout the day and, thus, throughout one's life.

The Christian tradition has a similar practice, known as the Liturgy of the Hours (or Divine Office). This practice grew from a combination of daily Church services and the monastic tradition. In the patristic Church, Christians gathered in the early morning and evening before and after their workdays. They sang hymns, chanted psalms, and prayed standardized prayers. The texts that they drew on were aligned to the time of day. Most Christians were illiterate, but memorizing the daily and weekly routine did not take one very long. There were even regular hymns sung every morning and evening, such as the Canticle of Zachariah (Luke 1:68–79) and the Magnificat (Luke 1:46–55).

In the monastic tradition of the patristic Church, monks came to their chapel regularly to worship God and be fed on God's word. The earliest tradition focused on chanting the Psalms; the practice was to chant all 150 of them daily. The monks did not pick Psalms that corresponded to the time of day, they simply prayed through the psalter. They gathered before dawn (*matins*), at dawn (*prime*), midmorning (*terce*), noon (*sext*), midafternoon (*none*), evening (*vespers*), and finally at the end of the day (*compline*). Their purpose was similar to what one sees in Islam, to consecrate the whole day to God. While Islam characterizes *salat* as standing before God throughout the day, the monks would more likely understand themselves as regularly chewing on the word of God throughout the day, thus coming to intimacy with God through his word.

This Christian practice of chewing on the word of God is known as *lectio divina*, or "divine reading." In *lectio divina*, one is not trying to learn something specific from the Bible. Rather, one cultivates receptivity to the word, so that the revelatory text can speak to the soul. In this way, one comes to a greater intimacy with God through meditating on his revealed word.

Franciscan monks pray in the refectory before lunch in Queretaro, Mexico, in 1996.

In both Christian and Muslim prayer traditions, the word of God is the centerpiece but in different ways. For Muslims, because the Qur'an is understood as the perfect word of God, recitation is a powerful expression of devotion. Muslims can be moved to tears just hearing the Qur'an recited. In addition, something about reciting it closes the distance between Muslims and the original revelation given to Muhammad. For Christians, the text becomes a vehicle for intimacy, for letting God speak through his revealed word.

Intimacy with God is central to Christian prayer. The following are a few famous definitions of prayer: "Prayer is the ascent of the spirit to God" (Martin Luther); "Prayer is an emotion of the heart within, poured out and laid before God" (John Calvin); and "Prayer is a surge of the heart . . . a cry of recognition and of love" (St. Thérèse of Lisieux). In all of these expressions, one sees that prayer is interpersonal, intended to deepen one's relationship with God. One also sees that the heart is crucial. In the *Catechism*, Catholicism offers a longer, formal definition:

> Christian prayer is a covenant relationship between God and man in Christ. It is the action of God and of man, springing

forth from both the Holy Spirit and ourselves, wholly directed to the Father, in union with the human will of the Son of God made man. In the New Covenant, prayer is the living relationship of the children of God with their Father who is good beyond measure, with his Son Jesus Christ and with the Holy Spirit. . . . Thus, the life of prayer is the habit of being in the presence of the thrice-holy God and in communion with him. This communion of life is always possible because, through Baptism, we have already been united with Christ.

— *CCC*, no. 2564

This is quite a dense description. Here, one finds the language of covenant. Christianity recognizes three primary covenants with God: Abraham's covenant, which focuses on faith; Moses' covenant, which focuses on obedience to Torah; and the eternal covenant in Christ, which focuses on divine communion. One sees in this definition that prayer comes from God's life already within us, drawing us to him. Prayer also expresses the authentic yearning of the soul for communion. The ancient Church described this union of one's will and action with God's movement within one as synergy. Finally, one sees that the purpose of prayer is intimacy with God: "it is a living relationship of the children of God with their Father . . . with his Son, and with the Holy Spirit."

In *Jesus of Nazareth*, Pope Benedict XVI's reflection on Christ, the pope suggests that the words of the Lord's Prayer, or Our Father, provide signposts to interior prayer. He begins by discussing how people are children of God, sisters and brothers of Christ, who have been given the blessing to call God "Father." One even finds a famous dictum in the spiritual tradition from Aelred of Rievaulx: *Deus amicitia est* (God is friendship).

Islamic spirituality also strives for nearness to God as it anticipates the possibility of heavenly gaze on the Divine Majesty. Islam insists, however, that God should never be imagined in form, or anthropomorphized. Of course, Islam recognizes divine attributes, especially compassion and mercy, and these are analogous to human understandings. Still, there is no Fatherhood of God, no King, and certainly no image of divine Husband as one finds in the Old and New Testaments. In this sense, Islam does not encourage a posture of divine familiarity. The contrast might be fairly framed as such:

Islam seeks to be before God in awe and Christianity seeks communion with God. Perhaps a gift that Christianity could give to Islam is an invitation to consider God as one who invites this manner of intimacy. Islam reminds one that it is also possible to be too casual with one's sense of God so as to forget that God is indeed awesome, transcendent, and absolute mystery.

Review Questions

1. What are the five pillars of Islam and how is each understood as multilayered?
2. Muhammad is regarded as a kind of living Qur'an and an archetypal human. What are the various ways that he operates as such for Muslims?
3. Why do Muslims and Christians believe that humans have a higher nature than angels?
4. What do Muslims believe about the nature of the Qur'an that cannot be accepted by Christians?
5. How is the concept of prayer both the same and different for Muslims and Christians?

In-Depth Questions

1. The chapter suggests that it is philosophically and even metaphysically problematic that Muhammad could receive the Qur'an in an unmediated way. How do you respond to the idea of revelation as so constricted?
2. Fundamentally, Muslims do not scrutinize their faith but emphasize submission. How can a Christian understand surrender to the Gospel when it is always being revisited and open for reinterpretation?
3. What might happen to the Christian soul if one were to imagine regularly through the day, even perpetually through the day, that one stands before the Divine Throne? Has the modern Christian lost the sense of awe?

Select Bibliography

Augustine, *The Confessions*. Henry Chadwick, trans. Oxford: Oxford University Press, 1991.

Benedict XVI, Pope. *Jesus of Nazareth*. Adrian Walker, trans. New York: Doubleday, 2007. This inspiring reflection on Jesus particularly references the centrality of Christ to authentic Christian piety.

Cook, Michael. *The Koran: A Very Short Introduction*. Oxford: Oxford University Press, 2000.

Dunne, John. *The Way of All the Earth: Experiments in Truth and Religion*. Notre Dame, IN: University of Notre Dame Press, 1978.

Esposito, John. *Islam: The Straight Path*, 3rd ed. New York: Oxford University Press, 1998.

Husayn, 'Ali ibn al-. *The Psalms of Islam*, 2nd edition. William Chittick, trans. Burmingham, UK: Al-Mahdi Institute, 2007.

Jeffery, Arthur, ed. *A Reader on Islam: Passages from Standard Arabic Writings Illustrative of the Beliefs and Practices of Muslims*. The Hague: Mouton, 1962.

Koran. N. J. Dawood, trans. New York: Penguin, 1990.

Morray-Jones, C. R. A. "Paradise Revisited (2 Corinthians 12:1–12): The Jewish Mystical Background of Paul's Apostolate [Part One]." *Harvard Theological Review* 86 nos. 2, 3 (1993): 177–217, 265–292.

Nasr, Seyyed Hossein, ed. *The Heart of Islam: Enduring Values for Humanity*. New York: HarperSanFrancisco, 2002. This is an excellent, accessible book on Islamic theology and spirituality.

———. ed. *Islamic Spirituality*. Vol. 2, *Manifestations*. New York: Crossroad, 1991.

———. *Islamic Spirituality*. Vol. 1, *Foundations*. New York: Crossroad, 1987.

Ruthven, Malise. *Islam in the World*, 2nd ed. Oxford: Oxford University Press, 2000. This is an excellent book on the history and theology of Islam, both sympathetic and challenging.

Sells, Michael, ed. and trans. *Early Islamic Mysticism: Sufi, Qur'an, Mi'raj, Poetic and Theological Writings*. Mahwah, NJ: Paulist Press, 1996.

Taft, Robert. *The Liturgy of the Hours in East and West: The Origins of the Divine Office and Its Meaning for Today*. Collegeville, MN: Liturgical Press, 1986.

CHAPTER SIX

Hinduism's Many Layers

FROM SACRIFICE TO BRAHMAN

Opening Word

The Hindu religious world is extraordinarily complex. Hinduism is really shorthand for pluralistic and varied expressions of Indian religiosity. One might be better served to think in terms of a broad Hindu religious tradition that shares some general agreement in cosmology (how the universe is structured) and soteriology (the nature of salvation).

A number of theories exist about how and when Hinduism began. Currently the most persuasive is that waves of Aryan migrants from southern Russia and Afghanistan intermingled with the indigenous culture in the Indus Valley around 2000 BCE. The consequence was a blending of religious values, gods, and social structure that progressively created the Indian civilization, including the caste system. Indeed, being Hindu is first and foremost identifying with this civilization, this culture. While dating ancient religious texts is controversial, one can safely place the production of the earliest Hindu texts, the **Vedas**, from about 1500 to 800 BCE. *Veda* means "knowledge," and the Vedas represent four major collections of sacred writings that reflect early Hindu thought. The earliest is the Rig Veda, which concerns praise of the gods. This is a crucial text, because it accounts for Hinduism's knowledge of the gods, early sacrificial material, and accounts of the origin and structure of the universe. Other Vedas are the Yajur Veda, containing recitation material for sacrifices, the Sama Veda, containing material regarding spiritual chants, and finally, the Atharva Veda, which consists of practical prayers, charms, and other spiritual practices. Further Hindu scriptures include the Brahmanas, which focus on detailed execution of sacrifices, and the Aranyakas, which involve spiritual and ascetical practices of those who left society for the singular pursuit of the spiritual life.

Gods and Sacrifice

The early texts are predominantly concerned about the role of the gods and sacrifices to them. The gods of ancient Hinduism represented both individual persons and the forces of nature:

- *Prajapati:* the creator god
- *Varuna:* the god of cosmic order
- *Indra:* the god of storm (and war)
- *Rudra:* the god of winds
- *Parjanya:* the god of the rain cloud
- *Mitra:* the sun god
- *Soma:* the moon god associated with ritual (psychotropic) drink
- *Agni:* the god of fire

Among the most important gods were Varuna, who ensured universal order (*rita*), and Indra, who lorded over the gods themselves.

Understanding sacrifice is crucial because of a direct relationship between sacrifice and its effect. The world of the Vedas is a causal world. If one acted appropriately in sacrifice, then one literally caused the result. It was as if the gods had to give the boon (benefit or blessing) sought, if the sacrifice was offered rightly. The proper function of the sacrifice aligned with *rita* and made the boon happen. This practice was not considered manipulative but quite pious. One was engaging the gods rightly, and both humans and gods are under the laws of *rita*. Central to *rita* is the law of karma. *Karma* means "action," and initially it referred to ritual action. Karma also refers to the result of that action. Some of the Brahmanas describe the primary spiritual agenda as engaging in karma for one's direct benefit; for example, rain for one's crops. The most important rituals were made with fire. Fire consumes the sacrifice and brings it to the gods in heaven. Agni, the god of fire, was understood as both the sacrificial fire itself and the one who brought the sacrifice to the appropriate god to whom it was directed. Agni could even be identified with the other gods: "You, O Agni, are Indra, the Bull of all that exists; you are the wide-striding Vishnu. . . . [Y]ou control sustenance" (Rig Veda, II.I.3, 4, 6). The reason for Agni's importance is that Agni represents actual and latent power inherent in reality. In some texts, the gods even appear to obtain their power from Agni (Rig Veda, VI.7). The sacred order of the universe, sacrifice, devotion, and the interconnection between the heavenly and earthly realms dominate the early Vedas.

Rebirth and Escape

In later Vedic texts, the same law of karma was understood as capable of effecting a better rebirth. No longer did this event occur through ritual alone, but more importantly, through morality. One's reincarnation, and the karma that produced it, were understood to be primarily affected by one's life of virtue and inner wisdom. The possibility of gaining an excellent rebirth became a central interest.

In the next layer of Hindu religious texts, the Upanishads (800–300 BCE), a shift in spiritual preoccupation develops. The belief in ritual was not challenged, neither was the law of cause and effect. The belief in reincarnation based on one's moral life also remained foundational. A great interest arose, however, in going beyond merely the excellent rebirth that comes by accruing good karma to escaping rebirth altogether. Extraordinarily devout and virtuoso meditators were challenged to engage in spiritual practices that brought them to the unmoving center of the universe, the center of the wheel of **samsara** (literally wandering from one life to another). Regardless of the wonderful rebirth that one might achieve, it would be temporary and, even in itself, not ultimately satisfying. Because no part of the created universe represents the Ultimate Truth, the universe is, in a sense, illusory (**maya**). The great religious quest, then, is to escape (**moksha**) the illusory world and to enter into that which is absolute and ultimate. The only reality that is not considered transient and ultimately illusory in Hinduism is the Atman, the inner, ultimate self. One might say that the Atman is one's soul, but if so, then it ought to be understood as lacking the personality of the individual. Depending upon one's school of thought, this self is a portion of or essence of Brahman, the uncaused Ultimate. Some Upanishads appear to identify the Atman as Brahman itself. Brahman is what one might legitimately call God. Much of Hindu Upanishadic thought is rooted in the conviction that everything has an Atman and that "Atman is Brahman." The transcendent essence of all that is particularly one's inner self is the Universal Divine Brahman. To know Atman as Brahman requires great asceticism and meditation.

Fire and Coolness

Return to the sacrificial image of fire. One might imagine that from the time of the Upanishads, religiously serious Hindus would have abandoned sacrifice as an archaic, early representation of Hindu religiosity. Perhaps one might think that, because Brahman is Absolute Reality, Hindus would have little interest in gods often associated with primitive religion. In reality, Hindu sensibility is multilayered and typically involves various levels of religious truth simultaneously. The Vedas were not abandoned, though their emphasis on the nature gods had been left behind. Rather, many Vedic insights remain in the Upanishads and, indeed, in modern Hinduism. Take the concept of fire or heat, for example. Consider the following:

> As the form of fire when latent in its source is not seen and yet its seed is not destroyed, but may be seized again and again in its source by means of the friction, so it is in both cases. The self has to be seized in the body by means of the syllable *aum*. By making one's body the lower friction stick and the syllable *aum* the upper friction stick, by practicing the friction of meditation one may see the God (Brahman), hidden as it were.

> — *Svetashvatara Upanishad*, I.13–14

In this example, fire is used as a description of how one ought to direct inner heat in order to realize Ultimate Brahman. Fire, however, is also used as a symbol for what keeps the soul in samsara, and many Upanishadic texts require dispassionate coolness. Even as the above citation instructs the soul to create interior friction, it also teaches what appears to be the opposite: "To him (Brahman) . . . do I eager for liberation, resort for refuge. To him who is without parts, without activity, tranquil, irreproachable, without blemish, the highest bridge to immortality like a fire with its fuel burnt" (*Svetashvatara Upanishad*, VI.18–19).

One might be tempted to say that focusing on the gods employs the metaphor of fire quite well, because fire and heat are connected to ritual sacrifice and emotional devotion to the gods. Additionally, one might imagine that movement into Brahman requires coolness and detachment. This is valid up to a point, but it is ultimately superficial. As shown previously, in approaching Brahman one needs to use some kind of interior heat. As shown in the above-cited text, worshipping the gods rightly often takes great equanimity, stillness, and detachment.

The relationship between worshipping the gods and uniting with Brahman is complex. Many Hindus, particularly the more urban educated, believe the gods represent an access to, or even a face of, Brahman, particularly Shiva or Vishnu. Some Hindus, such as the great philosopher Shankara (788–820 CE), believe that worshipping these gods merely prepares one for knowing Brahman. Many others believe that these gods are a manifestation of Brahman itself, as Saguna-Brahman, or Brahman with qualities. One of the Upanishads narrates an insightful debate between Vidagdha Shakalya and the wiser Yajnavalkya. Vidagdha asks how many gods there are, and Yajnavalkya replies that there are as many as the Vedas say, namely 3,306. Vidagdha seems unsatisfied and repeats the question: "Yes," he says, "but how many gods are there, Yajnavalkya?" Yajnavalkya's answer is then 33. Vidagdha asks the same question five more times to receive the answers of six, three, two, one and a half, and finally one. After explaining that these gods are all manifestation of divinity itself, Yajnavalkya finally declares, "Which is the one God? . . . He is Brahman. They call him that" (*Brihadaranyaka Upanishad*, III.9.1–9).

Hinduism has a religious tradition of great asceticism and meditative absorption. One must learn to dwell in detachment and cool equanimity. Hinduism also has a tradition filled with passionate love for the Divine as divinity is envisioned. Fire and coolness end up less as opposites than as partners. The great challenge is to know how and when to be on fire and how and when to be cool.

FINDING GOD AND SELF
Finding Self Is Finding God

Who are we? Who is God? What is our relationship to God? How can we find union with God? These four questions are foundational to many religions. Typically, the answer to any one of them implies answers to the others. Discovering the answers involves progressive insight into each question. In coming to know oneself, one discovers God already present. In coming to know God, one discovers who one really is. If the relationship to God is rightly understood, then one can develop some intimacy with God, which itself deepens self-knowledge and insight into the Divine.

As noted previously, the Upanishads are devoted to such questions, particularly to pursuing insight into the ultimate nature of reality and the ultimate nature of oneself. These texts are also devoted to facilitating one's break from samsara. Few doubt that if one leads a meritorious life, the karmic consequences would condition an excellent rebirth. However, this rebirth would be temporary and, if scrutinized, not as excellent as it appears. Consider the following text in which the holy king Brihadratha renounces his throne and begins a zealous commitment to spiritual practice. During that time, he meets a guru named Shakayana, whom the text describes as radiant and as a "knower of the self." The king tells Shakayana that he does not really know the self, but that he only knows what it is not:

> O Revered One, in this foul-smelling, unsubstantial body, a conglomerate of bone, skin, muscle, marrow, flesh, semen, blood, mucus, tears, rheum, feces, urine, wind, bile, and phlegm, what is the good of the enjoyment of desires? In this body which is afflicted with desire, anger, covetousness,

delusion, fear, despondency, envy, separation from what is desired, union with the undesired, hunger, thirst, old age, death, disease, sorrow and the like, what is the good of the enjoyment of desires? And we see that all this is perishing.

—*Maitri Upanishad*, I.2–4

Brihadratha then discusses animals, beings with spiritual bodies, and even gods. He recognizes that they too die and are thus caught in the endless cycle of rebirth. Finally he pleads to Shakayana to free him, and Shakayana agrees to tell him the truth about his self: "Now he who, without stopping the respiration, goes upwards, moving about yet unmoving, dispels darkness, he is the self. . . . Now that serene one, who, rising up out of this body reaches the highest light and appears with his own form, he is the self . . . that is the immortal, the fearless. That is Brahman" (*Maitri Upanishad*, II.12).

This is a rich text in many ways. As shown in chapter three, the role of the guru is critical. Brihadratha had been practicing yoga deeply and was ready to hear deeper truths. Shakayana is described not simply as someone with information, but also someone who has realized the truth. Thus, he is a reliable teacher, both in having true knowledge and as one who can facilitate a disciple's experience of that truth. Brihadratha disassociates his identity with his body. His description of the body is repulsive but accurate. Brihadratha's description of the psyche's relationship to the body is also off-putting, yet when is the psyche completely free from at least subtle qualities of lust, anger, fear, envy, and so on? Finally, Brihadratha recognizes that the cycle of rebirth is unsatisfying, even for the gods.

Shakayana's answer is most critical, because the entire dialogue culminates with his response. Shakayana teaches that there truly is an immortal self that underlies the body. Shakayana identifies the self with Brahman, Absolute Reality. Many of the Upanishads follow this same strategy. These Upanishadic narratives urge one to look closely at oneself. They teach one to scrutinize and reject superficial identifications of the self. The changing body or mental state cannot be an enduring self, one realizes. These texts invite the individual to go deeper still to the underlying reality grounding body and mind. This deepest reality is the true self. To see that self is to see Brahman.

Finding God Is Finding Self

One could approach the issue of discovering absolute truth from the other side. Instead of starting with oneself and finding Brahman, one could seek Brahman and, by doing so, see the very nature of one's self. The Chandogya Upanishad offers one of the most famous dialogues on the nature of Brahman and its relationship to the self: A famous **Brahmin** priest, Uddalaka Aruni, sent his son Shvetaketu to learn the teaching of the Vedas and ways of the priesthood. After twelve years of study, the son returned well read and well trained, yet exceedingly arrogant, for he had identified with his superior knowledge and position. "His father then said to him, 'Shvetaketu, since you are now so greatly conceited, think yourself well-read and arrogant, did you ask for that instruction by which the unhearable becomes heard, the unperceivable becomes perceived, the unknowable becomes known?' 'How, Venerable Sir, can there be such a teaching?'" (*Chandogya Upanishad*, VI.1.4).

At this point, Shvetaketu learns from his father about Brahman as Being itself, the source of all creation, and how creation developed into living beings. The essence of Being itself is Brahman; it pervades all beings. From this reference, the father offers a number of similes and metaphors on Brahman. After each explanation, the father says to the son, *tat tvam asi*, a famous, regularly used phrase in Hindu theological discourse, meaning, "you are that." The father describes the impossibility of tracing materiality to the source, as honey from the essences of many flowers cannot be traced to any single flower. The essence that is universal is Brahman—*tat tvam asi*. He then compares individuality to rivers that flow into the sea, are now the sea, and are no longer separate entities. The water's essence is that of the sea—*tat tvam asi*. Then the father compares sap that flows through a tree and gives it life, so Brahman flows everywhere throughout reality—*tat tvam asi*. He points to a fig seed and has Shvetaketu dissect it. There appears nothing inside, nothing to point to, yet it is the source of trees. So too Brahman, which cannot be seen or apprehended, is the source of all that exists—*tat tvam asi*. Finally, the father has Shvetaketu put salt into a glass of water and leave it overnight. The salt cannot be seen but permeates the water. So too Brahman pervades reality without being in any particular place—*tat tvam asi* (*Chandogya Upanishad*, VI.9.1–13.3).

Absolute identification between the self and Brahman is the minority position. According to the *Brahma **Sutras***, various interpretive possibilities are available. One is that the Upanishads are describing unity, not identity. Another theory holds that the Brahman is a kind of state of existence the self achieves when released from all limitations. Yet another theory holds that the self and Brahman share the same truth and experience, which is *satchitananda*. *Sat* refers to "being," *chit* to "absolute consciousness," and *ananda* to "pure bliss." The collective, unitive experience is *satchitananda*. A final position argues that a liberated self takes on the form of the Universal Brahman.

Hindu wisdom argues that the true essence of the self is something utterly transcendent. Thus, just as Ultimate Reality cannot be objectified, so too the truest, deepest self cannot be made into an object of observation, a thing. The Hindu phrase when attempting such is *neti-neti*, or "not this, not that." It is nothing that one can point to but dwells in the mystery of God.

Christian Reflection

Language that sounds like the soul's identification with God need not shock one; neither should one think that it is alien to a Christian perspective. Christianity retains a clear distinction between God and the soul, Creator and creature. Yet its biblical and theological tradition does point to kinds of identification as well. Genesis reflects upon the nature of humans and their relationship to God. In the first creation account, one finds that humans are made in the image and likeness of God (1:26). In the second account, one finds Adam created out of the earth and God's breath (2:7), that is, from materiality and God's Spirit. One is certainly not God, which is something Adam and Eve desired to become. Yet, one is created in some way with God's transcendence. Perhaps Adam and Eve's impulse to become like gods was based on the truth about one's soul, that living God's life is one's destiny. Of course, one cannot achieve such a transcendent possibility by deception, pride, presumption, and disobedience, which was their strategy. Rather it must come as gift, through honesty, repentance, humility, and obedience.

The New Testament is filled with suggestions, images, and outright teachings on actually sharing in God's life and in some ways with God's identity. Christians do not think that they become God by nature, for they always remain creatures living by his grace. However, as shown previously, distinctions can blur. Consider the following:

- Beloved, we are God's children now; what we will be has not been revealed. What we do know is this: when he is revealed, we will be like him, for we will see him as he is (1 John 3:2).
- We receive the Spirit and become coheirs, true children of God, sharing Christ's very glory (Romans 8:14–17).
- His divine power has given us everything needed for life and godliness . . . so that through them you may escape from the corruption that is in the world because of lust and become participants in the divine nature (2 Peter 1:3–4).
- He disciplines us for our own good, so that we may share his holiness (Hebrews 12:10).
- Love has been perfected among us . . . because as he is, so are we in this world (1 John 4:17). (See also, John 1:12–13; 1 Corinthians 15:28, 49; 2 Corinthians 3:17–18, 5:17, 21; Ephesians 1:22–23, 4:24; Colossians 3:10–11.)

In these biblical texts, it seems clear that the authors did not merely abstractly believe that the soul took on the life of God or was transformed to "share the divine nature." These authors surely experienced God and themselves in this way. Paul, for example, is obviously bursting with the knowledge of God's Spirit in his soul. And yet, the soul is Paul's too. The divine life really is his experience of his deepest self. By God's grace, Paul saw that everything he once identified with was worthless. Like Shvetaketu, Paul had identified himself with his status and religious zeal. He had every "reason to be confident in the flesh" for he was "blameless." "Yet whatever gains I had, these I have come to regard as loss because of Christ. More than that, I regard everything as loss because of the surpassing value of knowing Christ Jesus my Lord." Paul now regarded any ego-achievement "as rubbish" (Philippians 3:4–8).

In finding God, Paul found his true self, one that was not identified with his body, his thoughts, or his religious practice. Rather, it was a self that was located in the very mystery of God. One could also say that as he looked into his experience of himself, he discovered God's Spirit animating and transforming him. Some of this language of the soul's identification with God was also shown in chapter two.

This kind of language is not only the experience of mystics or great saints like Paul. It also is the formal teaching of the Catholic Church, a teaching shared by Eastern Orthodox, Anglican, and many Protestant Christians. The following texts come from the Second Vatican Council:

> For God has called man, and still calls him, to cleave with all his being to him in sharing for ever a life that is divine and free from all decay (*Church in the Modern World*, no. 18); In his wisdom and goodness the eternal Father . . . decreed that men would be raised up to share in the divine nature (*Constitution on the Church*, no. 16); God's will was that men should have access to the Father through Christ, in the Holy Spirit, and thus become sharers in the divine nature (*Constitution on Divine Revelation*, no. 2); The Son of God entered the world by means of a true incarnation that he might make us sharers in the divine nature.
>
> — *Church's Missionary Activity*, no. 3; cf. *CCC*, nos. 1988, 1996–1999, 2002, 2780

PASSIONATELY LOVING GOD

Bhakti: The Path of Devotion

Most Hindus believe that the spiritual universe is made of a variety of spiritual beings, including gods. These gods represent parts of the cosmic order. One might venerate one of the gods as a personal choice or to seek a particular blessing. For example, if one were to seek good fortune for a venture, one might make an offering to Ganesha, the elephant-imaged god who removes obstacles and ensures success in human affairs. Many Hindus focus on Vishnu, who particularly represents Saguna-Brahman, Brahman

Carved stone sculpture of elephant god Ganesha in Khajuraho temple, Madhya Pradesh, India.

IMAGE: © BORIS STROUJKO/SHUTTERSTOCK

with qualities. Krishna, who is usually understood as an incarnation or **avatara** of Vishnu, is also popular. One reason for Krishna's popularity is that, as an incarnation, he becomes God among us. That is, he is God that one can experience and know. In loving him as a human, one can experience the graces of his divinity.

Passionately Experiencing the Passionate God

One of the most famous expressions of Krishna devotion comes from the Bhagvata Purana. This story is known to virtually every Hindu, particularly the Rasa Lila, the passionate love dance. In it, Krishna grows up in the country with his identity as the incarnation of God hidden from the villagers. As a young man seeing the flowering of the jasmine flowers, he decides to entice all the women of the village with his flute playing. As they begin to come to the forest at the sound of his flute, he magically replaces them with a duplicate at home so that their fathers or husbands would not miss them.

> Then and there Krishna, surrounded by these jewels of women—so devoted to him and joyful—started the Rasa Lila as the cowherd girls linked their arms together. The joyous festivity of the Rasa Lila, embellished by the circle of the cowherd girls, was fully set in motion by Krishna, the Lord of Yoga, who entered the circle between the two members of each pair of cowherd girls, and put one arm around the neck of each cowherd girl, so that these women would think that he was in her presence alone; one Krishna for every women. . . . With the movements of their feet and the waving of their arms, the coquettish arching of their eyebrows accompanied by their breast-cloths, and with the swaying of their earrings against their own and his cheeks, these brides of Krishna, their faces perspiring, and the knots of their braids and girdles come loose, now say in praise of him as they flashed brilliantly. . . . Thus with embrace and with touches of his hands, with loving glances, unrestrained love-play and with laughter, the Lord of Rama [Krishna] enjoyed the delights of love with the

beautiful women. . . . After multiplying himself so that there were as many forms of him as there were cowherd women, this *Bhagavan* [Krishna] made love, playfully as in a game, with these women, even though his delight is in himself.

—cited in Dan Sheridan, *Loving God*, 67–68

The text goes on to describe that this event drew the attention of many gods and goddesses who were themselves carried away by the beauty and intoxication of the experience. While the language of the Divine sexually cavorting sounds striking or even scandalous, it contains a great richness for contemplation. *Eros*, the term we typically use for sexual love, is also the loving force for union. Thus, it represents a deeply profound interior energy that drives one to unite with what one most loves. In one sense, sexual energy appears to be fully utilized. These women are passionately in love with and sexually charged by Krishna. One could also imagine the sexual love that is being described is a metaphor for a deep spiritual desire for union. Mystical literature often imagines the soul as a bride and God as the divine groom. The text invites the reader to imagine a loving relationship with God that is irresistible, intoxicating, and filled with bliss beyond description. Could it be, as the Bhagvata Purana seems to say, that one's passionate loving relationship with God can be so profound that it actually stirs and instructs the gods themselves? Could a person be so taken with God that one experiences him as one's possession or that God could love a person so profoundly that he is fully and completely united to one in an absolute way?

Passionately Experiencing the Absence of God

Bhakti celebrates God's passionate love for humans and theirs for God. Experiencing God's personal, unitive love is ecstatic and beyond description. Texts representing these experiences are among the most beautiful and profound in religious literature. Bhakti also includes wrestling with one's passionate love for God during times when God is silent or apparently absent. In this situation, the soul, seduced by God's love, longs for him and languishes without him.

After the death of her husband, Mirabai, a sixteenth-century princess and poet, left the palace in order to devote her entire consciousness to developing intimacy with Krishna. In one of her famous poems, she describes herself as drunk on Krishna's love. He is, she says, her husband and lover. However, she often experienced divine absence rather than presence. In one of her poems, she writes, "Tortured by longing I cannot sleep, and the fire of love drives me to wander hither and thither. Without the light of the Beloved my house is dark, and lamps do not please me. Without the Beloved my bed is uninviting, and I pass the nights awake. . . . Who can quench my pain? My body has been bitten by the snake of absence . . ." (cited in Mary Pat Fisher and Lee Bailey, *Anthology of Living Religions*, 79).

Another famous poet, Andal, writes in the same vein and with the same anguish:

> I hunger and thirst for a sight of Krishna, my dark Lord,
> So don't stand there mocking me, friends!
> Your words sting like sour juice poured on an open wound.
> Go, bring me the yellow silk wrapped around the waist
> of the One who does not understand the sorrow of women,
> Fan me with it, cool the burning of my heart.

> I weep, I sing his glories, but he does not show me
>   his form,
> He does not say, "Have no fear," he does not come close,
> He does not caress me nor embrace me, he does not fill
>   me up.
> Through the leafy pastures where his cows graze
> The sound of the flute played by the dark Lord reaches me:
> go, bring me cool nectar from the lips of that flute,
> spread it over my face—that will revive me.

> —cited in Francis Clooney, *Hindu Wisdom*, 61

One must appreciate the languishing of Andal, who has known such profound joy and union with God and who now experiences only absence and her own bottomless hunger and thirst. What makes

Andal's poem particularly important is that she recognizes signs and hints of God's presence. These will not completely satisfy her, but they do bring some comfort. Krishna had left as a love token a waistband of yellow silk. By this, she asks her friends to fan her burning heart. She also hears his flute playing in the distance. The music that traditionally intoxicates his lovers is faintly in the air. She asks her friends to find his flute, another token of his presence, and bring it to her. As unappetizing as the image is in our culture, she wishes to take the saliva left on the flute and smear it over her face. This is part of Krishna; it is something to sustain her until he comes to ravish her again. We should note that this kind of love for Krishna as bride to groom or lover to beloved is a model for men as well as women. As we see below, this is also the case with Judaism and Christianity.

Christian Reflection

Christianity is replete with examples of employing the metaphor of sex and marriage to describe the relationship both the community has with God and the individual soul has with God in Jesus Christ. The Old Testament is filled with these images. Ezekiel allegorized Israel as a young virgin whom God has married. The idolatry practiced through Israel's history is not imaged simply as apostasy, but also as the adultery of an unfaithful wife having sex with other gods. Hosea was even called by God to marry a prostitute as a prophetic sign of Israel's condition. Yet God promised through both prophets a healing reunion: "You will call me *My Husband*" (Hosea 2:18). This reconstitution of Israel as a chaste virgin spouse to God is also taken up in Isaiah: "For as a young man marries a young woman, so shall your builder marry you, and as the bridegroom rejoices over the bride, so shall your God rejoice over you" (Isaiah 62:5).

For Christians, this messianic espousal was inaugurated with Christ. Jesus began his ministry with a sign of this new era at the wedding at Cana, and the book of Revelation makes the divine intention explicit. When the final victory over the forces of evil is complete, the whole host of believers will sing, "'Halleluia! The Lord our God the Almighty reigns . . . for the marriage of the Lamb has come and his bride has made herself ready'" (Revelation 19:6–7).

John of the Cross

From the early Church onward, the image of a bride wed to Jesus the divine groom has been a great source of meditation and inspiration. Origen, one of the early Church's greatest theologians, describes the Song of Songs as the biblical text that best represents mystical union with God. So profound is its meaning that he believed only the most mature and holy Christians should meditate on the text. Other theologians have followed. Bernard of Clairvaux, for example, preached a series of more than eighty homilies on the Song of Songs, and found it so spiritually rich that he never read past the third chapter of the biblical text. Many of his homilies were focused on just one verse: "Let him kiss me with the kisses of his mouth" (Song 1:2). Perhaps the most famous love poem written to Jesus is John of the Cross's "The Dark Night." In it, the bride steals away under the cover of darkness, guided only by the light of love burning inside her heart. One verse exclaims, "O guiding night! O night more lovely than the dawn! O night that has united the Lover with his beloved, transforming the beloved in her Lover."

What exactly is the dynamic being described? Is it an imagined actual sexual encounter between the Divine and a human? Surely, this is far-fetched, and even becomes an impossible interpretation when one reads other material from these same authors. Is it then merely a metaphor, one used perhaps because sexual union is such a profound image? Perhaps so, but again if one reads other writings from these saints and mystics, this interpretation seems to minimize the passionate love they have for God. What appears to be the case is that this intense love and union calls forth all the energies of the saint, including sexual energy, and directs it in total devotion to God.

As has been shown with the Hindu lovers of Krishna, such intense love can make the soul lovesick when one's sense of God is nothing but absence. In John of the Cross's famous *Spiritual Canticle*, he describes this aspect as well. The poem begins, "Where have you hidden, Beloved, and left me moaning? You fled like a stag after wounding me; I went out calling you, but you were gone." It should be noted that *The Spiritual Canticle* is forty verses long and ends with the bride and groom finding each other, and the bride's deep hunger and thirst for her divine groom fully satisfied.

Why does God put the soul in such a precarious situation, that having filled the soul with such spiritual delight and bonded the soul all the more deeply to him, he then withdraws, leaving the soul languishing? John of the Cross says that God does this ultimately for the soul's purification; that the soul, which he calls "the bride," may love God even more deeply and freely. The great problem in receiving such profound consolations from God is that the soul can love God primarily because of the gratifications God gives the soul. The spiritual life can easily become focused on these gratifications and not on God. Thus, this sense of God's absence and silence purges the soul to love God only for God's sake. In a word, nothing is enjoyable, gratifying, or even valuable in this experience except pure, naked devotion to God. The soul is stripped of all other props to lean on and all other joys. The soul encounters her own dependence and poverty, and her love for God is stretched to the hilt. If there is any sign that God is in fact not absent, it is that the soul, so advanced in the spiritual life, is filled with spiritual zeal to serve God. This tells the soul subtly that God may not be as far away as it seems.

While such passionate lovers of God in Hinduism or Christianity are rare, they provide a great lesson and challenge. They teach that it is possible to love God with all one's energies, indeed, with every aspect of one's psyche. They also challenge one to recognize the value of both presence and absence. The spiritual life is energizing when one experiences God's graces and blessings. This is good. Absence and spiritual dryness are good too, for they expose one's weaknesses and uncover every façade of piety that is not real devotion. The purification of love typically comes, not during times of consolation, but during times of desolation. During desolation, there is no self-serving reason to love God, but one loves God anyway, even and especially in one's periods of the dark night.

WITNESSING AN UNTAMABLE GOD
Introduction

When one looks at Hindu iconography, whether these are statues, paintings, murals, and so on, one cannot help but be a little unnerved by some of the images. Shiva, for example, is usually depicted with four arms, sometimes with a trident or sword in one of his hands and a snake garland around his neck. Kali, a divine mother, is more striking still. She is usually depicted with red, intoxicated eyes and a raging face. Her hair is wild and her mouth is filled with fangs. Her neck garland is made of human heads. Why would one want to be devoted to God under this image? What Hinduism witnesses is a reminder that God is overwhelming, wild, and untamable. Usual, and perhaps all too sanitary, depictions of God can serve to domesticate God. God, however, does not serve standard conventions; God breaks them.

Shiva the Dancer

Many depictions of Shiva show him dancing. On the one hand, Shiva is a destroyer God. He dances with a bowl of fire with which he will burn up the world. On the other hand, his dance represents unleashing creative energy and one of the great symbols of Shiva is a lingam, a sacred pole that must be seen as a phallic symbol. Thus, the process of life and death are in his hands. In the *Brahmanda Purana* is a myth called "Shiva in the Pine Forest." In this myth, devout ascetics and sages encounter Shiva and are scandalized by him. Shiva had intended to come to the forest to bless them, but they find him outrageous, fitting none of their religious categories. He appears as a naked man. Sometimes he laughs horribly, at other moments he sings, and he even dances erotically. The ascetics curse this scandalous stranger so that his penis will fall off. Shiva allows the curse, and his penis falls to the ground. He then disappears.

From this moment on, the sages lose their spiritual power and energy. Indeed the whole universe seems to have gone dark for everyone. These sages then appeal to the creator god Brahma. He advises them to worship the penis that has fallen off Shiva for the next year. It should be noted that the penis now had become transformed into a sacred pillar or lingam. At the end of the year, Brahma and Vishnu go to the site to see what has become of the lingam. They see that it has grown so large that it pierced the highest heavens where it then burst into flames that spread everywhere.

The witness of Shiva in the Pine Forest is the witness of a God who has no conventionality. The truly wise person needs to be open to the surprises and shocking revelation of the Divine. God is Other, and to accept this is to be open to, and transformed by, power that enflames the universe. To reject God's Otherness is not only to miss transformative possibilities but also to lose one's spiritual potency.

Kali the Raging Mother

The principal reason that Kali is depicted virtually as a raging demon is because she is a warrior against evil; she rages to protect the good and virtuous and to bless those who love her. In the *Markandeya Purana*, a battle between Kali and a great buffalo demon is told:

> When the fierce Goddess saw the great demon attacking, swollen with anger, she became frantic to slay him. She hurled her noose over him and bound the great demon. [The text goes on to say that he became a lion whereupon she cut off his head. Then he appeared as a man and she shot him with arrows, then an elephant whose trunk she cut, then he became a buffalo.] Enraged at this, the furious mother of the universe drank the supreme wine again and again; her eyes became red and she laughed. . . . She leaped up and mounted that great demon and kicked him in the neck and pierced him with her trident. . . . The Goddess cut off his head with her great sword, and he fell.
>
> —cited in Clooney, *Hindu Wisdom*, 89–90

The image of Kali is not a comforting one: she appears utterly vicious. Depicted with a garland of skulls and blood dripping from her mouth, she is certainly no conventional mother. Hindu wisdom points to the power in the Divine Feminine and challenges one to rethink attitudes about masculine and feminine.

Looking Inside Krishna

The experience of Krishna thus far has been under the auspices of *bhakti* or emotional devotion. Krishna is the divine lover and a human means to experience God. It should be remembered, however, that the Hindu tradition recognizes the divinity of Krishna as overwhelming too. Much earlier in the same myth where Krishna was seducing women, we find him as a little boy being raised by his adopted mother Yashoda. Krishna has been playing with other boys when it is reported to her that he has been eating dirt. She scolds him, though with teary eyes, but he assures her that he hasn't eaten dirt. He then invites her to look into his mouth to inspect for dirt. When she looks, she sees the whole universe within him and is completely overwhelmed, so much so that Krishna has to erase the specifics of the encounter in order to protect her psyche.

One finds a similar kind of overwhelming experience in the famous Bhagavad Gita. In this text, one no longer finds a child or lover, but a guru and warrior who teaches prince Arjuna the mysteries of the spiritual life. At a certain point, Arjuna believes himself ready to experience Krishna's divine form. Krishna agrees and gives him the gift of the *divine eye* to see him as he truly is. Arjuna cannot sustain such a disturbing and bewildering vision. He begs Krishna to return to a more manageable form.

> Krishna . . . revealed to Arjuna the true majesty of his form. It was a multiform, wondrous vision, with countless mouths and eyes and celestial ornaments, brandishing many divine weapons. Everywhere was boundless divinity containing all astonishing things. . . . If the light of a thousand suns were to rise in the sky at once, it would be like the light of that great spirit. Arjuna saw all the universe in its many ways and parts, standing as one in the body of the god of gods . . . [Arjuna says]: I see no beginning or middle or end to you; only boundless strength in your endless arms, the moon and sun in your eyes, your mouths of consuming flames, your own brilliance scorching the universe . . . seeing this awesome, terrible form of yours Great Soul, the three worlds tremble.
>
> —Bhagavad Gita 11:9–20

In the first case, Krishna is a lovely young boy, in the second, a handsome charioteer. Behind the façade, however, is something utterly awesome. One should not be fooled by the tame exterior. Underneath a seemingly gentle presence can be a divinity that overwhelms.

Christian Reflection

Hindu wisdom challenges one to take God's Otherness seriously. The issue is not simply that God is transcendent, and that divine images and concepts are only an analogy to what God is really like. The Hindu witness says much more. God is overwhelming, unpredictable, unmanageable, and unconventional. The Old Testament portrays a similarly awesome God. Exodus describes a glance from God throwing the whole Egyptian army into confusion (Exodus 14:24). In the Old Testament, one finds the divine warning that "no one shall see me and live" (Exodus 33:20, cf. Leviticus 16:1ff). In one particularly unnerving account, a pious Jew named Uzzah tries to steady the Ark that is falling off a cart and God strikes him dead (2 Samuel 6:6–7).

It can be tempting to imagine that Jesus replaced the terrifying image of God in the Old Testament with a compassionate (and tamed) image. However, one must be careful. God is fundamentally compassionate in the Old Testament and, in fact, Jesus can be condemnatory in the New Testament (Matthew 12:41–42, 13:41–43; Mark 8:38; Luke 11:42ff; John 8:24, 44–47). In both Testaments, one finds a God who will not be housebroken, who cannot be reduced to divine niceness. Both Old and New Testaments insist that God's supernatural quality is overwhelming, even awful. The New Testament regularly commends this sense. Christians are to "fear him who can destroy body and soul in hell" (Matthew 10:28) and realize that "it is a fearful thing to fall into the hands of the living God" (Hebrews 10:31), who is "a consuming fire" (Hebrews 12:29).

There is one striking difference between Hinduism and Christianity, which is that Hinduism tends to be more private. One can choose what gods one wants to be devoted to, and a central point of the spiritual life is creating the kind of karma for a better rebirth. As shown, it is not as though devout Hindus do not love the divine for divinity's sake. Still, it tends to be an individualistic religion. Such a focus tends to be less concerned with social justice issues.

Additionally, if one were poor or from a low caste, this is because of what one karmically deserved. Many devout well-born Hindus resist scrutinizing the root causes for such disparities.

In Christianity, God is most threatening precisely around issues of justice. This theme dominates the prophets who proclaimed that the only way to God's presence and favor was with justice (Amos 5:12–14); that sacrifices mean nothing without justice, which itself was the true sacrifice (Isaiah 1:11–18, 58:6–9); and that God would destroy them without a repentance of justice (Jeremiah 7:3–11). Justice and compassion dominate Jesus' preaching as well (Matthew 5:7, 9:13, 23:23; Mark 6:34; Luke 10:37).

Review Questions

1. How does the Hindu religious tradition develop from the time of the earliest Vedas to the time of the Upanishads in terms of the gods, sacrifice, karma, rebirth, and the nature of the self and Ultimate Reality?
2. Many of the Upanishads identify the self (Atman) with Ultimate Reality (Brahman). Why then do most Hindus argue that these two are not identical?
3. How does Karma work in terms of sacrifice and rebirth?
4. The sexual metaphor used to describe the relationship between the soul and God ought to be taken neither literally nor analogically. How should it be taken?

In-Depth Questions

1. Hindus are dualists and Christians are supposedly not. Do you believe that your body is part of your eternal self or something that your soul needs to deal with while on Earth? What are the implications of identifying with the body? What are the implications of not identifying with the body?

2. Is it really possible for someone to have a sexually passionate love with God in the manner addressed in the text? What is your reaction to such a suggestion?

3. Hinduism reminds not to housebreak God. Do you think that Christians typically do this, imagining God as merely nice?

Select Bibliography

Bernard of Clairvaux. *Bernard of Clairvaux: Selected Works.* G. R. Evans, trans. Mahwah, NJ: Paulist Press, 1979.

Bhagavad Gita. Barbara Stoler Miller, trans. New York: Bantam Books, 1986.

Clooney, Francis X. *The Truth, the Way, the Life: Christian Commentary on the three Holy Mantras of the Shrīvaisnava Hindus.* Louven: Peeters Press, 2008.

————. *Hindu Wisdom for All God's Children.* Maryknoll, NY: Orbis Press, 1998. This is an excellent series of reflections that show a dialogue between classic Hindu and Christian spiritualities.

Fisher, Mary Pat, and Lee W. Baily. *An Anthology of Living Religions.* Upper Saddle River, NJ: Prentice Hall, 2008.

Hopkins, Thomas. *The Hindu Religious Tradition.* Encino, CA: Dickenson, 1971. This is an excellent, short presentation of Hinduism, and all citations from the Rig-Vedas come from this volume, unless otherwise noted.

John of the Cross. *The Collected Works of John of the Cross.* Kieran Kavanaugh and Otilio Rodriguez, trans. Washington, DC: ICS Publications, 1991.

Klostermaier, Klaus. *A Survey of Hinduism*, 2nd edition. Albany: State University of New York Press, 1994. This is a much denser, longer, and more scholarly introduction to the massive Hindu religious tradition.

Mirabai. *Mira Bai and Her Padas.* Krishna P. Bahadur, trans. Delhi: Munshiram Manoharlal Publishers, 1998.

————. *The Devotional Poems of Mīrābāī.* A. J. Alston, trans. Delhi: Motilal Banarsidass, 1980.

Radhakrishnan, Sarvepalli, trans. and ed. *The Principle Upanishads.* London: George Allen Unwin, 1953.

Ramakrishna, Sri. *The Gospel of Sri Ramakrishna* (abridged edition). Swami Nikhilananda, trans. New York: Ramakrishna-Vivikananda Center, 1958.

Sheridan, Daniel. *Loving God: Krishna and Christ: A Christian Commentary on the Nāranda Sūtras.* Leuven: Peeters Publishing, 2007.

Thanissaro [Bhikkhu]. *The Mind like Fire Unbound.* Barre, MA: Dhamma Dana, 1993.

Vedic Hymns. Edward Thomas, ed. and trans. London: J. Murray, 1923.

CHAPTER SEVEN

Buddha's Revision

BUDDHA'S BIOGRAPHY
Birth and Enlightenment

As discussed in chapter six, the Upanishads taught that it is most desirable to escape samsara, the wandering from lifetime to lifetime of rebirths. Even the most gratifying existence such as a **deva** rebirth is pointless, subject to decay, and upon scrutiny, less excellent than it appears. One needs to find a way to escape (*moksha*), and such an escape requires higher knowledge and intensive meditational practice. This chapter investigates some of the technical specifics of such knowledge and practice as well as the Buddha's direct teaching via the Pali canon, the earliest recorded texts.

The Buddha (c. 563–483 BCE) shared many conventional Hindu beliefs about the problem of rebirth and the need for escape. He did, however, diverge from traditional Hindu thought in important aspects. While the Buddha agreed with his Hindu contemporaries that the body, thoughts, and emotions are nothing to be attached to or identified with, he also taught that there was no Atman, no enduring or eternal self underneath them. To seek some kind of eternal soul is a fool's errand, the Buddha believed. Further, to identify with this nonexistent delusion ensures more rebirths. The Buddha conceived of the mind and body as made up of five impersonal, impermanent aggregates of physical, perceptual, and mental operations. Unless one realized that there is no underlying Atman, or self, one could not become free. This belief contrasts with the Hindu's that one must discover one's ultimate self and associate it in some way to Brahman, the Eternal Absolute. The Buddha instead spoke about Nirvana, which had nothing to do with Atman or Brahman.

The Buddha's life story is part biography and part legend. It is also a myth, that is, a sacred story that freely uses metaphors and symbols to charge the spiritual imagination. Outside of piecemeal accounts in the canon, the first full-length biography of the Buddha, *Buddhacarita* (*Acts of the Buddha*), comes from the first-century CE Indian poet Ashvaghosha. Following is the broadly accepted version that includes both Ashvaghosha's poetic biography as well as occasional references from the canon itself.

Long before the Buddha became the Buddha, he lived in a specific heavenly realm (*tusita heaven*), awaiting the most auspicious time to be born and share the dharma (teaching). When the time became ripe for the reception of the dharma, he was born as the first son of a minor Indian king and queen, Shuddhodana and Mahamaya Guatama, in Northern India (now Nepal). His conception itself was miraculous. He mysteriously entered his mother's right side in the form of an elephant, an auspicious symbol of success. The legend goes that as soon as he was born, he faced north and uttered, "I am the highest in the world, I am the best in the world, I am the eldest in the world; this is my last birth."

When this young future Buddha was presented to the temple, the statues of all the gods fell at his feet and sang a hymn in his honor. He received the name Siddhartha, which means "goal attained." At that time, temple priests recognized thirty-two fundamental and eighty secondary signs of a great man and declared that Siddhartha would become either a universal sovereign or an extraordinary spiritual liberator. His father committed himself to assuring that he would be the former.

At the age of sixteen, Siddhartha married a neighboring princess, Yasodhara, who ultimately gave him a son whom he named Rahula, which means "fetter" or "impediment." Interestingly, the Buddha praised the monastic, celibate life as free from the fetters of this world.

From the time of Siddhartha's birth, his father was obsessed with keeping him from anything that would provoke religious consciousness. He ensured that Siddhartha would live in absolute opulence and comfort. He also tried to keep Siddhartha from ever experiencing anything disturbing. For example, whenever Siddhartha went out of the palace, his father ensured that he would not see anything that might make him ask ultimate questions about the nature of life and death. Everything had to be pleasant.

Despite these precautions, on four separate occasions, Siddhartha did leave the palace and witnessed three disturbing sights and one intriguing one: he saw an old man, a sick man, a corpse, and finally a holy man. Thus, he saw the realities of old age, sickness, and death, as well as an example of someone who strove to escape these ravages of the human condition. So it was that one night he stealthily left the palace forever, determined to confront life's great curses of aging, sickness, and death.

Having left the palace, Siddhartha found a great spiritual master who taught him *samkhya*, which represented an advanced form of Hindu psychology and metaphysics. Upon mastering *samkhya*, he then found another master who taught him advanced meditational techniques, which he quickly mastered as well. Giving up on these practices, he embraced severe asceticism—particularly fasting—in the hope this would bring him escape. He found this asceticism especially unhelpful, however. From that point on, Siddhartha could proclaim that he had mastered the best philosophy, yoga, and ascetic practices of the day, and found them all wanting. Finally, he accepted a pious woman's offering of boiled rice and milk. With his strength regained, he sat under a pipal tree, known henceforth as the *bodhi* (enlightenment) tree, and determined not to leave it until he became enlightened.

Mara, the tempter and personification of death, became unnerved by the possibility that someone could achieve full enlightenment and escape his realm or, worse yet, teach others to escape as well. He assailed Siddhartha with a terrifying army of demons, ghosts, and monsters, all to no avail. Next, he tried to overthrow Siddhartha from his seat, but Siddhartha's amassed merit protected him. Mara, as master over the realm of the created universe and thus Siddhartha's life, then challenged him directly. The soon-to-be Buddha touched the earth with his right hand and called on the earth to testify to his

In Ayutthaya, Thailand, the head of this sandstone Buddha image is entwined in the roots of the bodhi tree.

right to escape. The earth quaked in affirmation. Finally, Mara sent his three daughters, Discontent, Delight, and Thirst, to seduce him. Siddhartha remained unmoved.

On the night of his enlightenment, Siddhartha had three key experiences. On the first watch of the night, he recollected his past lives. During the second watch, he surveyed the entire universe and all beings in it. In doing so, he discovered that nothing exists that is substantial. He saw that all things are impermanent (*anicca*) and without a self (*anatta*). In the third watch, he saw the conditions that lead to death and rebirth, and he discovered the **Four Noble Truths**. Finally, as dawn approached, he attained all knowledge. From this moment on, Siddhartha became known as the Buddha, which means "awakened one." The Buddha then spent the rest of his life tirelessly teaching the means to awaken and escape samsara. He called this utter awakening Nirvana.

Considering the Story

Historians take some of the Buddha's story literally. Few doubt that he lived around the time that Buddhists claim, that he was the son of a king, that he went off to learn advanced spiritual practices, discovering their assets and liabilities, and finally, that he sat for many days under a pipal tree until he achieved full awakening. Other parts of the story are less accepted. Yet, even if the rest of the narrative is not historical, it is important. The Buddha's myth points to extraordinary intentionality and providence. Siddhartha Guatama is only one of many Buddhas who have lived through the eons, each emerging at his own discretion when the era is ripe for spiritual transformation. The Buddhist canon lists others by name and circumstance. It is believed the next Buddha, whose name is Maitreya, is already waiting in the *tusita heaven* for the right time to reveal himself in a future eon.

In Siddhartha's presentation and naming ceremony at the temple, the statues of the gods bow to him. This show of respect resonates well with Hindu cosmology, in which the gods also are created beings and have a limited time before they die and are reborn into some other form. Thus, also like other beings, the gods need the dharma, and indeed spiritual beings regularly came to listen to Siddhartha's message. The whole cosmos was in high anticipation for Siddhartha's presentation and naming. In bowing before the child Siddhartha, the gods (represented by the statues) recognized his spiritual superiority, even though his current rebirth was that of a mere human.

It is impossible to imagine that a twenty-nine-year-old married man and father had no idea that people aged, became ill, and died or that there are such people as spiritual seekers who try to liberate themselves from the rebirth. Surely, his father, in wanting to ensure that he would become a great king, would have trained him in politics, literature, philosophy, warfare, and so on. Prince Siddhartha would have been a savvy, well-educated young man. In this regard, Ashvaghosha's description is insightful: "When he thus gained insight into the fact that the blemishes of disease, old age, and death vitiate the very core of this world, he lost at the same moment all self-intoxication, which normally arises with pride in one's own strength, youth, and vitality" (cited in Conze, *Buddhist Scriptures*, 43). From an early age, everyone knows about death. However, rarely do people live as though they know about it. They take risks or follow ambitions as though they were creating something of lasting significance. It is this approach to life that Ashvaghosha describes as "self-intoxication."

Coming to terms with one's mortality is a critical moment in the spiritual life. Doing so is not merely conceding that people age and die. What is at stake is seeing the truth of one's mortality for what it is and incorporating that truth into one's life, living now in the context of this truth. To see aging, sickness, and death in this case is to realize fully their implications. To see a holy man seeking liberation is to recognize someone who has taken the issue of mortality seriously, a spiritual seeker who has placed himself in the very heart of life's truth and unflinchingly committed to stop living in delusion.

Reflecting on the Four Noble Truths

The Buddha preached the Four Noble Truths in his very first sermon. One could say that everything he taught over the many decades of his ministry could be traced to these Noble Truths. In brief, the Four Noble Truths are (1) life is suffering; (2) the cause of suffering is craving; (3) the cessation of suffering comes from the cessation of craving, which is Nirvana; and (4) the way to the cessation of suffering is the **Eightfold Path**. The Buddha phrased it more dramatically:

> This is the noble truth of suffering: birth is suffering, aging is suffering, illness is suffering, death is suffering, union with what is displeasing is suffering, separation from what is pleasing is suffering; not to get what one wants is suffering; in brief the five aggregates subject to clinging are suffering. This is the noble truth about the origin of suffering: it is craving which leads to renewed existence, accompanied by delight and lust, seeking delight here and there; that is, craving for sensual pleasures, craving for existence, craving for non-existence. This is the truth for the cessation of suffering: it is the remainderless fading away and cessation of the same craving, the giving up and relinquishing of it, freedom from it, non-reliance on it. This is the noble truth of the way leading to the cessation of suffering: it is the noble eightfold path.
>
> — *Samyutta Nikaya*, 5.56.11

This teaching may be striking to modern ears. Surely while life has suffering in it, is suffering an apt overall assessment? The

Buddha's teaching is actually more nuanced in this regard. The Pali term **dukkha** traditionally translates as "suffering." *Dukkha* is a term that can mean many things and indeed could literally mean suffering, though it could also translate as stress, unease, or dissatisfaction. To add to the complexity not all *dukkha* is the same. The most common form of *dukkha* is *dukkha-dukkha*, which refers to the experience of things that are literally painful, be they mental, physical, or emotional. Dropping a hammer on one's foot is *dukkha-dukkha*. A second kind of *dukkha* is *viparinama-dukkha*, which refers to the condition produced by change. Because everything is in flux, one can never enjoy anything in a sustained way. Even in enjoying a thing, there is something disquieting in its dissipation. Finally, there is *samkara-dukkha*, which refers to all conditioned states being relative and never being a true refuge for the soul. In the previous citation, when the Buddha mentions that the "aggregates subject to clinging are suffering," he was referring to the five parts of the human, all of which are impermanent and without an eternal self. Thus, seeking refuge or ultimate satisfaction in these impersonal and ever-changing parts that make up a human is bound to fail. Only the first form of *dukkha* is suffering outright. The second form corresponds to suffering only vaguely. The third form, *samkara-dukkha*, is more of an evaluation of the limited nature of reality. Still, it is difficult to imagine that most people resonate with this assessment, even with its nuances.

Adding to the dour diagnosis that life is *dukkha*, the Buddha also characterized the unawakened mind as conditioned by lust, ill will, and delusion. These qualities can be quite subtle. Encountering something pleasant conditions attachment (lust) and encountering something unpleasant conditions aversion (ill will). The Buddha also taught that one's experiences are rife with delusion. As there is no enduring self, whenever one identifies with an experience one is deluded. Humans are also deluded in other ways. Take lust, for example. It makes the heart restless, unhappy, and frustrated. Yet, humans still cultivate it. Consider resentment. Everyone knows that resentment is toxic, but people still cultivate it. Why perpetuate something that harms one? The only possible reason is that such a mental state also inflates the ego—the ultimate delusion.

Christian Reflection

Providential Birth

Just as Buddhists believe that the Buddha's birth entails providence, so Christians believe that Jesus' birth was providential. Christians have two short narratives concerning Jesus' birth, one from Matthew and the other from Luke. Usually they are blurred together to create a single nativity story, thus missing their unique insights.

In Luke's Gospel, the archangel Gabriel visits Mary. She is told, "The Holy Spirit will come upon you, and the power of the Most High will overshadow you; therefore, the child to be born will be holy; he will be called Son of God" (Luke 1:35). Gabriel's description of Mary being overshadowed corresponds to God's glory overshadowing the Ark of the Covenant in the desert (Leviticus 16:2; Numbers 9:15ff).

Mary then visits her cousin Elizabeth, the mother of John the Baptist, and powerfully witnesses to God, who raises the lowly, scatters the proud, fills the hungry, and remembers his promises (Luke 1:46–55). Mary's witness, modeled on the Old Testament songs of divine praise (e.g., 1 Samuel 2:1–10), describes the inversion of earthly circumstances in which one recognizes God's action. Mary, in her lowly estate, becomes a living symbol of divine liberation.

Because of a census, Mary and Joseph must travel to Bethlehem to register. There, they find no room at the inn and have to sleep in a barn. Jesus is delivered in the barn, while an angel informs shepherds of the event, and a multitude of angels praise God. The shepherds rush to the scene to see the baby Jesus. Eight days later, Mary and Joseph travel to Jerusalem (just six miles away) and have Jesus circumcised. They then return home to Nazareth. What we see in Luke's narrative is a way of framing God's plan, one that unites human lowliness with divine power and glory. As Buddha teaches the deconstruction of the ego unto liberation, Jesus' birth in Luke shows how God's typical way of salvation is through the gate of humility.

Matthew tells a different story. He begins with Jesus' genealogy, which shows a providential plan from God with fourteen generations from Abraham to David, fourteen from David to the Babylonian exile, and fourteen from the exile to Joseph. In Matthew's version,

Mary and Joseph are not from Nazareth; they only eventually emigrate there to avoid King Herod's son Archelaus (Matthew 2:22). It appears that they actually lived in Bethlehem, for they were dwelling in a house when the wise men from the East came to visit them (Matthew 2:11). Their gifts are symbolic: gold, reflecting Jesus' royal dignity; frankincense, reflecting his priestly dignity; and myrrh, anticipating his death on the cross. Matthew also tells a story of the forces of power fearing the truth of God and God's messiah. Herod plots the death of this newborn messiah and kills all the young boys in Bethlehem to make sure of it. God's protective care is at work, however, as Joseph is directed to take Mary and Jesus to Egypt.

In Matthew's narrative, the Old Testament prophecies are fulfilled, such as the messiah being from Bethlehem (Micah 5:2). Matthew also provides allusions to Old Testament history, from lamentations over the death of children in the exile (Jeremiah 31:15) to Jesus representing the whole people of Israel: "Out of Egypt I have called my son" (Hosea 11:1). Jesus fulfills prophecy and becomes part of God's great plan of universal salvation, a plan that even the stars announce (Matthew 2:2). Like Siddhartha, Jesus receives a providential name: *Jesus* means "God saves." In addition, Herod, like Mara for the Buddha, was extraordinarily alarmed, for worldly power is always threatened by spiritual truth. The lesson in both Buddhist and Christian narratives is that providence is stronger than its spiritual enemies.

Seeing the Obvious

Another parallel is that both Buddha and Jesus spent much of their ministries pointing out the obvious. For the Buddha, it was the truth of suffering. For Jesus, it was the inauguration of the kingdom of God. Even though Jesus' ministry clearly manifested spiritual power, some simply refused to believe what was before their eyes. Jesus once said, "When you see the cloud rising in the west, you immediately say, 'It is going to rain'; and so it happens. And when you see the south wind blowing, you say, 'There will be a scorching heat'; and it happens. You hypocrites! You know how to interpret the appearance of earth and sky, but why do you not know how to interpret the present time?" (Luke 12:54–56). "For, in fact," Jesus later says, "the kingdom of God is among you" (Luke 17:21). Signs of the kingdom were everywhere in Jesus' ministry. Jesus also revealed and expressed divine mercy and forgiveness (Matthew 9:2–8), and some of the worst sinners were converting (Matthew 21:31ff). These conversions should have pleased everyone, yet Jesus was derided as a "friend of tax-collectors and sinners" (Matthew 11:18). The contentiousness between Jesus and those who resisted the truth became so great that when Jesus freed those who were possessed by demons, he was accused of using the power of Satan to do it. Jesus responded by assuring his accusers that the kingdom had come upon them, and they now must decide about their relationship to truth and falsehood (Luke 11:14–23).

Both the Buddha and Jesus directly challenged their audience to open their eyes and hearts. In one collection of the Buddha's sayings, we read, "Ashamed of what is not shameful, and not ashamed of what is shameful; those undertaking wrong view go to a miserable existence. Being afraid of what is not frightful, and being unafraid of the frightful; those undertaking wrong view go to a miserable existence. Imagining fault in the faultless, and perceiving no fault in the sinful; those undertaking wrong view go to a miserable existence" (*Dhammapada*, nos. 316–318). It is one thing to be weak and to act unskillfully, but it is wholly another to become so habituated in sin as to lose one's moral foundations and believe evil to actually be good. The Church fathers referred to this mental disposition as *scotosis*, the systematic, intentional practice of keeping oneself from the truth. Jesus saw *scotosis* everywhere. He found that many religious leaders were "blind guides" and "blind fools" (Matthew 15:14, 23:16–17). Their greatest problem was that they refused to admit that they had a problem, that they needed reform. At one point, Jesus reminds them that if they recognized their blindness, they could be healed too. To insist that they were not blind was to ensure that they remained so (John 9:35–41). It was, in a sense, a commitment to blindness.

The Buddha Helping the Christian Hear Jesus

Buddhism points one's consciousness to the central truth that life is *dukkha*, painful or dissatisfying, and that this pain comes from a grasping, craving mind. In one fitting saying the Buddha declares: "Whatever an enemy would do to an enemy, a hater to one hated, worse than that is the harm a wrongly directed mind can do to one-self" (*Dhammapada*, no. 42). To look at one's own sinful inclinations as one's worst enemy draws one away from judging others and back to attending to one's own inner life. It can also bring one to recognize the need for universal compassion. One finds an example of this in Jesus' parable of the Pharisee and tax collector in the temple:

> Two men went up to the temple to pray, one a Pharisee and the other a tax collector. The Pharisee, standing by himself, was praying thus, "God, I thank you that I am not like other people: thieves, rogues, adulterers, or even like this tax-collector. I fast twice a week; I give a tenth of all my income." However, the tax collector, standing far off, would not even look up to heaven, but was beating his breast and saying, "God be merciful to me, a sinner!" I tell you, this man went down to his home justified rather than the other; for all who exalt themselves will be humbled, but all who humble themselves will be exalted.

—Luke 18:10–14

IMAGE: © CHRIS HELLIER/CORBIS

The Pharisee and the Publican pray in the temple.

In this well-known parable, the reader easily understands that the Pharisee is prideful and judgmental, while the publican is humble and thus forgiven; and indeed, that one should follow the humble example. The less obvious insight comes from a Buddhist analysis of the Pharisee, who is immersed in *dukkha*. His ego-inflation not only harms him in the future, but also it is causing him suffering at the moment, worse than an enemy could inflict. Of course, the Pharisee does not realize his situation, and his delusion makes him all the more tragic. There is an additional level of insight available: without awareness of suffering and its intimate relationship with a deluded ego, the reader ironically is likely to judge the judgmental Pharisee and take on his very toxic mental state. One can easily unwittingly become that same Pharisee. Buddhist wisdom does not then condemn the reader, but invites the reader to embrace the parable more fully and to cultivate compassion toward all who suffer delusion— Pharisee, publican, and oneself alike.

MEDITATION
The Buddha's Two Meditative Tracks

Certainly the core of the Buddha's message involves meditation. "Absorbed in meditation," the Buddha said, "with perseverance and constant effort, the wise touch Nirvana, that ultimate shelter" (*Dhammapada*, no. 23). There are two tracks of meditation in Buddhism, and both are crucial for different reasons. The first represents meditations that induce concentration or *samadhi*. These meditational forms cultivate a mind that is strong, pure, and filled with Buddhist values. The great Buddhist scholar Buddhaghosa (fifth century CE) delineates forty traditional meditational subjects. These include qualities of the Buddha, which inspire greater devotion to him as well as the cultivation of the kinds of spiritual qualities needed to become enlightened. They also include meditating on such things as decaying corpses, which instills a greater sense of impermanence and helps the meditator gain distance from sensual desires.

Four famous samadhi meditations represent what are called the Divine Abiding meditations. They are loving-kindness, compassion, sympathetic joy, and equanimity, and are some of the most highly praised and consistently used meditations. Collectively, these represent a balanced, highly skillful mind and way of relating to others. In loving-kindness, one meditates on wishing the universe and all in it to be well, happy, and flourishing. In compassion, one inclines toward all who suffer, filling one's mind with the desire that they be freed from what oppresses them. Sympathetic joy represents meditating on delighting in the success of others, without any sense of concern for one's own. And finally, equanimity is the meditation that infuses one with the conscious acceptance of the universe as it is, including others' own karmic responsibility. If one could meditate deeply on these qualities and hold them in balance, one would walk in the world filled with love, care, and support of others, with the freedom that accepts reality for what it is.

Samadhi meditations fortify and train the mind, and this makes them very important. But they are not curative; they cannot directly lead to Nirvana. "Neither by precept and virtue, nor by great learning," the Buddha proclaimed, "Neither by attaining samadhi, nor by solitary dwelling; not by thinking, 'I touch the happiness of renunciation, unknown to the ordinary,' do you, O monk, find contentment, if you have not attained the dissolution of the toxins" (*Dhammapada*, nos. 271–272). In samadhi the toxic qualities of the mind—lust, ill will, and delusion—are suppressed and in some sense counteracted, but they are not actually removed from the mind. This can only come with the second track of meditation, *vipassana* or insight meditation. The purpose of samadhi meditations is to strengthen the mind and make it more naturally wholesome. The purpose of *vipassana* meditation is to know the mind by direct observation and see that it and the body (and the universe by extension) are impermanent, selfless, and dissatisfying. There are different strategies in *vipassana* meditation. One is watching the ever-changing dynamics of the breath. Another is watching the arising and dissipation of mental states and discovering that they are empty of any real identity. Still another could be attending to one's body and deconstructing it by paying attention to its various parts. It is one thing to say that one believes in no-self or impermanence, it is another to deeply penetrate that truth by long, sustained meditative attention to these facts.

Christian Reflection

Buddhist meditation is very different from Christian prayer, including and especially contemplation. Buddhist meditation is a process of self-induced mental control. In contrast, Christians believe that God's Spirit guides prayer and that prayer is itself a response to the indwelling Spirit. We saw this in chapter five. Prayer is also an experience of intimacy with God. And the tradition widely proclaims that the deeper one goes into prayer, the clearer and more profound the intimacy with God is. We saw this witness as well in chapter six. Further, this intimacy is characterized by intense love. This is very different than the loving-kindness meditation that we saw above. The experience in Christian prayer is a love that has the potential to be overwhelming to the soul, even ravishing, and at times even heartbreaking. For Christianity, divine love is the agent of the soul's transformation, for "God is love" (1 John 4:8). In contrast, insight into the three characteristics of no-self, impermanence, and *dukkha* is the agent of transformation, according to the Buddha.

The above distinction is of crucial importance if we are to truly appreciate Buddhism and its uniqueness. Its very difference is what brings gifts and insights into the dialogue. For example, Buddhists have a tradition of distinguishing authentic and inauthentic mental states; the latter are often called the "near enemies." The near enemy of loving-kindness is a kind of attachment to the other, which is characterized by some kind of clinging or control. Compassion's near enemy is pity, which is really an expression of aversion to another's condition and considerable fear. While compassion leans into the suffering to be present to another, pity is far more reactive. Sympathetic joy's near enemy is comparison. Even as one celebrates another's good fortune, one does so as a comparative to one's own situation. Finally, the near enemy of equanimity is indifference. True equanimity allows one to enter into a situation with an open, spacious heart. This ensures that one's engagement is free and authentic. Pseudo-equanimity looks like acceptance, but actually distances one from the moment.

The tradition of the Divine Abiding meditations points to a healthy, balanced engagement in the world. In fact, some Christians involved in Buddhist-Christian dialogue practice them regularly. Collectively these mental states allow for a balanced, robust engagement with the world; one that seeks the peace and flourishing of all beings and has the composure to enter into the darkest suffering with care and not fear. The tradition also wisely demonstrates how unskillful mental states can masquerade as a spiritual value; where self-righteousness masquerades as religious confidence or religious myopia as deep devotion.

TWO CONFOUNDING QUESTIONS:
THE SELF AND NIRVANA
The Self and Anatta

The Buddha taught that one of the three characteristics of all phenomenal reality is *anatta*, **no-self**. His teaching of no-self was the great contrast to the Hindu dogma that the self (Atman) was Brahman. Who (or what) am I, if I am not a self? The Buddha's answer is that humans are nothing more (or less) than an impersonal collection of five interrelated aggregates: materiality, feeling, perception, mental formations, and consciousness. Buddhism teaches that humans live under the delusion that a stable, essential self exists underneath humans' experience. This delusion is brought on by failure to analyze the aggregates and their impersonal, ever-changing nature. In one sense, Buddhists can talk about a self as being one's own protector and liberator, or one's worst enemy. This use of the term *self* is conventional. In a famous dialogue with King Milinda, the monk Nagasena challenges him to explain a chariot, to which the king replies that it consists of an axle, wheels, a carriage, and so on. Nagasena presses to know what is the chariot's essence, to which the king replies that it has no essence. Nagasena agrees, because only by convention do humans call this collectivity a chariot. So it is, he argues, with the self; the conventional term is useful, but there is no essence underneath it.

The confounding paradox is as follows: what is the self that can liberate the self to see that there is no-self and thus attain Nirvana, the place of ultimate refuge for the self? One might also ask, why be compassionate if there is nothing personal to be compassionate toward? Indeed, if there is no-self, then who is being compassionate in the first place? Buddhists respond by insisting that a person is very real in the sense that these aggregates are real. Humans are sentient beings who suffer. Thus, compassion is the only appropriate response to that reality. Buddhists also say that doctrines are meant to bring one to Nirvana. That is, they have only an instrumental use: the only way to achieve Nirvana is to assess and analyze reality in this way (*anicca*, *anatta*, and *dukkha*). Finally, Buddhists might argue the following: there are two kinds of truths; one is conventional and relative (*sammuti-sacca*) and the other is ultimate (*paramattha-sacca*). The relative truth really is true, but only in terms of the phenomenal world and only on this side of Nirvana. Therefore, the teaching on no-self is part of *sammuti-sacca*. As far as *paramattha-sacca* is concerned, nothing can be asserted, particularly regarding the issues of self and no-self.

In a famous dialogue with the Buddha, the monk Malunkyaputta challenged the Buddha about why the Buddha never spoke about important philosophical concerns. Posed as questions, they would be the following: Is the world eternal or not eternal? Is the world finite or infinite? Is the soul the same as the body or different from the body? After death does a fully enlightened person exist, not exist, both exist and not exist, or neither exist nor not exist? The Buddha's defense of his silence was, "Because it is unbeneficial, it does not belong to the fundamentals of the holy life . . . to enlightenment, to Nirvana." The Buddha then likened such concerns to a man who was shot by a poisoned arrow. He refused treatment until he knew everything about his assailant's life and even the bow and arrow used. He concludes, "All this would still not be known to that man and meanwhile he would die" (*Majjhima Nikaya*, 63).

In one teaching, the Buddha explained dharma through the use of two similes—a poisonous water snake and a raft. One needs to grasp the dharma carefully and with great skill, like the snake. One clings to a raft only to get across to the other side of the river to continue one's journey, but then must let go. As the Buddha says, "The dharma is similar to the raft, being for the purpose of crossing over, not for the purpose of clinging" (*Majjhima Nikaya*, 22:11–13).

Nirvana

Just as problems exist with the issue of the self, so also there are problems in speaking about Nirvana. Etymologically, the word *nirvana* suggests blowing something out, such as a candle. Its opposite is represented by the craving, burning quality of an unawakened mind. Therefore, one way to understand Nirvana is in the context of the metaphor of fire:

> All things, O priests, are on fire. . . . The eye is
> on fire . . . forms are on fire . . . eye-consciousness is on
> fire . . . impressions received by the eye are on fire. . . .
> The ear is on fire . . . the nose is on fire . . . the tongue

is on fire . . . the body is on fire . . . the mind is on fire. . . . And with what are these on fire? With the fire of lust, with the fire of ill will, with the fire of infatuation; with birth, old age, death, sorrow, lamentation, misery, and despair are they on fire.

—cited in Burtt, *Teachings of the Compassionate Buddha*, 72–73, slightly adjusted

Nirvana is the blowing out of this fire, this craving, this life as it is characterized by lust, ill will, misery, and despair. Nirvana is not merely the absence of craving, but it cannot be described directly: it is *atakkavacara*, inaccessible to thought, and *avisayasmim*, beyond conceptual range, even for the Buddha.

In the *Aggivacchagotta Sutta*, the Buddha illustrates the enigmatic quality of final Nirvana in his conversation with his disciple Vaccha. In doing so, he focuses on the question of the self going to final Nirvana. Given that the Buddha rejected nihilism, the belief that after death nothing existed, he posited that something actually does happen after death. However, humans have no reference points.

"What do you think, Vaccha? Suppose a fire were burning before you. Would you know: This fire is burning before me?"

"I would, Master Gautama."

"If someone were to ask you, Vaccha: What does the fire burning before you burn in dependence on?—being asked thus, what would you answer?"

"Being asked thus, Master Gautama, I would answer: This fire burning before me burns in dependence on grass and sticks."

"If that fire before you were to be extinguished, would you know: This fire before me has been extinguished."

"I would, Master Gautama."

"If someone were to ask you, Vaccha: When that fire before you was extinguished, to which direction did it go: to the east, the west, the north, or the south?—being asked thus, what would you answer?"

"That does not apply, Master Gautama. The fire burned in dependence on its fuel of grass and sticks. When that is used up, if it does not get any more fuel, being without fuel, it is reckoned as extinguished."

"So too, Vaccha, the Buddha has abandoned that material form by which one describing the Buddha might describe him; he has cut it off at the root, made it like a palm stump, done away with it so that it is no longer subject to future arising [rebirth]. The Buddha is liberated from reckoning in terms of material form, Vaccha, he is profound, immeasurable, unfathomable like the ocean. The term 'reappears' does not apply, the term 'does not reappear' does not apply, the term 'both reappears and does not reappear' does not apply, the term 'neither reappears nor does not reappear' does not apply."

— *Majjhima Nikaya*, 72.19–20, trans. slightly adjusted

What does one do when no words, no thoughts, no concepts apply? It is clear in Buddhism: one lets go of the need to know and continues on the path.

Christian Reflection

The Buddhist take on Nirvana can be, in some respects, instructive for Christianity. On the one hand, Christians do claim to know something about heaven here on Earth. The apostle Paul described living in the Spirit as a foretaste and initial participation in one's future heavenly existence (Romans 8:23). Buddhist wisdom, however, teaches not to overplay one's hand. Christianity really does not know much about heaven. The specific evidence from the Bible on heaven itself is rather inconsistent. Take the question of what happens after death, for example. Some texts suggest that souls go right to heaven, such as the one in which Jesus tells the repentant criminal on the cross that he would be in paradise that very day (Luke 23:43). Paul suggests the same in Philippians 1:21–24. Yet, Paul also teaches in First Thessalonians that those who die in faith remain in a kind of sleep, or holding pattern, until the final day when all will be taken up to heaven collectively (1 Thessalonians

4:13–18). So, one would not know if those who have died are in heaven or resting in peace until the last day. Paul also gives an image of the whole physical universe being transformed into, and participating in, the glory of the Resurrection (Romans 8:19–21). In addition to these passages from Paul, one finds an alternative image of the universe consumed in fire and replaced by a spiritual universe (2 Peter 3:10–13).

And what of heaven? In the Book of Revelation, it is described as a new created universe with a new Jerusalem and temple (Revelation 11:19, 21:1–4). In contrast, Jesus describes living a life like the angels live (Mark 12:25). Elsewhere, one sees that heaven will be more like living God's life: holy as God is (1 Peter 1:15–16), reigning with him (2 Timothy 2:11–13), becoming as he is (1 John 3:2). Paul says that Jesus' resurrected body directly models humans' (1 Corinthians 15:49). He calls it a *soma pneumatikos* (spiritual body). While Paul is suggestive, he also believed that attempting a specific investigation or philosophical analysis to such a question was inappropriate. It simply cannot be answered because it is beyond conception: "But someone will ask, 'How are the dead raised? With what kind of body do they come?' Fool!" (1 Corinthians 15:35).

What shall one make of these images, many of which do not cohere with each other? It seems clear that in using a variety of images, metaphors, and symbols, the Bible is both firing one's spiritual imagination and telling one that the actual reality is beyond what the human mind can comprehend. Indeed, too much attention to this issue can take one away from what is crucial in following the path described in the Bible. In the Pauline tradition, believers are instructed to avoid considerations that "promote speculations rather than the divine training that is known by faith." Such is "meaningless talk." In contrast is instruction whose aim is "love that comes from a pure heart, a good conscience, and a sincere faith" (1 Timothy 1:4–7). The point is neither to equate resurrection and Nirvana nor to simply say that both are beyond conceptualization, and thus should not be addressed. Rather, like Buddhists before Nirvana, Christians are challenged by their tradition to be humble before their great mysteries of faith.

SHIFTS IN BUDDHISM
AND THEIR MEANINGS

Introduction

Early Buddhism is most clearly represented by the **Theravada** tradition, which one still finds dominant in Sri Lanka, Burma (Myanmar), Thailand, Laos, and Cambodia. The Theravada (way of the elders) school has a tradition that highly encourages the monastic way of life with the focus of seeking one's liberation. This way of life need not be seen as selfish, especially because the life of one who is awakened is characterized by selfless compassion. Seeking one's liberation is also seeking to be free from narcissistic craving and ignorance. The Theravada scriptures are filled with Buddha's defense of the monastic life. In the *Samannaphala Sutta*, for example, the Buddha responds to the challenge that the monastic life is a distorted and self-centered lifestyle. He describes the monastic life as one more spiritually skillful and truly free in contrast to a lay lifestyle "full of hindrances . . . a path for the dust of passion" (*Digha Nikaya*, 2). In another saying, one finds, "Those who are mindful depart; they do not delight in a house. They leave behind every home, like swans who abandon a pond" (*Dhammapada*, no. 91). As for the charge of selfishness, the Theravada tradition points to the holy witness of monks, the training they offer, the mutual support they give each other for the holy life, and that in contrast to material gifts (*amisa dana*), they offer to society their spiritual gifts (*dhamma dana*), something much more valuable.

Mahayana (big vehicle) Buddhism expresses a shift from the earlier tradition. Mahayana is "big vehicle" because it is more inclusive, holding great confidence that ordinary lay lives can be extraordinarily holy and awakened. In contrast to the Theravadin emphasis on withdrawal from engagement with life, Mahayana understands the Buddhist path to be a deep penetration in the context of life's complexities. Indeed, the lay life could even be better. Consider the following:

> At that time, there dwelt in the great city of Vaisali a wealthy householder named Vimalakirti. . . . [He resides] only for the sake of the necessary means to saving creatures . . . ever

careful of the poor, pure in self-discipline, obedient to all
precepts . . . removes all distraction [and] ignorance
by full wisdom . . . using the jeweled ornaments of
the world, yet adorned with spiritual splendor; though
eating and drinking, yet enjoying the rapture of meditation . . . having a profound knowledge of worldly
learning, yet ever finding pleasure in things of the spirit
as taught by the Buddha . . . Though profiting by all the
professions, yet far above being absorbed by them; ben-
efiting all beings, going wherever he pleases, protecting all
beings as a judge with righteousness.

—cited in Burtt, 215–217

Vimalakirti points to possibilities of extraordinary holiness in normal
lifestyles. Perhaps this example additionally suggests different ways
to consider one's relationship to the world. In the following two
sections, the doctrines of **dependent coarising** and the bodhisattva
vow will be discussed. Both doctrines are held by Theravada and
Mahayana traditions, yet both take on different perspectives as these
different schools advance them, which is highly instructive.

Dependent Coarising

The Buddhist understanding of the perpetual arising and dissipation
of any given thing is grounded in a concept called *paticca samupadha*.
Paticca means "having depended" and *samupadha* means "together
arising." In the Theravada tradition, dependent coarising refers to
the interconnected way in which all causes affect consciousness,
karma, rebirth, and death in a given person. It has ignorance as its
primal condition:

Ignorance conditions volitional [desire] formations,
Which conditions consciousness,
Which conditions mental-materiality,
Which conditions the six-fold base [of physicality],
Which conditions contact with the world,
Which conditions feeling,
Which conditions craving,

Which conditions clinging,
Which conditions becoming,
Which conditions birth,
Which conditions aging and death,
Which conditions sorrow and grief.

— *Visuddhimagga*, XVII.2

The only condition that can be successfully overcome is the first, ignorance. When ignorance is dispelled, a fully awakened person no longer craves and, thus, no longer creates karma. That alone would break down any future rebirths. Being attentive to the dynamics of dependent co-arising means focusing one's attention inward, seeing one's attachment to experience, and discovering the truth about no-self.

The Mahayana tradition interprets dependent co-arising differently. It refers to the interconnectedness, and indeed interpenetration, of the entire universe. While all Buddhists believe that there is no self or Atman underneath one's aggregates, the primary reason that Mahayana Buddhists maintain this position is that they believe there is no such thing as an independent being. Rather, all beings are part of each other and each other's spiritual path. Mahayana spiritual practice is inseparable from that of others in the same way that one's being is inextricably bound with all beings. There is little sense of personal enlightenment or awakening.

In Mahayana, compassion and wisdom involve transcending the notion of an individual self and breaking down the barrier between oneself and others. By seeing the delusion that radically distinguishes self and other, one also sees that the sufferings of another are one's own, and the eradication of another's suffering is the eradication of one's own. Of course, one realizes that conventionally one has a center of will and consciousness that is truly one's own. This conventional truth is important and helpful. Ultimately, however, it needs to be exposed as a limited and false view of oneself and the world.

One of the most inspiring meditational strategies in Mahayana Buddhism is the exchange of self for the other. One places all of one's spiritual interest and energy on that of another, even so far as taking on the other's negative karma as one's own in order to heal and purify it. The great Buddhist master, Shantideva, in his classic, *The Way of the Bodhisattva*, describes making the interchange of *I* and *other* as embracing the sacred mystery of happiness and truth: "All the joy the world contains has come through wishing happiness for others. All the misery the world contains has come through wanting pleasure for oneself" (8.129).

The Bodhisattva Vow

In the Theravada tradition, a bodhisattva is a being who is far advanced on the path but has not yet attained perfect enlightenment or Nirvana. This person (or *deva*) then vows to hold off on personally attaining Nirvana in order to develop so extraordinarily that he might become a future Buddha, and to do so strictly for the good of others. All those who have broken the chains of ignorance and craving attain Nirvana, but few of them would reach the profound excellence of being a Buddha. To become a Buddha would be to have attained the ten perfections (giving, morality, renunciation, wisdom, exertion, patience, truth, resolution, loving-kindness, and equanimity) to the highest possible standard. In the past lives of the historical Buddha, he could have attained Nirvana eons ago, but he forestalled this attainment for the sake of saving others as a Buddha. The bodhisattva vow is unique and relegated to those few extraordinarily developed beings that seek to become a Buddha.

The Mahayana tradition also has a bodhisattva vow, except that instead of taking it with the idea of forestalling Nirvana in order to become a Buddha, one vows to hold off attaining Nirvana until every sentient being attains Nirvana first. Further, many Mahayana Buddhists take this vow. Thus, a vast multitude of Buddhists have vowed to return again and again through innumerable eons in service for the salvation of all sentient beings. Until every single being is released, they remain in service. In doing so, they not only place themselves in almost eternal servitude, they also commit themselves to taking on the negative karma that others have created. The following expresses the spirit of the bodhisattva vow:

> A Bodhisattva resolves: I take upon myself the burden of all suffering. . . . At all costs I must bear the burdens of all living beings. . . . All beings I must set free. . . . I must

not cheat all beings out of my store of merit. . . . It is better that I alone should be in pain than that all these beings should fall into the states of woe . . . and with this my own body I must experience, for the sake of all beings, the whole mass of all painful feelings. . . . In reward for all this righteousness that I have won by my works. . . . May I be balm to the sick, their healer and servitor. . . . May I be in the famine of the ages' end their drink and meat . . . an unfailing store for the poor. . . . I have given them my body, why shall I care? . . . My foes . . . dwell in my spirit.

—cited in Burtt, 109–118

The bodhisattva vow is beyond extraordinary heroism. A curious question can be posed: If all people are interrelated, universally dependent coarising beings, is it possible that anyone could attain Nirvana before all attain Nirvana together? That is, if there is no discrete or separate self, as all beings interpenetrate, then no one *could* attain Nirvana until the entire universe attains it simultaneously. In one Mahayana text, the Buddha addresses the issue: "All these living creatures are my children to whom I will give equally the Great Vehicle, so that none will gain an individual Nirvana . . ." (cited in Burtt, 124). Is the vow then meaningless? Buddhists would say that the bodhisattva vow expresses proper and deep intentionality to one's existence, whereby one devotes one's existence to serving others and to remembering continually that one's fate is wrapped in the very fate of one's supposed enemy. As the previously quoted verse states: "My foes . . . dwell in my spirit."

Christian Reflection

While the Bible surely does not reflect eastern cosmology, the New Testament is filled with allusions to interrelatedness, such as in some of Paul's teachings. In Romans, for example, Paul writes that the entire created world will eventually participate in universal restoration, for it is all apiece (Romans 8:19–21). For Paul, the action of the resurrected Christ is to draw all things together into glory. This cosmic Christ is uniting all things in heaven and Earth (Ephesians 1:10), "that God may be all in all" (1 Corinthians 15:28).

Interrelatedness can also point to immediate experience. For example, someone's anger or love can literally fill a room, affecting everyone's thoughts and feelings there. One could ask, whose thought or feeling is this that I am experiencing? Of course, it is one's own but not as if separate from others' thoughts or feelings. Humans are interconnected.

One might also ask if the bodhisattva vow is really a profoundly Christian vow even as it is a profoundly Buddhist one. In this vow, one commits one's whole self to seeking the salvation of others, even to the point of suffering for the sins of others. This is what Christ did, dying to save humans from their sins. (John 6:51, 11:51–52; Romans 3:25; 2 Corinthians 5:14–15; 1 Timothy 2:6). Jesus is understood as mediating salvation as a sacrifice on the altar, a peace offering to God and a communion sacrifice (Matthew 26:26ff; Mark 14:22ff; Luke 22:14ff; 1 Corinthians 5:7; Ephesians 2:13). Jesus' sacrifice produces communion, according to Hebrews, because he has been accepted by God, has entered into heaven to secure eternal redemption (9:12) and make purification for sins (1:3, 10:11–14), thus bestowing sanctification (10:10) and enabling souls also to enter the sanctuary and approach God (10:19ff). The sacrifice of Christ is not to appease an angry God but to express God's love and to unite humans to the Father (Romans 8:32; John 3:16).

Jesus calls his disciples to imitate him in this regard: "If any want to become my followers, let them deny themselves and take up their cross and follow me" (Matthew 16:24); ". . . whoever wishes to be first among you must be your slave; just as the Son of Man came not to be served but to serve, and to give his life a ransom for many" (Matthew 20:27–28; see also Luke 22:26). This is Paul's vision as well. According to Paul, Christians are to have the mind and heart of Christ who emptied himself, taking the form of a slave (Philippians 2:5ff). It is striking that the bodhisattva vow represents exactly what Christ wants of his disciples.

Review Questions

1. What are the parallels between the Buddha's and Jesus' birth?
2. What are the Buddha's Four Noble Truths, and how do they relate to his assessment of the three conditions of all reality?
3. What is the difference in Buddhist teachings and the vision of holiness between Theravada and Mahayana schools?

In-Depth Questions

1. Consider three of your most pleasurable experiences in the last week. How long did each last? How did you feel when the pleasure was gone? Can you make a general statement about the extent that pleasures can satisfy?
2. Do you think that *dukkha* or dissatisfaction is an apt characterization of human existence? If so, why? If not, what would be a more incisive way to characterize it?
3. Are Christians too individualistic? If so, which Buddhist insights might draw Christians to become more broad-minded?
4. How far ought a Christian to take the Mahayana insight of dependent coarising? Just how interrelated are humans or all sentient life?
5. Is it possible that with respect to the crucial Christian teaching regarding imitation of Christ both as servant and as one who takes on the sins of the world, Mahayana Buddhists are more Christian than Christians?

Select Bibliography

Bailey, Greg, and Ian Mabbett. *The Sociology of Early Buddhism*. Cambridge: Cambridge University Press, 2003.

Buddhaghosa, Bhadantacariya. *The Path of Purification* [*Visuddhimagga*], 5th ed. Bhikkhu Nanamoli, trans. Kandy, Sri Lanka: Buddhist Publication Society, 1991.

Burtt, E. A., ed. *The Teachings of the Compassionate Buddha: Early Discourses, the Dhammapada, and Later Basic Writings.* New York: New American Library, 2000.

Buswell, Robert, and Robert Gimello, eds. *Paths to Liberation: The Marga and Its Transformation in Buddhist Thought.* Honolulu: University of Hawaii Press, 1992.

Collins, Steven. *Nirvana and Other Buddhist Felicities: Utopias of the Pali Imaginaire.* Cambridge: Cambridge University Press, 1998. This is a challenging and important guide to understanding the relationship between the pursuit of gratifying rebirth and that of Nirvana.

———. *Selfless Persons: Imagery and Thought in Theravada Buddhism.* Cambridge: Cambridge University Press, 1982. This is a highly accessible, scholarly introduction to Theravada Buddhism.

Conze, Edward, ed., *Buddhist Scriptures.* New York: Penguin, 1959.

Digha Nikaya: Thus Have I Heard: The Long Discourses of the Buddha. Maurice Walsh, trans. London: Wisdom, 1987.

Feldmeier, Peter. *Christianity Looks East: Comparing the Spiritualities of John of the Cross and Buddhaghosa.* Mahwah: Paulist Press, 2006.

Gombrich, Richard. *Theraveda Buddhism: A Social History from Ancient Benares to Modern Columbo.* London: Routledge, 1988.

Kugler, Peter. "The Logic of Nirvana: A Contemporary Interpretation." *International Journal for Philosophy of Religion* 53 (2003): 93–110.

Majjhima Nikaya. Bhikkhu Nanamoli and Bhikkhu Bodhi, trans. Boston: Wisdom Publications, 1995.

Rahula, Walpoloa. *What the Buddha Taught* (revised). New York: Grove Press, 1974. This is the most widely read and accessible introduction to Theravada Buddhism.

Samuels, Jeffrey. "Buddhist Theory and Practice: A Re-evaluation of the Bodhisattva-Shravaka Opposition." *Philosophy East and West* 47, no. 3 (1997): 339–415.

Samyutta Nikaya (2 vols.). Bhikkhu Bodhi, trans. Boston: Wisdom Publications, 2000.

Shanta Ratnayaka, "The Bodhisattva Ideal of Theravada." *The Journal of the International Association of Buddhist Studies* 8, no. 2 (1985): 85–110.

Shantideva, *The Way of the Bodhisattva.* Padmakara Translation Group, trans. Boston: Shambala Press, 1997.

Silva, Lilly de. *The Buddha and the Arahant.* Kandy, Sri Lanka: Buddhist Publication Society, 1996.

———. *Nibbana as a Living Experience.* Kandy, Sri Lanka: Buddhist Publication Society, 1996.

————. *The Problem of Self in Buddhism and Christianity.* Columbo, Sri Lanka: Study Centre for Religion and Society, 1975.

Thurman, Robert, trans. *The Holy Teaching of Vimalakirti: A Mahayana Scripture.* University Park: Pennsylvania State University Press, 1976. This is one of the most important Mahayana scriptural texts.

Wijayaratna, Mohan. *Buddhist Monastic Life.* Claude Gragler and Steven Collins, trans. Cambridge: Cambridge University Press, 1990.

Yoshinori, Takeuchi, ed. *Buddhist Spirituality: Indian, Southeast Asian, Tibetan, Early Chinese.* New York: Crossroads, 1995.

CHAPTER EIGHT

Zen Mind, Ordinary Mind

INTRODUCING ZEN

Why Zen?

It might seem odd to have an additional chapter on Buddhism, because no other religion has more than one chapter in this book. Indeed, Zen is perhaps the most well-known and widely engaged expression of Mahayana, a form of Buddhism that was already addressed. However, Zen has stripped from itself much of the Indian ethos that characterized the first thousand years of Buddhism. In addition, Zen is so unique and nonconceptual that some Christians even claim to embrace both Zen and Christianity at the same time. Forty years ago, widely respected Jesuit missionary priests, such as William Johnston, Hugo Enomiya-Lassalle, and Heinrich Dumoulin, were commending Zen insights and meditational practices for Christians. More recently, Father Robert Kennedy, SJ, Father Willigis Jäger, and Lutheran minister Gundula Meyer have each been officially designated as a *Roshi* (Zen master) and argue that a successful kind of unity can be made between Zen and Christianity. Such a unity is nonetheless controversial and not without its critics, both in the Christian and Zen communities.

On the surface, the fusion of any kind of Buddhism with Christianity seems simply impossible. Christians believe in God, while Buddhists do not. Christians believe in grace as the foundation for anything spiritually valuable, while Buddhists insist that all progress is due to one's own effort. Christians believe in an eternal soul that is unique and singular in this one life, while Buddhists claim no-self and rebirth over a myriad of lifetimes. However, Zen is unique in Buddhism, and its distinctiveness allows for cross-referencing that is far less problematic than with other Buddhist traditions.

To understand Zen, it may help to look at the development of Buddhism early in the Common Era. Mahayana Buddhism tends toward a kind of universal perspective as shown in chapter seven. The Mahayana version of dependent coarising, for example, represents the belief that all things interpenetrate, and thus, Nirvana is not something one could individually realize alone. Much of this perspective came from the great Buddhist scholar, Acharya **Nagarjuna** (c. 150–250 CE). Nagarjuna argued additionally that if the Buddha's teachings on impermanence and no-self were taken to their necessary conclusions, then everything is empty. Form, constantly in flux, is emptiness. Yet, even emptiness is not an absolute, because it expresses itself in form.

Nagarjuna wanted, above all, to take away any kind of dualism in Buddhism. There is no absolute subject-object dichotomy. There is only interpenetrating, ever flowing reality. To even consider Nirvana as a separate reality, Nagarjuna argued, is to create a dualistic mind. Nirvana is not some reality beyond Samsara. Rather, Nirvana and Samsara are one; Samsara is empty of itself even as Nirvana expresses itself in the context of Samsara. Nagarjuna writes,

There is no difference at all between Nirvana and Samsara. There is no difference at all between Samsara and Nirvana. . . . What is identity, and what is difference? What is eternity, what non-eternity? What do eternity and non-eternity being together mean? What does negation of both issues mean? Bliss consists in the cessation of all thought, in the quiescence of plurality. No separate reality was preached at all, nowhere and none by Buddha!

—cited in Burtt, *Teachings of the Compassionate Buddha,* 152–153, slightly adjusted

What does it really mean to say that Nirvana and Samsara are one? Does this suggest that they are two names for the same reality? Is there just one reality represented by different perspectives or different experiences of it? Is the Absolute Reality experienced in the context of the relative? Could it be that Nagarjuna was not even making a metaphysical claim but, rather, moving the religious seeker to a different mode of consideration? Is Nirvana really before everyone all the time, yet it is imagined somewhere else? Zen created a unique way of addressing these questions— one in which direct seeing and knowing ultimately replace doctrine and conceptualizations.

Zen practitioners often refer to an ancient story of one of the Buddha's sermons as exemplary of the essence of Zen and the true nature of enlightenment. The story says that the Buddha had gathered his disciples around him in order to teach them. Instead of speaking, however, he merely held up a lotus flower. Some were waiting for him to speak after this, imagining that patient attention was part of the lesson. Others imagined that the lotus flower was a metaphor and the essence of the teaching for the day. The lotus was often used in this way. It arises out of muddy waters, but its texture is such that none of the slime or mud sticks to it. Thus, the enlightened person remains pure in the midst of the world. It turns out that the Buddha neither intended to speak nor was he using the lotus flower as a metaphor for anything. Only one monk, Mahakashyapa, understood the teaching, and in doing so, became immediately enlightened.

What did Mahakashyapa see or understand? The lesson was nothing more or less than seeing the flower. The flower did not represent something else. It was not a symbol, it was a flower, and Mahakashyapa was simply engaged in the everyday, ordinary experience of life, directly and immediately. "No big deal," Zen masters say, "it is just ordinary mind, ordinary life; that is Zen."

Stories like this abound in the Zen oral tradition. One story has a monk ask a master, "What is enlightenment?" The master answers, "I chop wood. I carry water. What joy! What bliss!" Another story has two disciples of different spiritual masters talking. One boasts that his master is so spiritually advanced that he can be in two places at one time and can even foretell the future. The other disciple boasts that his master is even more advanced. "When he is tired, he just rests; when he is hungry, he just eats; and his mind is ever at peace." Hearing this, the first disciple abandons his master and becomes a follower of this latter master. One Zen master described enlightenment simply and elegantly: "Enlightenment is not something to be attained. If right now you bring forth this non-attaining mind, steadfastly not obtaining anything, then this is enlightened mind. Enlightenment is not a place to reside. For this reason there is nothing attainable" (cited in Takeuchi Yoshinori, *Buddhist Spirituality II*, 35). Simply chopping wood, just eating, or bringing forth a nonattaining mind requires extraordinary spiritual discipline and mental cultivation.

Historical Notes

Bodhidharma

Buddhism was introduced into China around the year 100 CE, but it was, at best, marginally successful. Due to its emphasis on solitary meditation, celibacy, monasticism, and renunciation of social classes, it ran counter to the Chinese Confucian culture. It took several hundred years for Buddhism to become a serious religious force. According to ancient tradition, **Bodhidharma**, the third son of an Indian prince, traveled to China in 527 CE and introduced a new form of Buddhism to China. He is also said to have been the twenty-eighth patriarch in a direct line of dharma transmission from the historical Buddha himself. The Buddhism that Bodhidharma introduced is known as *Ch'an*, a Chinese word for the Sanskrit, *dhyana*, which means "meditation" or "meditative absorption." *Zen* is the Japanese term for *Ch'an*.

Bodhidharma's biography witnesses to the importance of meditation. Upon Bodhidharma's arrival in China, the emperor asked that they visit. The emperor, a devout Buddhist, said, "Since I came to the throne, I have built countless temples, copied countless sutras [teachings], and given supplies to countless monks." Then he asked, "Is there any merit in this?" Bodhidharma replied, "There is no merit whatsoever." Then the emperor asked, "What, then, is true merit?" Bodhidharma replied, "True merit consists in the subtle comprehension of pure wisdom, whose substance is silent and void" (cited in

A statue of Bodhidharma, a Buddhist monk traditionally credited as the transmitter of Zen to China, at the Temple Kencho-ji in Kamakura, Japan.

John Wu, *Golden Age of Zen*, 34–35). Bodhidharma then went to the Shaolin monastery, where he spent the next nine years perpetually facing a wall, deep in meditation. According to one legend, he fell asleep seven years into his discipline and, in response, cut off his eyelids in order to stay awake. Miraculously, tea leaves formed to replace those eyelids. Thus began the practice of drinking tea in order to sustain mental alertness. According to the tradition, Hui-k'o, Bodhidharma's future disciple and second patriarch of Ch'an (Zen), tried desperately to get Bodhidharma's attention to no avail. Finally, Hui-k'o made Bodhidharma notice him by cutting off his own arm. When Bodhidharma saw this, he realized that Hui-k'o was truly serious, and he trained Hui-k'o in this new form of Buddhism. Surely, one need not imagine this narrative to be historically factual, but it does point to Ch'an's focus on meditation and the need to be utterly invested in the practice.

One of the most important Mahayana sutras, composed in the sixth century CE, was the Lankavatara Sutra, which taught that enlightenment is realized by doing away with all duality and rising above all distinctions. Further, it taught that the mind is inherently pure and indeed already enlightened. The challenge then is to realize this ever-present pure consciousness, what Zen will later call Buddha-nature, or the foundational reality and pure truth of all things. Such realization comes from seeing reality as it is, with no attempt to objectify anything. There is simply the flow of reality revealing Buddha-nature. This being the case, the Lankavatara Sutra also emphasizes the importance in not relying on words or concepts, which can create the mental distinctions that need to be unmasked in meditation. A text attributed to Bodhidharma expresses the core insight of Ch'an/Zen:

> A Special transmission outside the scriptures,
> Not founded upon words and letters;
> By pointing directly to one's mind;
> It lets one see into one's own true nature and thus
>   attain Buddhahood.
>   —cited in Heinrich Dumoulin, *Zen Buddhism*, 85

In China, Ch'an broke into various schools of practice and philosophies on how one ought to attain enlightenment. Of particular importance is the general division between the Northern School, which emphasized a gradual step-by-step approach to spiritual development, and the Southern School, which adopted the method of sudden realization. These schools are foundational reference points to the two major forms of Japanese Zen: **Soto Zen** and **Rinzai Zen**.

Soto Zen

While this new form of Buddhism entered Japan as early as the middle of the sixth century, the development of the Zen school of Soto is located in the twelfth and thirteenth centuries, particularly with Master Dogen (1200–1253). Dogen writes: "To study the Buddha Way is to study the self. To study the self is to forget the self. To forget the self is to be actualized by myriad things. When actualized by myriad things, your body and mind as well as the bodies and minds of others drop away. No trace of enlightenment remains, and this no-trace continues endlessly" (cited in Stephen Addis, *Zen Sourcebook*, 152). In this famous and somewhat enigmatic verse, one hears echoes of the historical Buddha's insistence on looking at oneself in order to realize that there is no eternal self at all (*anatta*).

Thus, paying attention to the self reveals no-self and allows one to stop identifying with one's experience and, thus, to stop craving. One also sees the influence of Nagarjuna, who insisted that form drops away into emptiness. Finally, one seems to see something new, even shocking: "No trace of enlightenment remains, and this no-trace continues endlessly." Why would no trace of enlightenment remaining be a good thing? Does one not want to find enlightenment? For Dogen, spiritual practice and enlightenment are not separate realities; one makes a crucial error if practicing to attain enlightenment. Enlightenment is right before one, only to be realized. To even mention enlightenment as if it were something other than the endlessly continuous flow of reality—something that has a trace—is to misunderstand the very nature of enlightenment. As Master Shido Munan once put it, "Enlightenment is the Buddha's greatest enemy." Dogen writes,

> Now, when you trace the source of the Way, you find that it is universal and absolute. It is unnecessary to distinguish between "practice" and "enlightenment." The supreme teaching is free, so why study the means to attain it? The Way is, needless to say, very far from delusion. Why, then, be concerned about eliminating the latter? The Way is completely present where you are, so of what use is practice or enlightenment? However, if there is the slightest difference in the beginning between you and the Way, the result will be a greater separation than between heaven and earth. If the slightest dualistic thinking arises, you will lose your Buddha mind.
>
> —cited in Addis, 141–142

In Zen, the interpenetrating, ever-changing universe is Buddha-nature always expressing itself. Thus to distinguish one's self from other things, to create subject-object distinctions, is to live in delusion. This insight can be particularly traced back to the fifth patriarch in China and his successor. The tradition states that Hung-jen (601–674 CE) invited his disciples to compose a poem that expressed the spirit of Ch'an. The winner would be given the patriarchal mantle and the title as Hung-jen's legitimate heir. Shinshu, the head monk and presumed heir, wrote the following poem and publicly posted it.

The body is the bodhi tree.
The soul is like a mirror bright.
Take care to keep it always clean.
Let no dust heap up little by little.

The next morning a counter-poem was posted next to the first:

The Bodhi is not the tree.
The mirror is nowhere shining.
There is No-thing from the beginning.
Where can any dust accumulate?

—cited in Xishan, *Paragon of Zen House*, 9

This second poem was written by Huineng, a humble, unassuming monk, whom Hung-jen realized truly understood the Buddha-dharma (absolute truth). While Shinshu's poem is beautiful and indeed wise, one still sees in it fundamental dualism. The body and soul are characterized as holy and need to be constantly attended to in order to retain purity; still they are posed as some specific entity in contrast to other things. Huineng won the contest because his poem challenges any duality, any separation among things. The challenge is not to keep the soul unstained; it is to realize that there is no separation or radical distinction in anything. *Bodhi* (enlightenment or awakening) is not a tree, it is the nature of the ever co-arising universe. Another way to reframe the issue of nonduality comes from Master Ch'ing-yuan:

Thirty years ago, before I began to study Zen, I said, "Mountains are mountains, waters are waters." After I got insight into the truth of Zen through the instruction of a good master, I said, "Mountains are not mountains, waters are not waters." But now, having attained the abode of final rest (awakening), I said, "Mountains are really mountains, waters are really waters." Do you think that these three understandings are the same or different?

—cited in Maseo Abe, *Zen and Western Thought*, 4

This first stage of consciousness represents understanding that differentiates. On the most obvious level, one recognizes that rational minds must make distinctions. There is the mountain; there is the stream. Words are only meaningful if they can reference different things. More deeply, one could also say that this is the stage of spiritual practice in which one recognizes that good and bad exist as well as right understanding and false view. Making these distinctions can be quite valuable.

Deep Zen practice, however, reveals that duality is a mental construct placed on the always flowing, interpenetrating universe. Objectification of the world, especially the self, is overcome. The radical distinctions between one and others are gone, and no-self is realized in the context of interrelatedness. With no duality, all is recognized as empty, even as the interrelated dynamism of reality reveals Buddha-nature. All views and evaluations seem to drop, because there is no exterior or eternal reference of assessment. Simply the interpenetrating flow of all reality exists.

In this third stage of realization, one sees that emptiness reveals itself in form, and that there can be a kind of affirmation of things in the context of their relativity. The truly awakened self delights by experiencing the true dharma in the wonder of mountains and streams. However, one does not revert to the initial perspective but experiences absolute truth in the context of conventional truth and the ultimate dimension in the context of the relative dimension; indeed, they are one. One's Buddha-nature is ever revealing and expressing itself, always free, always without craving, always filled with compassion. Now, fully enlightened, one can simply chop wood, just eat, and express nonattaining. This is "ordinary mind," yet it is anything but typical.

Rinzai Zen

The Soto school is identified with a gradual approach to enlightenment. One cultivates a spacious mind and heart and allows the dharma to reveal itself. As Dogen says, "[Zazen] is simply the easy and pleasant practice of a Buddha, the realization of Buddha's wisdom" (cited in Addis, 142). In contrast, the Rinzai school was derived from the philosophy that the best way to attain enlightenment was by creating a kind of mental pressure cooker, in which *satori*, an enlightenment experience, explodes in the mind. Rinzai was named after the Chinese patriarch, Lin-Chi (d. 866). The center of his training was the use of impossible questions or puzzling dialogues. In Japanese, these are known as **koans**. One famous *koan* states: Two hands clap, and there is a sound. What is the sound of one hand? Another famous *koan* says: A disciple asked his master, "Does a dog have a Buddha-nature?" The master answered, "Wu." "But what do you mean by this?" The master responded, "That is what a dog would say if you asked it."

To an outsider, such expressions appear meaningless. Is there a right answer that is being sought? In fact, there are "traditional answers" (*kenjo*) to many *koans* that are preserved as exemplary responses by excellent students. Yet, the point is not to give the master a particular answer, one that may be true but not actually experienced as such by the disciple. The real point is to evidence to the master that one has grasped the state of mind expressed by the *koan* itself. This state of mind transcends linear thinking.

Consider the question of a dog having a Buddha-nature. The master's response allows a number of possible interpretations. One is that *wu* in Chinese is a prefix of negation. Perhaps the master's response was simply, "No." However, the Zen tradition already widely asserts all things have a Buddha-nature. How could the answer be no? Perhaps the master intended to shock the student out of a speculative framework. Perhaps, because emptiness and form are related, he was asserting the emptiness quality. Perhaps his response was simply a joke. One way that some dogs bark is to make a sound very much like *wu*. (Dogs certainly cannot make the *ef* sound in *woof*.) That is, a dog would bark at such a question and not answer it at all. Perhaps the master was telling the disciple to look at and listen to a dog being its natural self; by barking, it was expressing its Buddha-nature. The master could have meant any, all, or none of these.

The point of *koans* is to approach the state of mind of the master who is posing the questions. The master is not really seeking an insightful response. Rather the master is using the *koan* to force the disciple's psyche into another paradigm of consideration, and in doing so to provoke a profound experience. Thus, masters were forcing students to use their minds in order to transcend their minds. The great fifteenth-century master Koin Jokin wrote,

. . . apply yourself wholeheartedly to the task of holding on to your koan, never letting it go off the center of your consciousness, whether you are sitting or lying, walking or standing still. . . . [T]he time will most assuredly come to you when it is absolutely impossible for you to go on with your inquiry, as if you had come to the very foundation of a stream and were blocked by the mountains all around. This is the time when the tree together with the entwining wisteria breaks down, that is, when the distinction of subject and object is utterly obliterated, when the inquiring and inquired are fused into the one perfect identity. Awakening from this identification, there takes place a rare *satori* that brings peace to all your inquiries and searchings.

—cited in D. T. Suzuki, *Essentials in Zen Buddhism*, 313

Zen exposes a great problem in the human condition: making objects of one's reality, particularly of oneself. Say someone asks an individual how that person is, and the person pauses to reflect, actually asking himself or herself, "How am I?" In this reflection, who is asking whom about what? Without realizing the traps of dualistic thinking, one creates a subject-object, oppositional perspective on reality, including one's self. Given that, one can boldly approach the question of the sound of one hand clapping. Working the *koan* day and night with particular intensity in *zazen* (formal meditation), one starts living inside the *koan*. Eventually, the *koan* and the practitioner become one and oppositional thinking dissolves. The two hands have become one, and no difference exists between the sound of two hands clapping or the sound of one hand. What would be the right answer that the master would then accept? Many responses could be legitimate. The master is not looking for a right answer but for indications that the disciple's mind is opening to its own Buddha-nature. Here are some other famous koans:

• What is your original face before your parents were born?
• If you meet the Buddha, kill him.
• Master: I don't like to hear the word *Buddha*. Disciple: Do you help people or not? Master: Buddha! Buddha!
• Disciple: In the day, there is sunlight; at night, there is firelight. What is "divine light"? Master: Sunlight, firelight.

- Disciple: Who is the Buddha? Master: Three pounds of flax.
- Disciple: When not a thought is stirring in one's mind, is there any error here? Master: As much as Mount Sumeru.
- Disciple: What is the meaning of the first patriarch's visit to China? Master: The cypress tree in the front courtyard.
- Disciple: What are honest words? Master: Eat an iron stick!

Final Note

What then is Zen? Is it a particular sect in Buddhism? Is it the essence or core of Buddha's message? Is its fundamental message and practice something that has transcended the specifics of Buddhism and even religion completely? In this latter possibility, one could say that Zen is beyond books and beyond beliefs. It is simply reality as it is and the existential awakening to one's true self. One's response to this issue may determine whether and how one might incorporate Zen wisdom into a Christian spiritual horizon.

Christian Reflection

Jesus was not a Zen master, yet he did seem to reflect some of the wisdom of Zen. The great theme in Jesus' preaching was the kingdom of God. In Matthew's Gospel alone, Jesus addresses this theme fifty-six times. The kingdom of God represents God's active lordship and saving power, and it is available to any. Jesus' fellowship with sinners expresses the kingdom's radical inclusivity (Mark 2:16–19). While the kingdom often refers to a future reality (Matthew 6:10), it also represents God's truth and life here and now (Romans 14:17). Jesus proclaimed that the kingdom was near (Matthew 10:7; Luke 10:9–11), among his listeners (Luke 17:21), and even upon them (Matthew 12:28; Luke 11:20).

Perhaps two particularly helpful points can be made. First, the kingdom did not represent some kind of utopian social or religious program. It was a transcendent mystery that could be known but not observed (Luke 17:20). Jesus used metaphors and similes (Matthew 13:1–53). He could provoke one's imagination to engage the kingdom, but the kingdom could not be accessed directly. The Zen tradition emphasizes this concept: in pointing to the moon, do not confuse the finger for the moon. Second, Jesus commanded believers to receive the kingdom like children (Matthew 18:3–4; Mark 10:15; Luke 18:16–17). In Jesus' day, children had no status or rights; they could claim nothing. They are the kind of "poor in spirit" who gain the kingdom (Matthew 5:3). A child also represents openness, wonder, and a spontaneous, unguarded approach to life. These qualities are the very ones commended in Zen. One has to divest oneself of any attachments or ego identifications and live with a childlike immediacy.

An additional interesting parallel between the Gospel and Zen is the use of the paradox of losing oneself to find oneself. Frequently Jesus preached this paradox: "For those who want to save their life will lose it, and those who lose their life for my sake will save it" (Luke 9:24, cf. Matthew 10:39; Mark 8:35; Luke 14:26; John 12:25). Jesus' paradox works like a perplexing *koan*. If a person ultimately wants to save one's life, then that person is told to lose it. However, if the intention is to preserve it by losing it, then has one really given it away? One could easily imagine a Zen master saying to a disciple: "Live and you die; die and you live." Jesus personally and dramatically witnessed this paradox. On the cross, he draws all to himself (John 12:32), expresses his glory (John 17:1), and even identifies himself with God's Old Testament name as the "I AM" (John 8:28). His true glory is in his emptiness. Saint Paul also understood Jesus' glory as intimately associated with his act of self-emptying (Philippians 2:5–11).

The wisdom of emptying oneself of all things to become filled with God is witnessed throughout the Christian tradition. Bonaventure writes, "For by transcending yourself and all things, by the immeasurable and absolute ecstasy of pure mind, leaving behind all things, and freed from all things, you will ascend to the superessential ray of darkness" (*The Soul's Journey into God*, 115). Meister Eckhart challenges everyone to leave behind all notions or thoughts of God so that they might know God:

> Men's last and highest parting occurs when, for God's sake, he takes leave of God. St. Paul took leave of God for God's sake and gave up all that he might get from God. . . . In parting from these, he parted with God for God's sake and yet God remained in him as God is in his own nature . . . but more as an "is-ness," as God really is. Then

he neither gave to God nor received anything from him, for
he and God were a unit, that is, pure unity.

— Meister Eckhart, 204

Finally, John of the Cross describes the ascent to union with God as
climbing a mountain: "The path of Mount Carmel, the perfect spirit:
nothing, nothing, nothing, nothing, nothing, nothing, and, even on
the Mount, nothing" (John of the Cross, *Collected Works*, 111). Even
union is characterized as nothing one can point to or claim; union is
"nothing." Yet, as discussed in chapter two, the soul and God seem to
cohere so radically that one cannot draw the line between oneself and
God. John of the Cross writes, "As soon as natural things are driven
out of the enamored soul, the divine is naturally and supernaturally
infused, since there can be no void in nature" (199). When Zen masters say that emptiness is fullness and fullness is emptiness, perhaps a
legitimate Christian parallel could be emptiness is **divinization** and
divinization is emptiness.

Chapter one identified the Christian understanding of God's
grace as God's loving, saving presence in human lives. God's presence is actively part of every person's life. Christianity broadly agrees
that God's grace precedes all good works and is active in those good
works. This is not to suggest that God's grace causes one to love, care,
forgive, express compassion, and so on. This doctrine points out that
God's presence is the foundation for all good. God is good, God is
love, and God is truth. Thus, to act in goodness, love, or truth is to
necessarily be grounded in and cooperate with God. God's grace is
both the foundation and ultimate horizon for all goodness and truth.
When a person loves, is God loving through that person or is the
person loving? Christianity teaches that in truth, the answer must
be both. Conceptually, one can distinguish God as supernatural and
humans as part of created nature. However, such a distinction is really
quite abstract to the lived experience of loving. In the actual dynamic
of love, the Absolute (God) and the relative (human) become the
same act of love, the same expression of truth.

Christianity believes that Jesus models the radical union of the
relative and Absolute in his very identity as both human and divine.
He is with God, and is God (John 1:1; 10:30), and his being is one
with the Father (John 14:10–11; 14:20). Yet Jesus is also a servant of

the Father, his will emptied to that of the Father (John 5:36, 10:38, 12:49–50). Interestingly, the Church has taught that what Christ is by nature, human and divine, Christians will become by grace— still human but participating in God's life in the same manner that Christ does.

One of Zen's great gifts is its insistence of being present at every moment. God, truth, beauty, and so on, are right before everyone. This is the great witness of Thérèse of Lisieux. The goal of her famous "little way" was to offer herself in love at every moment. She was looking for nothing more than the present moment to empty herself lovingly. She writes: "Yes, my Beloved, this is how my life will be consumed. I have no other means of proving my love for you than that of strewing flowers, that is, not allowing one little sacrifice to escape, not one look, one word, profiting by all the smallest things and doing them through love" (*The Story of a Soul*, 196). Similar to Zen's insistence that emptiness is fullness, Thérèse lived in radical, spiritual poverty of self-offering, and paradoxically she lived fully and richly:

IMAGE: BRIDGEMAN-GIRAUDON/ART RESOURCE, NY

St. Thérèse of Lisieux (1873–1897), photographed in 1895.

> Living on Love is giving without limit
> Without claiming any wages here below.
> Ah! I give without counting, truly sure
> That when one loves, one does not keep count! . . .
> Overflowing with tenderness, I have given everything
> To his Divine Heart . . . lightly I run.
> I have nothing left but my only wealth:
> Living on Love.
>
> — *The Poetry of St. Thérèse of Lisieux*, 90

One sees in this passage from St. Thérèse that her being in the moment is an expression of devotion and love to God. In Zen, this posture of being in the moment is quite different. Zen invites one to be engaged in the world, but with a great sense of the transience of the world and a bit of a detachment. Recently, during a question-and-answer period in a Zen community, one of the *sangha* members asked the teacher about how she might deal with a coming family event. The questioner described deep family dysfunction and her fears about the many landmines she might step on. By the time she finished, she was in tears. The response from the Zen teacher was illustrative: "Remove your preferences." This was the master's entire answer. This advice aligned to not being swept up in the futility of trying to control others. It was Zen-code for walking with a spacious, open mind. It called for her to be available to whatever came in a nonreactive way. This was a good response to her question. In addition, it was a very Zen response.

One need not imagine that Zen's understanding of such things as the unity of the absolute and the relative, Nirvana and Samsara, and practice and enlightenment are exactly represented in the relationship between nature and grace or humanity and divinity. Nonetheless, the associations are striking. God's presence penetrates all things without being any one of them. The Divine is always everywhere and nowhere, because it is not a thing to be pointed to as if part of the created universe. The Divine fullness only exists in the context of its being empty of all things. One can know it in any moment, any context, even as it is confoundingly elusive.

SPIRITUAL PROGRESS IN ZEN
Zen Ox-Herding Pictures

Zen insists that Nirvana and Samsara are one, that enlightenment is already before us, and that our Buddha-nature is our intrinsic ever-present truth. To know this, however, requires extraordinary spiritual intention and intense, skillful practice. Deconditioning the conditioned mind is a long, slow process of awakening. One of the most famous expressions of the development of that process is *The Ten Ox-Herding Pictures*. These ten pictures represent the relationship between the ox and the spiritual aspirant. The ox represents one's Buddha-nature, enlightenment, and even Zen practice itself, all of which enfold each other. A number of artistic renditions and poetic reflections on these pictures exist. Despite this variety, however, there is a great deal of regularity and even agreement about successive steps one must take to realize one's true nature. Below is one typical series (illustrations p. 187):

1. *Searching for the Ox.* One undertakes intentional spiritual practice. Most people do not really want to find their true self. They are happy being normally neurotic, intent on dressing up their prison cell, rather than actually escaping it. Undertaking Zen is not a self-improvement program for better adjustment. It is a rigorous search for one's self.

2. *Finding Traces of the Ox.* One has let go of distractions and has started making some progress on the path. Slowly the path begins to reveal itself. The revelation can still be somewhat of an intellectualization of the practice, and the newness can even be a bit romantic. However, one cannot help but be excited to receive hints of one's true self that are periodically revealed. During this stage, gentle perseverance is particularly imperative.

3. *Seeing the Ox.* The ox is one's true nature, and at this point, one has spotted it much more clearly. The truth about oneself is no longer an idea but a lived experience. However, staying stuck in conceptualizations can be a danger. Wisdom does not fit thought patterns, and one has to trust this direct experience.

4. *Catching the Ox.* The ox represents wisdom that is hard to hang onto or incorporate into one's life. Yet, wisdom is directly encountered. A danger at this point is that one can become spiritually inflated, thinking one has accomplished something. Until the ego is completely dismantled, it will regularly attach itself to and identify with spiritual attainments.

5. *Taming the Ox.* Master Kuoan's poetic reflection on this picture begins, "The whip and tether cannot be put aside or the ox may wander into mud-filled swamps" (John Daido Loori, *Riding the Ox Home*, 35). The Zen practitioner becomes relatively clear about how his mind works, but still needs to continue rigorously undoing the patterns of the conditioned mind. Without constant practice and discipline, one's ego-self or false-self will cloud one's Buddha-nature.

The Ten Ox-Herding Pictures, attributed to the 15th-century Japanese
Rinzai Zen monk Shubun.

IMAGES: WIKIMEDIA, PUBLIC DOMAIN

6. *Riding the Ox Home.* At this point, one travels with ease and
effortless activity, which represents living with extraordinary
freedom. There is no ego to advance or protect. The three poi-
sons of the conditioned mind, which Zen identifies as greed,

anger, and ignorance, are now becoming transformed into non-attachment, compassion, and wisdom. The developed Zen mind is practiced in being one with the dharma. No distinction lies between dharma and self in an interpenetrating world in which emptiness is form and form is emptiness.

7. *Forgetting the Ox.* Practice now is all the more joyful and effortless. Any sense of self is utterly let go. There is no place, conceptually or otherwise, to locate one's true self. The self is forgotten. Some Zen masters describe this stage of the practice as having the danger of renouncing the world. One realizes that the self is empty as is the world. So why bother?

8. *Transcending the Ox.* Recall the earlier discussion where one experienced the fusion of all things, in which mountains are not mountains and waters are not waters. This stage of spiritual progress expresses such an insight. From Nagarjuna on, Mahayana Buddhists have called this the principle of *shunyata*—"emptiness." Even considering such things as Nirvana, Buddha-nature, or Enlightenment suggests that there is a separate, objective reference to these words, a reference outside of the fundamental emptiness of reality. Transcending the ox represents letting go of these concepts.

9. *Returning to the Source.* Consider this the final stage of mountains again being mountains and waters again being waters. A highly developed Buddhist recognizes not only that form is emptiness, but also that emptiness is form. One arrives at the end of the journey and discovers that home was never left, yet sees it now for the very first time. Buddha-nature has been along all the time as one's true self and the true self of the universe. Master Kuoan's verse to this picture is extraordinary:

> Having returned to the source, effort is over.
> The intimate self sees nothing outside, hears
>   nothing outside.
> Still, the endless river flows tranquilly on.
> The flowers are red.

> —ibid., 62

There is nothing to attain, nothing to strive for. The enlightened self knows the truth of the entire universe within and constantly participates with that truth. Embodying the truth, then, the entire universe is within, not outside. The third line seems to represent the constant flow of an impermanent world. The sparse final line seems to reflect reality simply as it is. Just as Mahakashyapa saw the lotus flower held by the Buddha for what it was, so too does the enlightened person see the flowers in this verse: the flowers are red.

10. *Entering the Marketplace*. The final picture is most important. Again Master Kuoan's rendering:

> Entering the Marketplace barefoot and unadorned;
> Blissfully smiling, though covered with dust and
> ragged of clothes;
> Using no supernatural power;
> You bring the withered trees spontaneously into
> bloom.

—ibid., 67

The profoundly developed spiritual master enters the world humbly and unassumingly. Ever skillful and wise, the true Zen master's presence is naturally healing, with compassion being the premier expression of Buddha-nature. One walks without what is sometimes called "the stink of holiness." On a personal note, I once had an opportunity to know an unassuming Zen master over the course of a weeklong conference. On the last day, I asked her to give me a teaching. She demurred. "I have no special insight for you," she said. Then she started to speak casually about taking on a holistic spiritual perspective. Whatever she said drew me to say things about my spiritual life that were hidden somewhere in my consciousness but not fully clear to me. These insights into my life somehow emerged now with great clarity, and they became foundational for my spiritual development over the next several years.

Christian Reflection

A plan, or outline, of spiritual progression is nothing new in the Christian tradition. Among the desert fathers one finds such descriptors as Evagrius Ponticus's five stages to divine union, John Cassian's four stages of prayer, and twenty-six steps to holiness in John Climacus. In the medieval West, one has Walter Hilton's famous *Scale of Perfection* and Jan Ruysbroeck's *Seven Steps of the Ladder of Spiritual Love*. Perhaps the most important descriptor in the West has been Teresa of Avila's *Interior Castle*. In this classic text, Teresa imagines spiritual progress as that of entering a castle with a concentric series of dwellings. Each kind of dwelling represents a stage in the spiritual journey, particularly as it refers to the life of prayer. In some ways, the castle also represents one's soul, as one enters ever deeper to discover God at its center.

Teresa refers to her first dwelling as self-knowledge. This is when people confront their life starkly and recognize the prevalence of sin. They honestly face their soul and recognize its need for God. This is the moment in which they need to plunge decisively into spiritual life. The second dwelling represents those who have begun to live a morally integrated prayerful life. The great issue at this point is the will, because persons here have not advanced enough to resist sin easily. Effort and perseverance is the key. Teresa also insists that believers ought to be gentle with themselves, because they are likely to fall a number of times. Self-judgment should give way to self-kindness, even as people strive to be disciplined. The third dwelling represents those who are now practiced in the life of prayer. They easily become recollected in prayer and are happily inclined to perform works for the sake of the Gospel. Teresa encourages these souls simply to persevere. At this stage, she does not believe they will easily lapse into sin. However, they could become attached to delightful spiritual experiences. When these satisfactions dry up, they could feel discouraged. Teresa also notes that many souls are afraid of progressing further, and most do not. They are content to experience God through the mediation of inspiring thoughts and spiritual practices. They love God and desire to serve God, but they are ambivalent about the cost of full-blown discipleship.

The fourth dwelling represents a transition from experiences of God that are mediated, or indirect, to knowledge of God as directly dwelling in the soul. Teresa describes the "prayer of recollection," whereby God introduces souls gently to contemplation. People stop thinking about God and focus on simply being present to the divine within. From here, God draws them into the "prayer of quiet," which is a far more extraordinary understanding of God. Souls feel dramatic expansion that includes greater freedom and joy. Any worldly distractions to spiritual progress are distasteful. The fifth dwelling place is aligned with the fourth. The soul has become contemplative, knowing God with absolute surety—as discussed in chapter two. Teresa characterizes the fifth dwelling as that of experiencing the "prayer of union." It represents overwhelming encounters with God and a profound overflowing love for others.

Teresa regularly uses the metaphor of marriage for union with God. The fifth dwelling represents deeply committed love; the soul is in courtship. The sixth dwelling metaphorically represents becoming engaged. Such a stage is full of extraordinary experiences. This is the period when souls know the greatest spiritual darkness. God is purifying souls of every attachment they may have, particularly attachments to the spiritual consolations experienced. Whether the soul feels God profoundly or is plunged into great inner darkness, the result is the same—utter humility.

The final dwelling is that of mystical marriage. In this abode, souls are, on some level, always aware of God's direct presence in their life. Teresa describes this period as one of perfect self-forgetfulness and detachment. Souls see as God sees, love as God loves, and live in perpetual tranquility. They also have extraordinary energy to serve God, the source and center of their life.

In many ways, what Teresa describes is very different from the progress shown in *The Ten Ox-Herding Pictures*. For Teresa, everything rides on a deepening union with God through love. The soul recognizes God as divine love, as that supernatural Other that calls and leads the soul. Love is the source, the path, the agent of transformation, and the true completion of the soul. Even in its most apophatic expressions, Christianity is a relational religion. However, God as the Divine Absolute is also the soul's true resting place and the soul's truth. To become completely united to this absolute is to share many of the same characteristics of the Zen master who has completed the tenth stage. This master, now utterly humble and selfless, becomes an embodiment of compassion and wisdom, intent on serving all beings as a natural expression of Buddha-nature. For Teresa too, the soul has simply become love and acts accordingly everywhere.

There are other interesting similarities between Zen progression and Teresa's model. The spiritual path begins with a stark look at oneself and one's state. Whether one calls a spiritually undeveloped existence the life of sin or that of greed, anger, and ignorance, it amounts to the same thing: what is being addressed is a life that is controlled and tragically imprisoned. Both call for great self-awareness and honesty, and the stern commitment to embrace the spiritual path seriously. The earlier stages in both models represent the same virtues of perseverance and discipline. One is to be gentle yet firm with oneself. As one progresses, the path becomes easier, more natural, and more rewarding. Yet, the stakes also become higher. One confronts not being the center of the universe and that the self one has been clinging to is an illusion. The remedy is self-emptiness and availability to the Ultimate Truth that increasingly envelops the self.

Last Word

Zen, as a sect of Mahayana Buddhism, is a fascinating dialogue partner for Christianity. If, however, Zen transcends religion, as some claim; if Zen is nothing other than the awakening to one's true nature in the flow of life, then it may not be a counterpoint to Christianity or any other religion. It could represent a way of being or thinking that augments or deepens any religious faith. The possibility of fully uniting Zen to Christianity or another tradition is controversial and a minority position among scholars. Probably a good starting point would be caution. At the same time, one ought to be open to the possibilities. Jesuit Father Robert Kennedy Roshi writes,

> I never have thought of myself as anything but Catholic and I certainly never have thought of myself as a Buddhist. . . . What I looked for in Zen was not a new faith, but a new way of being Catholic. . . . Yamada Roshi [his master] told me several times that he did not want to make me a Buddhist but rather he wanted to empty me in imitation of "Christ your Lord" who emptied himself, poured himself out, and clung to nothing. Whenever Yamada Roshi instructed me in this way, I thought that this Buddhist might make a Christian of me yet!

—Robert Kennedy, *Zen Spirit, Christian Spirit*, 13–14

Review Questions

1. Describe the development of Zen Buddhism, from the Buddha's teaching to Nagarjuna to Bodhidharma to Dogen.
2. What is the difference between the Southern School (Rinzai) and the Northern School (Soto) in enlightenment philosophy?
3. Explain how Zen understands the spiritual progression: (1) Mountains are mountains; waters are waters; (2) Mountains are not mountains; waters are not waters; (3) Mountains are really mountains; waters are really waters.
4. What are the similarities between the ox-herding pictures and Teresa of Avila's spiritual progression in *Interior Castle*?

In-Depth Questions

1. Jesus' paradoxical challenge to lose oneself to find oneself is like a *koan*. Can you conceive of any other "Christian" *koans*?
2. The kingdom of God is like the oneness of Nirvana and Samsara in that the kingdom is mysterious and cannot be objectively pointed to, and it is something to realize yet before us now. Further, the childlike posture of receiving the kingdom is much like that one would need to realize Buddha-nature. Is it possible that entering the kingdom of God is fundamentally the same as Zen enlightenment?
3. Given this chapter's presentation of Zen, do you believe that one can fully embrace Zen and also be an uncompromised Christian?

Select Bibliography

Abe, Maseo. *Zen and Western Thought*. Honolulu: University of Hawaii Press, 1985.

Addis, Stephen, et al. *Zen Sourcebook: Traditional Documents from China, Korea, and Japan*. Indianapolis: Hackett Publishing, 2008. This is a wonderful collection of classic Zen sources.

Bonaventure. *Bonaventure: The Soul's Journey into God; The Tree of Life; The Life of St. Francis*. Ewert Cousins, trans. Mahwah, NJ: Paulist Press, 1978.

Chetwynd, Tom. *Zen and the Kingdom of Heaven*. Boston: Wisdom Publications, 2001.

Dumoulin, Heinrich. *Zen Buddhism: A History*. Vol. 1, *India and China*. James Heisig and Paul Knitter, trans. New York: Macmillan, 1999.

Eckhart, Meister. *Meister Eckhart: A Modern Translation*. Raymond Blakney, trans. New York: Harper Torchbook, 1957.

Enomiya-Lassalle, H. M. *Zen Meditation for Christians*. John Maraldo, trans. LaSalle, IL: Open Court, 1974. This book represents one of the first modern attempts to see possibilities in Zen that augment and support Christian piety.

Heine, Steven. *Zen Skin, Zen Marrow: Will the Real Zen Buddhism Please Stand Up?* Oxford: Oxford University Press, 2008.

John of the Cross. *The Collected Works of St. John of the Cross*. Kieran Kavanaugh and Otilio Rodriguez, trans. Washington, DC: Institute of Carmelite Studies, 1991.

Johnston, William. *Christian Zen: A Way of Meditation*. San Francisco: Harper & Row, 1971.

Joshu. *The Recorded Sayings of Zen Master Joshu*. James Green, trans. Walnut Creek, CA: AltaMira Press, 1998.

Kapleau, Philip. *The Three Pillars of Zen* (revised). Garden City, NJ: Anchor Books, 1980. This famous book addresses Zen from a theoretical level as well as provides personal accounts of Zen practice and experience.

Kennedy, Robert. *Zen Gifts to Christians*. New York: Continuum, 2004. Kennedy's Christian voice in American Zen is both modest in scope and critically important to Zen-Christian dialogue.

———. *Zen Spirit, Christian Spirit*. New York: Continuum, 1995.

Loori, John Daido. *Riding the Ox Home: Stages on the Path to Enlightenment*. Boston: Shambala, 1999.

Suzuki, D. T. *The Essentials of Zen Buddhism*. Bernard Phillips, ed. Westport, CT: Greenwood Press, 1962.

———. *An Introduction to Zen Buddhism*. New York: Grove Press, 1964.

Teresa of Avila. *The Collected Works of St. Teresa of Avila*. Vol. II. Kieran Kavanaugh and Otilio Rodriguez, trans. Washington, DC: ICS Publications, 1980.

Therese of Lisieux. *The Poetry of Saint Therese of Lisieux*. Donald Kinney, trans. Washington, DC: ICS Publications, 1996.

———. *The Story of a Soul*. John Clark, trans. Washington, DC: ICS Publications, 1975.

Wu, John. *The Golden Age of Zen.* New York: Image Books, 1996.

Xishan. *A Paragon of Zen House.* O'hyun Park, trans. and commentator. New York: Peter Lang, 2004.

Yokoi, Yuho, and Daizen Victoria, trans and ed. *Zen Master Dogen: An Introduction with Selected Writings.* New York: Weatherhill, 1990. This masterful collection of the most important voices in Zen Buddhism is made with competent, though challenging, commentary.

Yoshinori, Takeuchi, ed. *Buddhist Spirituality: Later China, Korea, Japan, and the Modern World.* New York: Crossroad, 1999.

CHAPTER NINE

The Chinese Spirit

CHINESE RELIGIOSITY

The Chinese Religious Culture

Chapters four through eight have dealt with specific religions, their beliefs, practices, and spiritual imagination. This chapter will discuss China as a whole. It will also address individual religious traditions, much like in the previous chapters, but that will not be the emphasis here. This chapter is principally dedicated to the religious character that permeates much of the Chinese mind and heart. Exploring this religious ethos, or spirit, is more important in understanding the Chinese soul than analyzing a particular religion. Arguably, China's size, population, and dramatic economic expansion make it the most important new cultural and political force in the early twenty-first century. Because of its emerging importance on the world scene, one would be wise to understand something of its religious sensibilities. In terms of Christian engagement, this chapter will reflect less on particular religious claims than on the Chinese way of thinking religiously.

Understanding Chinese religiosity is no easy task. Recent surveys on Chinese religious affiliations are wildly divergent and unreliable, fundamentally because most Chinese people do not identify with a specific religion, in contrast to other religions. If being religious means embracing a particular religious community, specific notions of God and revelation, and rites that are exclusive, then most Chinese people would not look religious. However, most of the Chinese population thinks of itself as very religious. In the Chinese culture, life is an aesthetic act. Living richly and artfully in ways that elevate the soul and give it meaning is being profoundly religious. The Chinese people are grounded in tradition, community, family, and history, all of which is sacred. Thus, the usual questions of whether Confucianism or Daoism is a bona fide religion can be disregarded. Chinese religiosity addresses questions such as, how does the universe work? What is the nature of the human? What does human flourishing mean? These are religious questions indeed. One should also note that Buddhism is very much a part of the Chinese spiritual landscape. However, because Buddhism was already dealt with in the two previous chapters, it will not be addressed overtly in this one.

Chinese Language and Metaphysics

One of the challenges to understanding classical Chinese religious texts is that, until recently, translations have striven to align them to the western reader's religious horizon. Doing so can be misleading or at least a bit distorting. For example, consider the standard and alternative translations of the words in the following chart:

	Standard Translation	Alternative Translation
Tien	heaven (as distinct from Earth)	transcendental continuity
y'i	righteousness	optimal appropriateness
li	ritual	propriety in roles and relations
dao	Way (often capitalized as a transcendent principle or Chinese version of God)	way-making or skillful engagement

The standard translations of these words are not wrong, but they can prejudice the reader. Some of the translation decisions have to do with the complexity of the Chinese language and its difference from

A statue of Confucius.

English. There are, for example, no articles (*the*, *a*, *an*) in Chinese. In English, nouns, verbs, adjectives, and adverbs are clearly distinguishable; in Chinese, they are not. A character such as *dao* would represent all of the following at the same time: way, quality of way, way-making, and way-making dynamic. Thus, to translate *dao* as "the way" might be accurate but also limiting.

One's beliefs about the universe relate dynamically with one's language. English, for example, is a language of substance and essence. For the Chinese people, reality is less understood as concrete things and more as fluid events within relationships. For the Chinese philosopher **Confucius** (551–449 BCE), humans express their unique personhood not by individuation—how one is different from all others—but by creative ways they interact with others. For example, in a father-son relationship, one finds the Chinese characters *fufu* "fathers should father" and *zizi* "sons should son." A son "son-ing" sounds very foreign to

CHANGES IN TRANSLITERATION

There is a transition underway in English transliterations of Chinese characters, from the Wade-Giles method to the Pinyin method. This latter method is preferred in China and now being used extensively in the West because it is closer to Chinese pronunciations. For example, Lao Tzu is now typically rendered **Laozi** and his classic *Tao Te Ching* is now typically *Dao De Jing*.

English speakers because it reflects a different way of considering the universe and a human life in that universe. In classical Chinese, the subject is even frequently omitted, which strengthens the eventful reading of a sentence. Persons are not merely separate individuals, as if agents who stand independently from others. People are also considered ongoing events, defined by their roles and relationships.

Basics in Traditional Chinese Religious Culture

Spirits and Ancestors

Early Chinese belief was polytheistic. The universe was filled with spirits. Good spirits brought health, wealth, long life, and fertility. Pious or thoughtful people venerated these good spirits and performed rituals that attempted to garner their support. Bad spirits could cause accidents, bring sickness, and create natural disasters. These spirits were placated by ritual as well, and eventually harmony would be ritually restored. Ancestors were also venerated, and functionally they were identical to the gods or spirits—that is, they could bless or curse depending on how they were dealt with. Ancestors were believed to be ghosts who dwelt in a sphere that was not completely separated from the world. One might burn money for one's ancestor to use in the spirit world or offer food that the spirit could consume. Venerating one's ancestors was not only considered pious, but also it was a good investment. Well-attended-to ancestors blessed their families, while neglected ancestors cursed their progeny.

The god who ruled all the gods, and ultimately the world, was a shadowy figure named *Shang-Ti*, or simply *Ti*. The dead spirits could intercede with him on one's behalf. By the time of the Chao Dynasty (1100–222 BCE), *Ti* and *tien* (heaven) were used interchangeably. The practice of ancestor veneration and the belief in a variety of spirits continues into the modern period. One can think of Pearl S. Buck's culturally revealing novel, *The Good Earth*. In it, the Chinese farmers consider the gods and spirits to be completely responsible for rain, drought, harvest success, and so on, and regularly offer incense to them and try to stay out of a malevolent spirit's way. In a telling

200 · ENCOUNTERS IN FAITH

moment, the protagonists Wang Lung and O-lan had been boasting about how excellent their newborn baby was:

> And then as he exulted he was smitten with fear. What a foolish thing was he doing, walking like this under an open sky, with a beautiful man-child for any evil spirit passing by chance through the air to see! He opened his coat hastily and thrust the child's head into his bosom and he said in a loud voice, "What a pity our child is a female whom no one could want and covered with small pox as well! Let us pray it may die." "Yes—Yes—" said his wife as quickly as she could. . . .
>
> — *The Good Earth*, 50–51

Yin and Yang

After 1000 BCE, the Chinese people believed that the universe expressed itself in complementary principles, yin being the receptive, and yang the assertive. These principles have a dynamic relationship with each other, represented in the Daoist symbol:

On the top of the symbol, the yang is prominent, and the yin gives way; the contrast appears at the bottom of the symbol. Within each energy exists a small circle or presence of the other. The relationship between yin and yang is one of harmony and a developed cultivation as to which energy is called for at a given moment. Collectively, yin represents such things as darkness, night, cold, Earth, winter, female, silence, death, and stability, while yang represents light, heat, heaven, summer, male, sound, birth, and dynamism.

THE DAOIST CONTRIBUTION
Laozi (Lao Tzu) and Zhuangzi (Chuang Tzu)

The story goes that in the early sixth century BCE a scholar named **Laozi** spent much of his life as a state archivist or librarian. He became disenchanted with culture and decided to leave society altogether. Traveling to the West, Laozi encountered a border guard who agreed to allow him passage only after he wrote down his wisdom. Laozi produced a short text, *Dao De Jing* (*Tao Te Ching*), which is recognized as a spiritual masterpiece. Three hundred years later the philosopher **Zhuangzi** produced a similar text, simply known as *The Zhuangzi* (*The Chuang Tzu*), which filled out the religious significance of the *Dao De Jing*. It is doubtful that a single author produced the *Dao De Jing* alone. Its writing style is varied, there is no clear order, and there is a great deal of repetition. As for *The Zhuangzi*, some doubt that twenty-one of its twenty-eight chapters originated from Zhuangzi. Should these suspicions undermine the texts' authority? That both may have multiple authors, and that Laozi could even be a mythical figure, may actually strengthen their authority by suggesting these classic books came from a larger religious tradition.

The *Dao De Jing* and *The Zhuangzi* invite the reader to consider the universe and transcendence differently than one might otherwise. Traditionally, the Western mind thinks of the universe as divinely governed by natural and moral laws, and that these laws are intelligible. Without even thinking, one assumes many ancient Greek philosophical notions. From God (*theos*) comes an underlying creative organizing principle (*logos*) that reflects divine order and law (*nomos*). Plato believed morality, law, and aesthetics had nothing to do with cultural customs. Rather, they were grounded in universal, divinely ordered truths. In contrast, the Chinese Daoist point of view is virtually *acosmic*; that is, there is no concept of a coherent, single-ordered world. The closest Chinese word for *cosmos* is *yuzhou*, which expresses the interdependence between time and space. Further, there is no permanent reality or eternal substratum behind appearances, such as in the Hindu notion of Brahman. There is just the ceaseless flow of life. Even things are more like events that are intrinsically related to other events. The shape of things and what they do are real, but they are interdependent, mutually determining realities caught in a wide-ranging flow. This approach is found in Mahayana Buddhism as well, and Ch'an/Zen Buddhism is particularly influenced by Daoist principles.

Dao

Rather than God, one finds *dao*. *Dao* is a combination of two characters: *shu* (foot—meaning to pass over, go, or lead through) and *shou* (head—meaning foremost or leading). What is being addressed by *dao* is a "way," "guidance in forging a new way forward," and "way-making" in terms of actively moving (skillful momentum). *Dao* represents the nature of authentic life movement. Yet *dao* is also mysterious and references something transcendent. Consider two translations of the opening chapter of the *Dao De Jing*:

> The *Tao* that can be told is not the eternal *Tao*. The name that can be named is not the eternal name. The nameless is the beginning of heaven and earth. The named is the mother of ten thousand things. Ever desireless, one can see the mystery. Ever desiring, one can see the manifestations. These two spring from the same source but differ in name; this appears as darkness. Darkness within darkness. The gate to all mystery.
>
> —Feng and English trans., no. 1

> Way-making (*dao*) that can be put into words is not really way-making, and naming that can assign fixed reference to things is not really naming. The nameless is the fetal beginnings of everything that is happening, while that which is named is their mother. Thus, to be really objectless in one's desires is how one observes the mysteries of all things, while really having desires is how one observes their boundaries. These two—the nameless and what is named—emerge from the same source yet they are referred to differently. Together they are called obscure. The obscurest of the obscure, they are the swinging gateway of the manifold mysteries.
>
> —Ames and Hall trans., no. 1

The Feng and English translation sounds quite mystical. One can recognize theistic themes and detect Christian principles. The eternal *Dao* is beyond categories and cannot be named, while the *Dao* that can be named is the source of creation. This *Dao* could easily correspond to God as absolute mystery and Jesus as *logos* through whom the universe was created (John 1:1). As already shown, approaching divine things with true detachment and emptiness is the dark apophatic road of contemplation. A kataphatic expression is also valid in dealing with God, whom one knows conceptually. Both the apophatic and kataphatic authentically witness to the same divine mystery (the same source) but also differ. Knowing God thusly, one enters the gate of divine mystery. Perhaps one could also make associations with Nirguna-Brahman and Saguna-Brahman in Hinduism; that is, Brahman beyond concepts and form and Brahman with concepts and form.

The Ames and Hall translation points one down a different road. What that version addresses is a meditation on how experience is always in process. The fluid quality of experience does not allow for absolute naming of things, even as names are conventionally important. To be objectless in one's desire is to stop trying to manipulate reality but to allow it to unfold. Yet, to have some kind of intention can be valuable in skillfully engaging that same reality. The challenge is to learn how to balance knowing and unknowing, or conceptualizing and recognizing the limitation of creating concepts. Knowing how to embrace both postures at the same time is the door to wonderment in the world.

Wu-forms

The world is an ever-changing expression of continuity and novelty. The great challenge is to know how to work creatively with both simultaneously. One of the most important ways to ensure skillful engagement with the world is embracing the principle of *wu*. This Chinese word first appeared in chapter eight, with the *koan* about the dog having a Buddha nature. *Wu* is a prefix that acts as a negation. *Wu-wei* (no-action) points to the value of being nonimposing in one's activity. One does not force something, but learns to work with the energy at hand. *Dao* acts noncoercively, and humans must likewise. In acting thusly, humans become more true to the moment. A regularly associated characteristic to *wu-wei* is *ziran* (what-is-spontaneously-so). Nonimposing activity does not suppress spontaneity; it acts as a condition for being spontaneous. *Dao* works like the most skillful rulers:

> With the most excellent rulers, their subjects only know that they are there. The next best are the rulers they love and praise. Next are rulers they hold in awe. And the worst are the rulers they disparage. Where there is a lack of credibility, there is a lack of trust. Vigilant, they are careful in what they say. With all things accomplished and the work complete, the common people say, "We are spontaneously like this."
>
> —Ames and Hall trans., no. 17

The excellent rulers are vigilant, that is, mindful and prudent. They are not lax, but their activity is *wu-wei*, and thus their creative, moral presence is not even noticed. They are so aligned with the energy around them that the people's flourishing seems utterly natural.

Wu forms free energy and allows one to be unencumbered by artificial concepts or contrived moral precepts. Another important concept, *wuzhi* (no-knowing), refers to letting go of any artificial mental constructs that would blind one from the uniqueness of the new moment. Often humans name something in order to control it. *Wu-yu* is best translated as the "objectless desire." If everything is changing, then to desire something is to lose one's enjoyment in the moment. A Daoist worldview has desires or interests in personal flourishing, of course. Such a worldview can only be achieved, however, if one lets go of the neurotic need to be attached to some unchanging agenda. The universe is an evolving mystery unfolding before one. The best experience is to participate in it as it is, constantly changing. These and many other *wu* forms dispose the soul to embrace life as art. They teach a mental and spiritual habit that allows one to optimize creative possibilities without trying to manipulate one's experience. Zhuangzi writes,

> Let your mind wander in simplicity, blend your spirit in the vastness, follow along with things the way they

are, and make no room for personal views—then the
world will be governed. I take inaction [*wu-wei*] to be
true happiness, but ordinary people think it is a bitter thing. . . . The inaction of Heaven is its purity,
the inaction of earth is its peace. So the two inactions
combine and all things are transformed and brought to
birth. . . . I say, Heaven and earth do nothing [*wu-wei*]
and there is nothing that is not done. Among men, who
can get hold of this inaction?

—Burton Watson trans., 91, 112–113

From the *Dao De Jing*,

Extend your utmost emptiness as far as you can, and do your
best to preserve your equilibrium. In the process of all things
emerging together, we can witness their reversion. Things
proliferate, and each again returns to its root. Returning to
the root is called equilibrium. Now as for equilibrium—this
is called returning to the propensity of things, and returning
to the propensity of things is common sense. Using common sense is acuity, while failing to use it is to lose control.
And to try to do anything while out of control is to court
disaster. Using common sense is to be accommodating;
being accommodating is tolerance; being tolerant is kingli-
ness; being kingly is heaven-like; being heaven-like is to be
way-making; and the way-made is enduring. To the end of
one's days one will be free from danger.

—Ames and Hall trans., no. 16, slightly adjusted

What is found in these texts is a number of paradoxes enfolding
themselves. People are challenged to empty themselves so as to allow
a spacious mind and heart. Witness how flowering energy (yang)
returns naturally to its silent rooted energy (yin). A balance and
constant flow come about as things reveal their nature or propensity.
One does not have to do that much, the energy is already inside.
The paradox is that the very act of trying to control is how one loses
control. Accommodating to the unfolding reality before us is being
tolerant—with associations of royalty, heaven, and *dao*.

Daoist Mysticism?

Is Daoism mystical? Is it theistic? Many Western readers of the past have imagined *dao* as the Chinese version of God. After all, it represents an absolute reference point. It existed before heaven and Earth. It is soundless, formless, without beginning or end, and transcends all. *Dao* cannot be spoken of directly or understood conceptually, but its truth can be pointed out by analogy. Religions of the West discuss God and Hindus describe Brahman in such a way. Daoist religious tradition sought ways to experience a kind of eternal life by embracing principles and procedures derived from classic Daoist thought.

These associations, however, have been a bit too romantic and have even skewed the texts' translations to look more aligned than they really are. *Dao* does represent a kind of eternal principle, yet it also simply expresses how reality goes and how one ought to conform oneself to reality. Perhaps the answer to this question is that Daoism reflects a religious sensibility that does take one to a dimension beyond conventional life—a dimension that is truly transcendent and spiritual even if not ultimately located in a clear sense of divinity. Laozi writes, "Thus, only when we have lost sight of *dao* is there excellence; only when we have lost sight of excellence is there authoritative conduct; only when we have lost sight of authoritative conduct is there appropriateness; and only when we have lost sight of appropriateness is there ritual propriety" (Ames and Hall trans., no. 38). Zhuangzi states, "He who has a clear understanding of the virtue of Heaven and Earth may be called the Great Source, the Great Ancestor. He harmonizes with Heaven; and by doing so he brings equitable accord to the world and harmonizes with men as well" (143). Both Laozi and Zhuangzi addressed something religiously profound.

Christian Reflection

Another Possibility for Moral Discourse

In many ways, Daoist sensibilities contrast a great deal with Christianity. Christianity is convinced that there is a Creator God who is known as love. This loving God desires a personal relationship with humans, and ultimately to draw humans to himself eternally. This God is not *dao* at all. Most Christians also imagine that the substructure of the universe entails a moral law that comes from God and reflects God. These laws are written on our hearts, are understandable, communicable, and can be recognized by all people of good will and intelligence. Most Christians also believe that the natural law cannot be violated, because it reflects God's intrinsic design for the universe.

Daoism has no absolute order and argues that imagining such an order actually reduces human dignity and compromises flourishing. For Daoism, the moral life is an art in perceiving the most appropriate response in an ever-changing universe. One might ask oneself if that is a better way to approach reality or morality. Surely Daoists are not moral relativists; they do not believe that there is no right or wrong. Yet, in contrast to a Western way of conceiving reality, Daoists might say that a "one-size-fits-all" moral structure wrongly presupposes a static universe.

One Western bridge to Daoist sensibilities might be Aristotle, who seems to hold the moral fluidity of Daoism with a version of the natural law. Aristotle believed in absolute, eternal virtues, such as courage, temperance, and fortitude. For him, however, the virtuous person does not simply take a moral precept and apply it to every situation. In the same way, morality is not a matter of do's and don'ts. Rather, morality consists in learning how to apply these virtues prudentially to new situations. Morality is learning the art and practicing the habit of appropriately responding to every unique situation.

Yin-Yang and Appropriating the Wu Forms

Chinese spiritual wisdom invites the Western mind to consider the nature of harmony and the interrelationship between complementary energies. In one sense, Chinese sensibilities make contrasts. Yin represents feminine, receptive, dark, silent, and so on, while yang represents masculine, assertive, light, sound, and so on. The same can be typical in some Christian dialogue. Pope John Paul II, for example, regularly contrasted the feminine with the masculine. The genius of women was understood as expressions of receptivity, watchfulness, contemplation, and nurturance, which can be contrasted with the nature of men, who are more overtly involved in the world but less relational or emotionally integrated. Some have argued that such distinctions artificially stereotype men and women and that these characterizations make women and men unequal.

The Chinese wisdom of yin and yang recognizes distinctions without suggesting that they act as absolute reference points. In fact, they do the opposite. As yang asserts itself, it naturally ends up receding into yin. Out of yin's contemplative receptivity comes assertion again. One can see assertion and recession in spiritual development. The great depth psychologist Carl Jung argued that the premier task of midlife for men is to attend to their anima, their feminine principle, and to become less assertive and more contemplative. In contrast, women are challenged to discover hidden, creative gifts and to find more fully their self-authorizing voices. Chinese wisdom respects various postures for what they are and names them stereotypically. Yet, people are also challenged to rethink their patterns. All women and men must act in ways both yin and yang.

The Chinese spirit also bids one to listen to the wisdom of the *wu* forms. Christianity has no exact correlation here, but in no way would these principles compromise Christianity. The *wu* forms cultivate an open, spacious mind and heart, respectful of the reality unfolding before one. A great temptation in Christian pastoral ministry is to impose an agenda on others. Perhaps the congregation is not vibrant at, say, a wedding. The pastor might want to pump up the energy. All such a situation does is to guarantee that the minister and congregation are out of sync. *Wu-wei* (nonimposing action) suggests entering the energy that exists and working skillfully with it, not against it. Perhaps a minister meets a parishioner in crisis. He or she may be uncomfortable with the pain or ambiguity of the situation. The principle of *wu-yu* (objectless desire) leads the minister to stop seeking a personal agenda and to be present as the suffering person needs one to be present. One does not have to come into the situation imagining that its conclusion will be joy, surety, or healing. While all are laudable goals, they are imposed goals. *Wu-yu* tells one to be authentic in the moment, but indeed someone may need to grieve a long time or remain for a time in doubt. These feelings can be respected.

A minister celebrates a marriage. A minister skillfully engaging the energy of the couple and the congregation at such a celebration might be said to be embracing the principle of *wu-wei*.

IMAGE: © BILL WITTMAN

THE CONFUCIAN CONTRIBUTION

Confucius

Confucius (Kong Fuzi—Master Kong) is widely recognized as China's greatest teacher. His religious, social, and political sensibilities laid the groundwork for what is known as Chinese culture—and virtually Korean, Japanese, and Vietnamese culture as well. Confucius was born in the kingdom of Lu during a somewhat chaotic, but formative, period in Chinese culture. He founded a kind of school or academy in Lu and later acted as an independent philosopher, traveling from state to state seeking royal benefactors and trying to persuade political leaders of the practical means for social and political order. Confucius attracted a large number of students through the years. His academy inculcated students with both knowledge and refinement, including the six arts of ceremony, music, archery, chariot riding, writing, and arithmetic.

After Confucius died, some of his students wrote down what they remembered the Master had said to them. The tradition is that at least ten books encompassed his life and teaching by the beginning of the fourth century BCE and an additional twelve more a century later. These collections became the *Analects*, or "Sayings of Confucius." The fixed status of the text is now later, perhaps 150 BCE. The most influential developers of Confucius's tradition were Mencius (fourth century BCE) and Hsun Tzu (310–219 BCE). During the Han Dynasty (206 BCE–220 CE), Confucianism became the official philosophy of the state. This tradition survived for two thousand years. In fact, during a particular renaissance of Confucian thought in the Sung Dynasty (960–1279 CE), a new commentary on the *Analects* by the Confucian scholar Chu His (1130–1200 CE) became the basis for all of Chinese education.

Confucian Spiritual Principles

While not a religious leader per se, Confucius's philosophy profoundly influenced the Chinese religious spirit. He claimed that everything he taught came from the earlier tradition (VII.1), including belief in *dao*, the celestial gods, veneration of ancestors, ritual action, and so on. These traditions were not, however, spiritually transformative. Confucius took this rather superstitious and dry tradition and infused it with deep religious significance. Unlike Laozi, Confucius believed that the universe did have an inherent moral order. This he characterized as the way (*dao*) of heaven; and the way of heaven informs humanity on how to live righteously and harmoniously. Crucial to the Confucian spirit is the principle of *tiaren heyi*: the harmonious oneness of heaven and humanity.

In many ways, Laozi represented a philosophy that was antilearning and antiritual. One can be slightly suspicious of this approach. The *Dao De Jing* is quite an intellectual text. Still, it regularly warns of the dangers of being caught in constricting mental or ritual forms of life. To lose *dao*, Laozi believed, is to fall to excellence, then to fall into authoritative conduct, then to appropriateness. The final and worst fall is to ritual propriety. Confucius took an opposite view, arguing that ritual propriety conforms one to heaven and Ultimate Truth. Confucius perceived an alignment between cosmic structure and ritual structure, between harmony in heaven and harmony on Earth. The truly superior person conforms oneself to ritual as part of becoming authentic: "Having a sense of appropriate conduct as one's basic disposition, developing it in observing ritual propriety, expressing it with modesty, and consummating it in making good one's word: this then is an exemplary person" (*Analects*, Ames and Rosemount trans., 15.18).

For Laozi, cultivating wisdom through learning can be a trap: "Exterminate the sage, discard the wise, and the people will benefit a hundredfold" (Lau trans., no. 19). In contrast, Confucius was convinced that cultivating learning was key to interior development:

> Love of goodness without love of learning degenerates into silliness. Love of wisdom without love of learning degenerates into utter lack of principle. Love of keeping promises without love of learning degenerates into villainy. Love of uprightness without love of learning degenerates into harshness. Love of courage without love of learning degenerates into turbulence.
>
> —Waley trans., 17.8

If Daoism is fundamentally interested in harmony with nature and attending to emerging energy and forms before one, Confucianism is fundamentally concerned with harmonious relationships. The five great relationships constitute the fundamental social culture. They are,

1. *Father-Son:* The father is responsible to the son's development, and the son is respectful and obedient. This relationship also includes employer-employee relations.
2. *Elder-Younger Brother:* The elder brother, while a kind of peer, is also responsible for guiding the younger.
3. *Husband-Wife:* Although a hierarchical relationship, it also demands mutual solicitude.
4. *Elder-Younger:* This represents a kind of respect that all youth should show to their elders, including teachers and mentors.
5. *Ruler-Subject:* Similar to the father-son relationship, it is extended to the political realm.

Most all relationships in China (as well as in Japan and Korea) fall into one or more of these categories, even if by analogy. These five great relationships are then infused with Confucian virtues of *ren* (sympathy or consideration), *li* (propriety), *shu* (reciprocity), *xiao* (devotion to family and ancestors), and *wen* (aesthetics). In a Confucian worldview, one learns the art of becoming a morally, relationally cultured person. Relationships are infused with a kind of religious ritualization. Confucians do not consider rituals stultifying to creativity, neither should the relationships become rigid. Instead, they become infused with order, intentionality, respect, generosity, and mutual responsibility.

There is a kind of mystical element to Confucianism, whereby when one aligns with *tien* (heaven or transcendence), one becomes united to the spirit of the universe or, perhaps, the spirit underlying the physical universe. Mencius writes, "All the ten thousand things are present in me. There is no greater happiness for me than to find, on self-examination, that I am true to myself" (*Mencius*, 7A.4). Hsun-Tzu, who had a very different temperament than the joyful, optimistic Mencius, reflects the same: "Emptiness, unity, and stillness—these are qualities of great and pure enlightenment. . . . He who has such enlightenment . . . has a penetrating insight into all beings . . . and masters the great principle and all that is in the universe" (*Hsun-tzu*, 131). Medieval Confucian master Chang Tsai (1022–1077 CE) sounds virtually pantheistic: "Heaven is my father and Earth is my mother, and even such a small creature as I find an intimate place in their midst. Therefore that which fills the universe I regard as my body and that which directs the universe I consider as my nature. All people are my brothers and sisters, and all things are my companions" (cited in Wing-Tsit Chan, *Sourcebook in Chinese Philosophy*, 497).

Confucianism slumped tremendously in the twentieth century. In the New Culture Movement (1916), it was roundly criticized for virtually enslaving women and subjugating sons and subordinates to tyrannical fathers and elders. Above all, it was accused of keeping a stagnant culture alive. Mao Zedong, the leader of the Communist takeover of China, further undermined Confucianism by characterizing it as feudal, patriarchal, and that which imprisoned the Chinese people, especially the peasants. Confucianism has fared far better in Korea, where it still flourishes.

While Confucianism has taken some blows in its authority to guide Chinese spiritually, it is now making a remarkable comeback. Given the moral and spiritual vacuum left after the demise of Maoism, Confucian spirituality is returning—with the Communist authority's support. For example, in 2005 more than 2,500 people, including high-ranking Communist Party members, made a pilgrimage to Confucius' traditional birthplace. The Communist leaders are seeing in Confucian ideals a way to address increased social restlessness and widespread greed as China has embraced the free market. The resurgence of Confucianism is not a wholesale restoration movement. It is a rediscovery of Confucian values that can help redefine cultural identity and guide social and economic development. Confucianism is also reemerging in education. While in the last few decades it was derided as backward, disconnected with job skills, and antiscientific, today it is looked upon as a valuable resource in cultivating the kind of moral person who can learn job skills and know how to work in a fully humane way.

Daoism is also being officially reconsidered as well. Dr. Zhou Zhongzhi, professor of law, economics, and politics at Shanghai Normal University, has called for Chinese ethics to reground itself in a Daoist vision:

> As China enters the twenty-first century, it enters an era calling to build a harmonious society. . . . According to the idea of the unification between man and universe, Daoism believes that man, as the organic part of nature, is inalienable from it. . . . As a result of China's rapid economic growth, the ecological environment in China is now at risk. China's present effort in enhancing harmony between man and nature should absorb the ethical nourishment of Chinese Daoist ecological wisdom. Moreover, the Daoist school advocates avoiding selfishness and limiting desire . . . , which is evidently beneficial to the society for China in refraining from consumerism. . . . The Daoist view [is] to maintain a harmony between material and spiritual life.

> —cited in Fisher and Bailey, *Anthology of Living Religions*, 183–184

Uniting Religious Considerations

This chapter began by suggesting that most Chinese people consider themselves spiritual but hesitate to identify with a religion. Rather, religious or spiritual sensibilities are part of the air that they breathe, which has been the case for centuries. Consider the following:

Emperor Ziaozong: Use Buddhism to rule the mind, Daoism to rule the body, Confucianism to rule the world.

Philosopher Liu Mi: Although the three teachings are different in the arguments put forward, they are one.

Philosopher Lin Zhao-en: If someone is a Confucian, give him Confucius; if he is a Daoist, give him Laozi; if he is a Buddhist, give him Shakyamuni; if he isn't any one of them, give them their unity.

—Timothy Brook, *Rethinking Syncretism*, 17, 18, 22

The most intentional effort to harmonize and unite the religions came in the Ming Dynasty (1369–1644), when many great religious thinkers sought to combine the best features of them all into a kind of synthesis. A modern movement known as *Yiguandao* (unifying dao) now strives explicitly to unify Daoist, Buddhist, and Confucian teachings. Such an initiative is probably unnecessary. The Chinese spirit seems to naturally experience unity anyway by allowing different traditions to influence various parts of Chinese life.

Christian Reflection

Form and Creativity

The Chinese emphasis of deference toward others and the rich Chinese tradition of empathetic respect is something that Christians can learn from and relate to. Christians can ask about their solicitude toward their leaders. Is it respectful and rightly ordered? They might also ask how their leaders actually lead. Are these leaders open to new experiences or insights, or are they rigidly stuck to forms that are less and less appropriate and life-giving? Forms and rules are important, even crucial; this is the particular insight in Confucian thought. With its Daoist influence, the Chinese spirit invites believers to be open to novelty and creativity. Christianity is called to be open and available to the Holy Spirit. Paul reminds worshippers that "the letter kills, but the Spirit gives life," and that "where the Spirit of the Lord is, there is freedom" (2 Corinthians 3:6, 17).

One might look at a Christian example of such creativity. The spirituality of Francis de Sales (1567–1622) and Jane de Chantal (1575–1641), known as Salesian spirituality, is one. Francis and Jane met when Francis was the bishop of Geneva and Jane was a widowed baroness with a number of young children. Francis became her spiritual director, and as the relationship developed, they obviously had a mutual influence on each other. Jane told Francis that she had a burning desire to become a nun but that she was still called to directly care for her children. Conventionally at the time, doing both was impossible. A nun by definition was cloistered in a monastery and had to leave her family behind. In fact, embracing a monastic life and doing any kind of active ministry in the world was considered impossible for women. There were no models for it. Motherhood and consecrated sisterhood simply did not go together.

However, Francis encouraged Jane to take the movements of the Holy Spirit in her heart seriously. Jane and Francis spent six years imagining what God could be doing. In 1610, they cofounded the religious order known as the Visitation of Holy Mary, a congregation for women who felt a great need to live in community and follow a simplified monastic routine, and who believed that their mission was to be a visible ministerial presence in society. This dual vision, utterly new to vowed, religious women, captured the spiritual imagination of the French Catholic Church. Jane directed the establishment of more than eighty communities of the Visitation.

In many ways, Francis and Jane embraced seventeenth-century Catholic piety. They respected its forms, structures, possibilities, and limitations. This structure they called the "will of God's good pleasure." In the context of this already established form, they listened to the Holy Spirit, who seemed to be challenging them to stretch outside of the boundaries. They called their personal challenge, or movement of the Spirit, the "signified will of God," that is, something God is personally saying to one's soul. If the will of God's good pleasure and the signified will of God appear to be in conflict, it could be that God is drawing one to be particularly creative.

Even in Christianity, there is something of the Chinese spirit—one that respects ritual, form, structured roles, and traditional values, all the while being sensitive to the newness of the moment (literal or historical) and how the Spirit might be guiding the Church into something new.

Is the Chinese Spirit Missing Anything?

This chapter began by recognizing that many Chinese people believe themselves immersed in the spiritual life. At the same time, many do not believe in God or think that such a notion is not very interesting. The contradiction can be striking to one's ears. Even as one strives to respect another approach to religion and spirituality, it is difficult not to find such a religious posture inadequate. Most religions and spiritualities understand some kind of spiritual absolute reference. Additionally, most religions have an endgame. The Upanishads taught Hindus to unite Atman with Brahman; the Buddha taught full awakening or liberation from samsara; and Christ taught about heaven and union with the triune God. Any analogous interest seems to be missing in what has been discussed here about Chinese religiosity. From a Christian point of view, one might challenge this gap. While appreciating and honoring the truly sacred quality of engaging human relationships as if ritually understood, and while learning the importance of being available to and harmonious with the subtle energies around one, still one might ask of Chinese belief: shouldn't there be more?

Review Questions

1. Most Chinese people would avoid professing a religion and yet most think of themselves as very religious. How is this conclusion framed in the text?

2. In this chapter, *dao* has been shown as both mystical (as the West has often assumed) and not really mystical at all. How can it be approached from both perspectives?

3. Laozi and Confucius are often depicted as representing opposite approaches to a flourishing life. What assumptions and principles do they agree on, and where do they differ?

4. How and why is modern China embracing Daoist and Confucian principles?

In-Depth Questions

1. Can you think of how *wu-wei* (nonimpositional activity) or *wu-yu* (objectless desire) could be lived in your life? How might they be lived more broadly in Christianity?

2. Daoists believe that a one-size-fits-all moral structure presupposes a static universe, something they reject. How morally static is the universe? Is there a stable moral order? Is stable different from static?

3. According to Catholicism, the natural law should be obvious to everyone who is intelligent, reflective, and moral. Why then are there disagreements among thoughtful people about weighty moral issues?

4. Some in China argue that the five great relationships are veiled expressions of patriarchy and relationships of subservience. Others argue that these relationships provide a culture of deference, responsibility, and mutual respect. Would you want to live in a culture based on these kinds of relationships? What would be the assets and liabilities for you or for society?

Select Bibliography

Brook, Timothy. "Rethinking Syncretism: The Unity of the Three Teachings and Their Joint Worship in Late-Imperial China." *Journal of Chinese Religions* 21 (Fall 1993): 13–44.

Buck, Pearl S. *The Good Earth.* New York: Washington Square Press, 1931.

Chan, Wing-Tsit, trans. and ed. *A Sourcebook in Chinese Philosophy.* Princeton: Princeton University Press, 1963.

Ching, Julia. *Chinese Religions.* Maryknoll, NY: Orbis Books, 1993. This book is a good source for understanding the spirit of Chinese religiosity.

Chuang Tsu [Zhuangzi]. *Chuang Tsu: Inner Chapters.* Gia-Fu Feng and Jane English, trans. New York: Vintage, 1974.

Chuang Tzu [Zhuangzi]. *The Complete Works of Chuang Tzu.* Burton Watson, trans. New York: Columbia University Press, 1968. A delightful classic text, it complements the *Dao De Jing*, in which Chuang Tzu challenges Western conventional thinking with stories, images, and a great deal of humor.

Confucius. *The Analects of Confucius: A Philosophical Translation.* Roger Ames and Henry Rosemont Jr., trans. New York: Ballantine Books, 1998.

Confucius. *The Analects.* Arthur Waley, trans. New York: Alfred A. Knopf, 2000.

Fisher, Mary Pat, and Lee Bailey, eds. *An Anthology of Living Religions*, 2nd edition. Upper Saddle River, NJ: Prentice Hall, 2008.

Hsun-tzu. *Hsun-tzu: Basic Writings.* Burton Watson, trans. New York: Columbia University Press, 1963.

Katz, Steven, ed. *Mysticism and Religious Traditions.* Oxford: Oxford University Press, 1983.

Lao Tzu [Laozi]. *Tao Te Ching.* Gia-Fu Feng and Jane English, trans. New York: Vintage, 1972.

———. *Tao Te Ching.* D. C. Lau, trans. New York: Penguin. 1963. This is the most standard translation of the classic *Tao Te Ching.*

Laozi. *Dao De Jing: "Making This Life Significant," A Philosophical Translation.* Translated and commentary by Roger Ames and David Hall. New York: Ballantine Books, 2003. This is a dramatic revision of the *Dao De Jing* [*Tao Te Ching*] that is making inroads in Western Daoist studies. It is also being well received by scholars in China.

Mencius. *Mencius* (revised). D. C. Lau, trans. New York: Penguin Books, 2003.

Watson, Burton, trans. and ed. *Basic Writings of Mo Tzu, Hsun Tsu, and Han Fei Tzu.* New York: Columbia University Press, 1967.

Yao, Xinzhong. *An Introduction to Confucianism.* Cambridge: Cambridge University Press, 2000. Both student and scholar alike will find this book an excellent overview of Confucianism.

CHAPTER TEN

Indigenous Traditions
The Primal Voice

WHY NATIVE TRADITIONS MATTER
Shifts in Consideration

Mircea Eliade, one of the great pioneers in modern research of world religions, persuasively argued in academia that indigenous or native traditions were extremely important for understanding the spiritual life and, indeed, the way of the universe. Fifty years ago, he and others like him battled ignorance and bias to insist on including native traditions because scholarship had shown little interest in them to that time.

One of the many biases against studying native traditions was that they were simply too small, idiosyncratic, and numerous to contribute significantly to the wider world of knowledge. In North America alone, there are hundreds of Native American nations and more than fifty language groups. Given that native traditions were local, their language, rites, and beliefs seemed only meaningful to those who shared their specific subculture. In addition, native traditions are not text-based, and academia developed as a text-dependent enterprise, as written materials traveled well and could be widely disseminated. Many native communities also frustrated would-be inquirers by not admitting them. For many natives, their rites and beliefs are so sacred that it was a sacrilege to share them with those deemed not to have the proper respect or cultural-religious initiation.

One academic bias against native traditions was particularly strong: they seemed too primitive. They were believed to be unsophisticated and superstitious. Thus, these traditions might be interesting as curiosities, but they were not believed to be resources in understanding profound religious truth or spiritual transformation. Consider the evaluation of the great William James in his classic *The Varieties of Religious Experience*: "In the 'prayerful communion' of savages with such mumbo-jumbos of deities as they acknowledge, it is hard for us to see what genuine spiritual work—even though it were work only relative to their dark savage obligations—can possibly be done" (386–387).

Voices such as Eliade's helped to address such prejudices. Eliade argued that, instead of imagining these traditions as primitive, they should be regarded as primal. Obviously, these two terms are variations of the same root, *prime* or *first*. *Primitive* has the connotation of being simplistic or crude. *Primal*, on the other hand, speaks of something ancient and core. Eliade argued that native traditions preserve something about the religious human condition (*homo religiosus*) that is primordial to the human soul. Academia ignores their voices, he argued, to its peril.

The modern interest in native traditions could not be timelier for several reasons. One is that original native cultures are being diluted by the spread of mainstream cultures, and their ancient languages, rites, and wisdom are becoming lost. One Lakota holy man, **Black Elk**, for example, was so alarmed by the loss of his Sioux culture in the late nineteenth and early twentieth century that he was willing to share his autobiography with the world—the most mystical aspects of which were unknown even to his family—and also Lakota sacred rites, so that their practice and the wisdom therein would not be lost forever.

Modern respect for native traditions matters because such traditions came from tribal cultures that realized a harmonious and respectful relationship with nature. Given the ecological crisis that humans now face, listening to native wisdom and its posture toward nature may be the only way to ensure the future of humankind. Related to this is that native voices are unique in their own versions of interrelatedness. That is, many native traditions do not have strict lines of demarcation between human, animal, and plant life. Such blurring of lines not only emphasizes the need for harmony, it also challenges one's way of thinking about life itself, from a perspective centered on humanity (anthropocentrism) to one in which humans are part of a flowing universe of living creatures, all of whom share the same intrinsic dignity.

Leaving Anthropocentrism Behind

All Are Relatives

Harmony with Earth, the blurring of lines among creatures, and a holistic approach to religion dominates the ethos of many native traditions. Consider the following excerpt of a well-known speech by Chief Seattle in 1855:

> The president in Washington sends word that he wishes to buy our land. But how can you buy or sell the sky, the land? The idea is strange to us. If we do not own the presence of the air and the sparkle of the water, how can you buy them? Every part of the earth is sacred to my people. Every shining pine needle. Every sandy shore. Every mist in the dark woods. Every meadow. Every humming insect. All are holy in the memory and experience of my people. We know the sap that courses through the trees as we know the blood that courses through our veins. We are a part of the earth and it is part of us. Perfumed flowers are our sisters. The bear, the deer, the great eagle, these are our brothers. The rocky crests, the juices in the meadow, the body heat of

Chief Seattle, at about age 78, for whom the city of Seattle, Washington, was named.

IMAGE: © MUSEUM OF HISTORY AND INDUSTRY/CORBIS

> the pony, and man, all belong to the same family. . . . The
> water's murmur is the voice of my father's father. The rivers
> are our brothers. . . . So you must give to the rivers the
> kindness you would give any brother. . . . Will you teach
> your children what we have taught our children; that the
> earth is our mother? What befalls the earth befalls all the
> sons of heaven. This we know. The earth does not belong
> to man. Man belongs to the earth. All things are connected
> like the blood that unites us all. Man did not weave the web
> of life; he is merely a strand to himself. One thing we know,
> our God is also your God. The earth is precious to Him.
> And to harm the earth is to heap contempt on its creator.
>
> —cited in Joseph Campbell, *Transformations*
> *of Myth through Time*, 28–29

If a modern Anglo gave this speech, most would believe that the images, beautiful as they are, should not be taken at face value. The poetic identifications might be inspiring, but certainly not real. The flower is not one's sister and the bear is not one's brother. Yet Seattle meant it, even if in a nuanced way.

Chief Seattle was not alone in his thinking. Black Elk, in describing consecrating the universe through the smoke of the sacred pipe, said, "its fragrance will be known by the wingeds, the four-leggeds, and the two-leggeds, for we understand that we are all relatives . . ." (Joseph Epes Brown, *The Sacred Pipe*, 12). One sees that birds, wild animals, and humans are distinguished not by levels of consciousness but only by how they move about. Of course, the people of these traditions recognized that they were not biological sisters and brothers with animals or plants. Surely, they confronted that they had to hunt, fish, and harvest grains to survive. Yet, they did so recognizing the sacred gifts plants and other animals were and that they owed them veneration and respect. Indeed, many native myths concern ancient agreements between animals and humans that allow for the hunt. Thus, there is a kind of spiritual symbiosis between the people and the living things around them. Interestingly, when Black Elk was an adolescent, he had a profound mystical experience during which he saw a spiritualized version of all living animals. After this experience, it took him a long time to return to hunting at all.

Black Elk's Sacred Pipe

The sacred pipe is a sacramental that is used to mediate the sacred for many North American native traditions. It serves as an excellent illustration of the spiritual unity that Native Americans have with all living things. Black Elk describes the tradition of his tribe's receiving the sacred pipe from a mythical White Buffalo Cow Woman. She was sent by God, who is *Wakan-Tanka* (Great Mysterious or Great Sacred), and is understood as the ultimate Grandfather and Father. As Grandfather, he is Absolute Transcendence, and as Father, he is Creator. Earth, in counterpoint, is Grandmother as ground and potentiality of life, and Mother as producer of all living things. Black Elk identifies Earth as so holy that every step taken on it should be as a prayer. He describes the pipe in this manner:

> The bowl of the pipe is of red stone; it is the Earth. Carved in the stone and facing the center is this buffalo calf who represents all the four-leggeds who live upon your Mother. The stem of the pipe is of wood, and this represents all that grows upon the Earth. And these twelve feathers which hang here where the stem fits into the bowl are from the Spotted Eagle, and they represent the eagle and all the wingeds of the air. All these peoples, and all the things of the universe, are joined to you who smoke the pipe—all send their voices to *Wakan-Tanka*, the Great Spirit.
>
> —Joseph Epes Brown, *The Sacred Pipe*, 6

Virtually every major ceremony of the Lakota involves the sacred pipe. These rituals begin by offering the pipe to all four directions, which collectively symbolize the entire universe. It is first offered to the west, which represents completion and fullness; then to the north, which symbolizes purification; then to the east, which represents new life and spiritual guidance; and finally to the south, which represents the power that guards the right path. The powers of all the directions are invited into the pipe. In one ritual, when the preliminary rites are finished, the holy man takes the pipe and says, "This pipe which you have brought to me is really as sacred as the original pipe which was given to us by the White Buffalo Cow Woman. Indeed, to one who understands, they are really the same. But this pipe which you have now brought is especially sacred, for I see that there has been placed within it the whole of the universe" (ibid., 22). Those who smoke the sacred pipe, if their souls are pure, ingest the sacredness of the universe as well. The sacred pipe acts as a communion ritual as well as a petition for transformation by God. Are they communing with God or with the forces of the universe and all the creatures therein? To the pious Sioux, such a question suggests a false dichotomy. While the Sioux recognize *Wakan-Tanka* as God and the only One who should be worshipped, nonetheless, they would say that the essence of everything is *wakan* (sacred).

Speaking for a Sacred World

In 2004, a Peruvian shaman and leader of the Zapara people, Gloria Ushigua, addressed the UN Permanent Forum on Indigenous Issues. In a follow-up interview, she described the change in the life of her tribe over the past one hundred years. A century ago, there were twenty thousand members of the Zapara people who lived in the Amazon forest. They enjoyed clean waters, a healthy ecosystem, and perhaps the greatest biodiversity on the planet. Then the rubber companies arrived. They enslaved the Zapara and killed those who resisted the incursion. Following the rubber companies were the oil companies. Collectively, the environmental degradation caused by these companies was beyond imagination. Fascinatingly, decades before the arrival of these companies, the shamans of her tribe had prophesied that this would happen. The Zapara has dwindled to 350 members. Gloria was sent by her tribe to speak to the world before it was too late for her people and, indeed, for the world.

Gloria Ushigua's is not a singular voice. Other native wisdom figures have spoken to the world on behalf of Earth. One shining example is Thomas Banyacya, a Hopi elder and longtime advocate for world peace and environmental harmony. The following is a small part of the speech he gave in 1992 to the United Nations. Before he began, he sprinkled cornmeal next to the podium of the General Assembly, in order to consecrate the podium for this sacred purpose.

> My name is Banyacya . . . and I am a member of the Hopi sovereign nation. . . . The traditional Hopi follows the spiritual path that was given by *Massau'u*, the Great Spirit.

We made a sacred covenant to follow his life plan at all times, which includes the responsibility of taking care of this land and life for his divine purpose. . . . Our goals are... to pray and to promote the welfare of all living beings and to preserve the world in a natural way. . . . In the Earth today, humans poison their own food, water, and air with pollution. Many of us, including children, are left to starve. Many wars are being fought. Greed and concern for material things is a common disease. . . . Nature, the First People and the spirit of our ancestors, is giving you loud warnings. Today, December 10, 1992, you see increasing floods, more damaging hurricanes, hail storms, climate changes, and earthquakes as our prophesies said would come. Even animals and birds are warning us with strange changes in their behavior. . . . Why do animals act like they know about the earth's problems and most humans act like they know nothing? If we humans do not wake up to the warnings, the great purification will come to destroy this world. . . . If we return to spiritual harmony and live from our hearts, we can experience a paradise in this world. If we continue only on this upper path [of separation], we will come to destruction.

—Thomas Banyacya, "The Hopi Message"

The night before Banyacya's speech and those of other native wisdom figures, there was a total eclipse of the moon over New York City, and the sky was exceptionally clear. The night after the speech, rain fell so hard that New York experienced the worst flood in modern memory. The subfloors of the United Nations building were flooded. On the ground floor meeting room, Banyacya called all the participants gathered to form a great circle to pray. The storm quickly subsided. It could all have been a coincidence, but it was certainly uncanny.

Christian Reflection

The Christian relationship to the created world is varied. Some Christians, especially those who believe that Christ's return is imminent, imagine that God will soon destroy the world, and thus it is expendable. Several Christian denominations, such as the Seventh Day Adventists and Jehovah's Witnesses, began in the nineteenth century on the premise that Christ would soon return. While this expectation seemed to die down in the first half of the twentieth century, a modern revival of the expectation of Christ's imminent return has emerged, particularly among some Evangelical Christians. It started in the 1970s with books such as Hal Lindsey's *The Late Great Planet Earth*. Lindsey and others argued that biblical prophesies are now being fulfilled that are signs of the second coming. The *Left Behind* series of novels is based on this premise as well. One sees this expectation with high-profile Evangelical preachers such as Pat Robertson (b. 1930), Oral Roberts (1918–2009), and Robert Schuller (b. 1926). For these Christians, the great need is to convert souls and not to care about an environment that will be irrelevant within the next several decades. Most Christians, however, take a more attentive posture toward the environment.

Fundamentally, all Christian traditions ground their understanding of the relationship between humans and the rest of the world in Genesis. After God had created all things and saw that they were good, he created humankind:

> Then God said, "Let us make humankind in our image, according to our likeness; and let them have dominion over the fish of the sea, and over the birds of the air, and over the cattle, and over all the wild animals of the earth." So God created humankind in his image, in the image of God he created them; male and female he created them. God blessed them and said to them, "Be fruitful and multiply, and fill the earth and subdue it; and have dominion over the fish of the sea and over the birds of the air and over every living thing that moves upon the earth." God said, "See, I have given you every plant yielding seed that is upon the face of all the earth, and every tree with seed in its fruit; you shall have them for food. And to every beast of the earth, and to every bird of the air, and to everything that creeps on the earth, everything that has the breath of life, I have given every green plant for food." And so it was.
>
> —Genesis 1:26–30

What does one make of these verses? *The New Jerome Biblical Commentary* states the following: "The nuance of the verb is 'to master,' 'to bring forcefully under control.' Force is necessary at the beginning to make the untamed land serve humans. . . . Humans are the pinnacle of the created world, the world is made for man and woman" (11). *The Oxford Bible Commentary* reads, "The ordinance that mankind is to rule over the animal kingdom (1:26, 28), like the statement that the sun and moon are to rule over the day and night (1:16), determines mankind's function in the world. . . . Mankind is, as it were a manager or supervisor of the world of living creatures" (43). In both commentaries the authors go on to explain that the world is not to be exploited and even that it appears the text intends humans to be vegetarians (modified after the flood [Genesis 9:2–5]). Still, one cannot help but see the differences between commentaries. Is the world and are all creatures made for humans, or is humanity to act as stewards working on behalf of God and his creation?

What is true in both commentaries is that humanity is seen somehow as different from other creatures. Perhaps this is why Christianity has been a small voice in challenging environmental degradation; Christians do not identify with creation or other creatures directly. Christianity has also been late and relatively impotent in speaking out against global warming. While the World Council of Churches has had a department to specifically investigate climate change since 1990, it has done very little. In April 2007, the Vatican organized a conference on climate change. Pope Benedict XVI charged that abuse of the environment was against God's will, and he called for a global respect for all of creation. In the United States, the U.S. Conference of Catholic Bishops has produced several documents about ecology. These documents involve the culture of consumerism and the relationship between climate change and health care. Collectively, this appears to most readers as a rather tepid response to an approaching crisis.

A more powerful vision came from the Evangelical Lutheran Church of America in 1993. Its document, "Caring for Creation," characterized consumerism as a kind of captivity to demonic powers and destructive greed. In contrast to a posture of exploitation, it asserted that God loves and cares for all creation and creatures and that humanity is intimately related to creation; indeed all creation is interdependent. This means, the document stated, that in light of the principle of solidarity, all of creation stands together. Interestingly, the document also imagined Christ's final redemption as including all of creation, citing Paul's statement in Ephesians that Christ will unite all things in heaven and on Earth (Ephesians 1:10). As noted in chapter seven, one biblical expression also holds that all of creation will participate in Christ's redemption (Romans 8:19–21). What is interesting is that the bishops of the Lutheran Church decided to claim this approach rather definitively.

Anthropocentrism (human-centeredness) takes different forms. One end of the continuum is that creation was made only for humans and that nothing really matters but humans. Perhaps the middle position would say that humans are ultimately the only things that matter, because only humans have souls and can be saved. Still, humans should love and respect Earth and all its creatures, because they are gifts from God and intrinsically good. On the other end of the spectrum might be that, because humans are created with more spiritual importance, they have a higher responsibility to care for the world. The Lutheran bishops appear to be suggesting a step beyond this—that humans are a part of a larger salvific plan by God. If other animals are to be saved, then perhaps humans should not be the center of the universe. If Christians were to take seriously any position besides the most heavy-handed form of anthropocentrism, they would have to strive vigorously for animal rights. It is difficult, for example, to imagine that industrial farming practices in developed countries are anything but grossly cruel, inhumane, and a violation of the Christian faith.

Broadly speaking, native spirituality offers a vision in which humanity does not take center stage at all, even as environmental stewards. Life is an interrelational, spiritually alive, and fully conscious reality in which no one thing should be central.

SPIRITS AND SHAMANS
The Shaman

A central figure in many native traditions is the shaman. Native religions typically take for granted that a powerful, influential spirit-realm exists. They believe that the boundary between the physical and spiritual worlds is a permeable one in which spirits can affect the natural world, especially humans. Humans likewise can affect the spirits. Negotiating between worlds is the special role of the shaman. Broadly speaking, the shaman is a combination theologian, demonologist, healer, sorcerer, and psychologist. The common thread in those native traditions that have shamans—and most do—is that shamans have access to, and knowledge of, other orders of reality.

Shamans become who they are variously. In some traditions, shamans are part of a family of shamans. Just as musical or athletic gifts are regularly inherited, so it is believed are spiritual depth and psychic abilities. Such shamans learn the trade through years of watching and assisting their relatives. A disposition to spiritual depth may well be hereditary. Gloria Ushigua was part of a family of shamans for the Zapara community. Other shamans personally choose the path or are recognized by their tribe as having this gift. Still others may be spontaneously elected by the spirits. Such was true of Black Elk, who was carried off by the spirits and initiated by a lengthy, complex vision.

A future shaman's initiation is often overseen by elder master shamans and by the spirits of deceased shamans. The future shaman often singles him- or herself out by strange behavior. The initiate becomes a dreamer, sings during sleep, desperately seeks solitude, and often has visions. Sometimes he or she will go into fits that result in unconsciousness. There tends to be a kind of madness in future shamans, and this psychic chaos signifies that the initiate's ordinary identity is about to dissolve into a new identity, one that can unite both physical and spiritual worlds.

Shamanic initiation requires entrance into the spirit-world. Here the shaman needs to become familiar with the souls of the living and the dead, with demons and gods, and with all the innumerable figures that are invisible to the rest of humanity. Often, shamanic initiates become caught in a trance or lie unconscious for days while their souls travel to the spirit-world. Some have been found to have virtually stopped breathing. When they are resuscitated, they revive as a shaman.

What happens during that period of blackout? The occurrences vary drastically, depending upon the tradition. According to the Yakuts of northern Asia, for example, the spirits carry the future shaman's soul to hell and imprison the initiate there. That is where he or she undergoes initiation. Demons cut up his spiritualized body and give the pieces over to different spirits of illnesses. When reassembled, the initiate physically understands the nature of each illness. The spirit of each illness is now recognizable, and the shaman understands what a sick member of the tribe needs for healing. In some North American communities, the ancestral shamans pierce the future shaman's spiritualized body, cut the flesh, and pull out bones. They then eat the flesh and drink the blood. This surely symbolizes becoming one with the past shamans. Having communed with shamanic ancestors, the reassembled shaman has absorbed their wisdom and spiritual depth. Whatever the initiation process is specifically, shamanic induction is widely understood as a dramatic experience of death and rebirth. When shamans return from their spirit initiation, it is typical then to undergo a lengthy period of apprenticeship from elder shamans in the community.

Shamans have a crucial place in the tribal community. They can provide a safe passage for dead souls to negotiate the underworld. They can bring messages from those souls or to them from living relatives. They know the access points to ascend into heaven to seek a boon from the spirits, such as rain in time of drought or where game has gone in time of scarcity. Most of all, they are healers. They are the antidemonic champions who combat the spirits of physical, mental, and spiritual illness. They defend life against death, health against illness, and light against darkness. In a native worldview, humans are not alone, but are surrounded by spirits. Shamans are specialists in seeing what is invisible to others. Their presence not only confirms and fortifies the structures of traditional native religion but also nourishes the tribe's religious imagination and opens the windows to larger spiritual possibilities.

Another Form of Engaging the Spirits: Voodoo

Is the universe so full of spirits, and can one really regularly commune with them? One religion, **voodoo**, is a most dramatic expression of spirit communication. Voodoo is the name of the religious tradition in Haiti that is principally an African import. *Vo* means "introspection" and *dou* means "into the unknown." Thus, voodoo is looking into that unknown world of the spirits. Voodoo practitioners believe in a transcendent God whom they call *Bondye*. However, voodoo practitioners do not focus much of their energy on God. They are more interested in *Iwa*, who are spirits. It is the *Iwa* they believe can help them with day-to-day life. The *Iwa* work on humans'behalf when properly attended to and can also bring misfortune if ignored or insulted. In this sense, they look much like the spirits and ancestors in ancient China, which were discussed in chapter nine. Like those ancestors, *Iwa* can also be fed, offered gifts, and so on.

At this point, however, the comparison stops. *Iwa* want and need to be part of human lives. They come to people in dreams, trances, and bodily possessions. They warn their followers about approaching harm, they gossip about neighboring tribes, and they even scold their believers. Some spirits are relatively universalized throughout Haitian voodoo. *Legba*, for example, serves as the gatekeeper between the two worlds and needs to be placated before any of the other *Iwa* can be contacted. *Dahbala Wedo* is the most important *Iwa* and the most powerful. *Agwe* is the sovereign of the sea, and *Ogou* is a hero warrior. Each individual, family, or tribe has its own particular *Iwa* or combination of *Iwa* that it is particularly interested in or fascinated by. Priests typically associate with generally revered *Iwa* or those who are particularly important to their tribe.

While there is no set liturgy for invoking the *Iwa*, rituals usually involve drums, fire, dancing, and trance possession. Each voodoo temple is also autonomous and free to carry on the voodoo tradition according to how the priest interprets the instructions of the spirits. In a voodoo ceremony, the *Iwa* are invoked. At some time, a given *Iwa* takes over the body of the priest or another worshipper and then speaks to the community through the worshipper, who is in a trance state. Those possessed take on the personality traits of the given *Iwa*. They show the preferences, style of walking, and speaking pattern that is specific to that *Iwa*. These preferences might even include drinking alcohol or smoking tobacco. All of this is distinct from the personality of the possessed person. It is part of voodoo theology that the *Iwa* need to return to the flesh from time to time; the possessions somehow fortify them.

Some of the more devout worshippers can undergo a kind of mystical marriage. These devotees are called ***serviteurs***, and they can initiate a marriage proposal to the *Iwa*. If the *Iwa* accepts (through the mediation of someone possessed), then the *serviteur* will remain celibate and profoundly devoted for a lifetime. Sometimes, under the form of possession of another, the *Iwa* might personally make the proposal. In such an instance, the *serviteur* may be allowed to be married but must devote an evening per week to spend with the (disembodied) spirit. The marriage ritual is the same as it would be for people, except that the *Iwa*, as either bride or groom, has possessed the body of someone to walk down the aisle and make the vows. Once the *Iwa* is recognized as having taken over someone, then the wedding ceremony can begin. The couple exchanges vows, rings, and signs a wedding contract. In the marriage, the *Iwa* promises to protect the spouse and bring good fortune, while the *serviteur* promises to fulfill his or her rightful obligations to the *Iwa* as well.

Christian Reflection

Is Shamanism Spiritually Valid?

Shamanic mediation plays no central role in mainstream Christianity, but it does have some resonance in charismatic or Pentecostal forms. In these traditions, members describe being "baptized in the Holy Spirit," as when they become supernaturally empowered by God. Additionally, there are some forms of spiritual gifts (*charismata*) that are particularly astounding. Some are given the powers of prophecy, healing, or exorcism. Some claim the ability to read souls and to sense angels and demons and their activities.

The belief that the universe is filled with spirits, both benign and malevolent, has been part of the Church since its beginnings, as discussed in chapter three. Therefore, being able to discern good spirits from evil ones was crucial. Perhaps the most detailed instructions on discerning spirits come from the desert father, Evagrius Ponticus. His analysis of the ways of evil spirits grounded much of the patristic Church's understanding of them. What is interesting is that, from a modern point of view, they are described essentially as psychological dispositions. Ponticus shows how some thoughts and temptations are related to others. He also distinguishes personality types and the kinds of demons that favor each one. Even today, his insights seem psychologically sophisticated and insightful.

In considering shamanism, one cannot help but ask whether or not the universe is really that filled with spirits. On the one hand, does one demythologize them to one's spiritual peril? So serious is Roman Catholicism about the possibility of demon possession that every diocese designates one of its priests as an official exorcist—usually a very holy and insightful person who is able to discern mental illness from something demonic. Most Christians believe that Satan and supernatural evil are real. On the other hand, is it naïve and even paranoid to imagine demons active in and affecting our lives? Modern medical science operates on such a different level of assumptions about sickness that it makes it impossible to identify, as ancient religions tended to do, the cause of illness as supernatural. Germs and viruses are simply not demons.

A book titled *Ritual for Exorcism and Prayers for Particular Circumstances* is seen as priests listen to a lesson on satanism for clergy at Rome's Regina Apostolorum Pontifical Academy, Thursday, February 17, 2005. Worried about the lure of the devil, the Vatican-linked university debuted its latest course offering a class on satanism, black magic, and exorcism.

To read accounts of shamanic initiations one can easily imagine them to be psychotic episodes. Are they real, and do shamans actually gain spiritual power and healing insight? In Black Elk's case, his initiation into the spirit-world included prophecies about the future of his people that came true. Additionally, he began to heal people almost immediately after he returned from his mystical vision. He also devised healing dances and rites later in his life that corresponded to his original vision and seemed to have dramatic healing properties. On one occasion, many years after his vision, members of his tribe were very sick with an illness that no one could identify. Black Elk remembered seeing this sickness prophesied in his original vision. In that vision, he was instructed to use the herbs growing in a valley he was shown. While in prayer these many years later, he was directed to that unknown valley and found unidentifiable herbs that looked like those in the original vision. He used them to cure his people. What is particularly interesting about this story is that Black Elk, while recounting his life as a healer—a position he never rejected—was a Roman Catholic catechist. Even after his conversion to Christianity, he never doubted that the ancestors had called him to be a shaman.

Shamanism and Christian Cosmology

Chapter three gave a short synopsis of various cosmologies. Typically, Christians and Jews recognize the existence of only good and evil angels. Muslims add a category of Jinn (genies). If one were to embrace the East, it would include many more beings, from *devas* (gods) to hungry ghosts. What should one make of those shamans who enter the underworld? In some tribal traditions, shamans have to negotiate with complex spirits, some of whom are said to have a malevolent or trickster side.

Shamanism challenges one to stretch one's religious imagination, to see the spirit-world seep into the world of everyday. Accomplishing this challenge could open one to another realm that a modern scientific worldview has blocked. Surely, however, one need not take every claim at face value. Additionally, even if aspects of shamanism are real, they do not necessarily have to be associated with, much less affirmed. The Bible clearly condemns the practice: "You shall not practice augury or witchcraft" (Leviticus 19:26); "A man or a woman who is a medium or a wizard shall be put to death" (Leviticus 20:27). In Second Kings, one also sees Josiah's religious reforms phrased thusly: "Josiah did away with the mediums, wizards, teraphim [household gods], and idols, and all abominations that were seen in the land of Judah and in Jerusalem. . . . Before him there was no king like him, who turned to the Lord with all his heart, with all his soul, and with all his might according to all the law of Moses" (2 Kings 23:24–25). In the New Testament, Paul identifies sorcery as behavior that keeps one from inheriting the kingdom of God (Galatians 5:20–21), and in the Book of Revelation Jesus casts sorcerers into hell (Revelation 21:8).

That Black Elk, Gloria Ushigua, and Thomas Banyacya are holy people is not in question here. In addition, they learned some of their powers of healing from the spirit-world. Still, shamanism seems quite contrary to authentic Christian faith—particularly in terms of working with compromised or compromising spirits. Consider, for example, the experience of Dr. Mark Plotkin, an ethnobotanist who befriended several shamans in the northwest part of the Amazon rain forest during a decade of research there. Under their tutelage, he learned about natural ways to cure an enormous number of illnesses. He describes one particularly learned (and feared) medicine man of the Wayana tribe named Grandfather. At one point, Plotkin's elbow became injured. It was very painful and simply not healing. Grandfather performed a healing ritual on him. Briefly, the ritual went as follows: He laid Plotkin on a table, blew tobacco smoke on his elbow, and began chanting, which summoned the spirits. After a period of quiet, the walls of the hut began to shake violently as though something was passing through them. Then Grandfather conversed with the spirit for what seemed like hours. Plotkin then entered into a dreamlike trance and experienced again a violent shaking of the walls as though the spirit was departing. Grandfather blew smoke on his arm again and massaged his elbow. He then returned to chanting. Plotkin describes being lifted outside of his body and briefly dwelling on the top of the hut. Looking down, he saw the shaman blowing smoke over his physical body. Further chanting brought his spirit back to his body, and eventually, he was awakened as from a sleep.

Grandfather later explained that his spirit-body had a soft spot at the elbow and that evil spirits were attacking him from that point of weakness. In the ritual, he patched the soft spot and vanquished the evil spirits. Grandfather knew all about the evil spirits because he was also capable of using them to curse others, including a neighboring rival tribe. It was widely believed, and Grandfather slyly confirmed, that he sent evil spirits to attack the tribe of Black Jaguar, a shaman whom he blamed for an earlier curse on his tribe. One might note two things about Dr. Plotkin's experience with Grandfather as a shaman. First, his elbow was healthy and free of pain immediately after the ceremony and never bothered him again. Second, Black Jaguar's son committed suicide three days after the curse was supposed to have been laid on the village.

Most students who read about *Iwa* possession simply shake their heads in dismissal. They liken it to something psychosomatic, a product of the imagination. Considering that voodoo adepts believe in *Iwa* passionately, that their rites involve rhythmic dance, song, and drums, such trancelike possessions might, in fact, be little more than the psyche fooling itself. Modern theories of hypnosis give great respect for the power of suggestion. Most also find the theological claims in voodoo absurd, such as spirits who periodically need to take on flesh and who can effect religious and material boons for a community. To believe in, venerate, and even marry spirits who like to drink, smoke, and gossip about other tribes simply seems foolish. Others imagine that these phenomena are all too real, and that what is really being experienced is demon possession. For those who are disturbed in this regard, a deeper investigation into voodoo would be all the more alarming. For example, some voodoo adepts practice **sympathetic magic**, in which they take objects that represent another person. To these objects, they ritualize a blessing or (more likely) a curse that is supposed to directly affect the actual person. This is the origin of the voodoo doll. Can one commend any of this?

Review Questions

1. Until recently, indigenous religions have been ignored by academia. What are the reasons they have been ignored and why is study of them now considered far more valuable?
2. What are various expressions of Christian anthropocentrism and how do native traditions offer an alternative point of view?
3. What are the four ways given in the text by which a shaman is chosen, and how might these be related to the various ways a shaman is initiated?

In-Depth Questions

1. Native traditions imagine a world in which humans do not have a qualitatively distinct value over other animals. Do you think this is a wiser perspective than western anthropocentrism? Why or why not?
2. Do you think animals have souls? Are animals saved? On what basis would you respond to these questions?
3. Do you believe shamanic healing or spirit possession is psychosomatic? Explain.
4. How does one really know what beings are in the spirit-world? What claims should one accept or dismiss and why? Should Christians dismiss everything that does not appear in their religious tradition simply because it does not?
5. Is involvement with spirits or other supernatural beings compatible with Christian teaching? Explain.

Select Bibliography

Banyacya, Thomas. "The Hopi Message: An Address by Thomas Manyacya," December 11, 1992, at *www.welcomehome.ord/rainbow/prophecy/hopi.html*, accessed July 25, 2009.

Barton, John, and John Muddiman, eds. *The Oxford Bible Commentary.* Oxford: Oxford University Press, 2001.

Brown, Joseph Epes, ed. *The Sacred Pipe: Black Elk's Account of the Seven Rites of the Oglala Sioux.* Norman: University of Oklahoma Press, 1953. This is a superb expression of Sioux rites given by Black Elk with some helpful explanatory notes by Brown.

Brown, Raymond, et al., eds., *The New Jerusalem Commentary.* Englewood Cliffs, NJ: Prentice Hall, 1990.

Campbell, Joseph. *Transformations of Myth through Time.* New York: Harper & Row, 1990.

Cannon, Dale. *Six Ways of Being Religious.* Belmont, CA: Wadsworth Publishing, 1996.

Cohen, Daniel. *Voodoo, Devils, and the New Invisible World.* New York: Dodd, Mead & Company, 1972. This is a popular and well-researched investigation on modern esoteric movements from the occult to theories of ancient alien visitations.

Costello, Damian. *Black Elk: Colonialism and Lakota Catholicism.* Maryknoll, NY: Orbis Books, 2005.

Driscoll, Jeremy. *The Mind's Long Journey to the Holy Trinity: The "ad Monachos" of Evagrius Ponticus.* Collegeville, MN: Liturgical Press, 1993.

Eliade, Mircea. *A History of Religious Ideas: From Muhammad to the Age of Reforms.* Alf Hiltebeitel and Diane Apostolos-Cappadona, trans. Chicago: University of Chicago Press, 1985.

Evangelical Lutheran Church of America. *Caring for Creation: Vision, Hope, and Justice.* Minneapolis, MN: Division for Congregational Ministry/ Augsburg Fortress, 1993.

James, William. *The Varieties of Religious Experience.* Cambridge, MA: Harvard University Press, 1985.

Landon, Mary Kay. "Marrying Spirits in the Flesh." *Parabola* 29, no. 1 (2004): 73–79.

Metraux, Alfred. *Voodoo in Haiti.* Hugo Chareris, trans. New York: Schocken Books, 1972. A superb anthropological text on Haitian voodoo, the description of which can be eerie and grotesque.

Neihardt, John, and Nicholas Black Elk. *Black Elk Speaks.* Lincoln: University of Nebraska Press, 2000. Originally published in 1932, this biography of a Lakota holy man is a classic.

Plotkin, Mark. *Tales of a Shaman's Apprentice.* New York: Penguin, 1993.

Ushigua, Gloria, with Brian Keane. "Calling Back the Boas." *Parabola* 29, no. 3 (2004): 34–37.

CHAPTER ELEVEN

The New Age Message

WHAT IS NEW AGE?

This chapter is unlike the others in that it is less intent on investigating the insights of its subject—in this case, New Age religious expressions—than on offering a critique. As the reader will see, this author is less sympathetic toward the New Age religious movement than the other religious traditions discussed in this book. But I believe that it is important to reflect on New Age sensibilities, which are both instructive and problematic, so as to get a good sense of the contemporary religious world and also how one might skillfully address the underlying issues that have created New Age religions.

In 1971, Charles Reich wrote a now classic book called *The Greening of America*. In it, he offers a political and social critique of the postindustrial West as well as a vision of a new worldview. Reich signaled by the term *green* his intent to address the ecological crisis; however, he also meant something far greater: a spiritual renewal, one in which ecological harmony would be grounded in a higher sense of spiritual integration. Interestingly, when Al Gore published *Earth in the Balance: Ecology and the Human Spirit* (1993), he echoed Reich. Gore described the current cultural condition of the world as void of a center and in spiritual crisis. This kind of thinking represents a core

A worshipper of the pagan Wiccan religion, left, and a friend stand near the ancient stone monument of Stonehenge, as access to the site is given to druids, New Age followers and members of the public to mark the annual Winter Solstice, in Wiltshire, southern England, Friday Dec. 22, 2006.

characteristic of New Age spirituality, a religious phenomenon that acts as an active critic of modern society and mainstream religion and speaks to a void of spiritual meaning in today's culture.

A precise description of *New Age* is difficult, because the term refers to a great deal. For example, in John Button and William Bloom's *The Seeker's Guide: A New Age Resource Book*, a partial list in the table of contents includes Goddess Spirituality, ESP, Neo-paganism and Wicca, Native American Spirituality, Channeling, Herbalism, Acupuncture, Altered States of Consciousness, Near Death Experience, Jewish Kabbalah, Shamanism, Astrology, Transpersonal Psychology, and Ecofeminism. This is a dizzying variety of topics. All do, however, have one thing in common: they represent alternatives to the traditional culture and standard forms of religiosity. They also represent something of what was discussed about postmodernity earlier in this book. That is, the topics of *The Seeker's Guide* are part of a larger cultural movement that tends to favor pluralism, eclecticism, relativism, and personal choice. Today, many people feel free to mix and match beliefs and practices according to their inclinations or spiritual intuitions. Religion, like everything else, is no longer something one inherits, but something one chooses for personal fulfillment.

There is a context to New Age, and part of it is that Americans are far less "churched" than they were just a couple of generations ago. For example, 86 percent of Christians in the baby-boom generation (born 1944–1960) received religious training from their parents, but only half of these same boomers gave religious training to their children. Before 1940, most Americans lived in small towns, where church membership was often one part of a larger sense of belonging and meaning. Sociologists of religion have noted that most people in 1950 were not deeply introspective about their faith; it was taken for granted as part of their sense of home. For many, religious life was secure but flat. By the 1950s and 1960s, more Americans lived in suburbia, where lifestyles were increasingly a matter of choice and people experienced far less pressure to conform—religiously or otherwise. Thus, in the past fifty years, Americans have become less grounded in their traditional faith and more intentional about what to think and how to live religiously.

Given the baby-boomer context, New Age religiosity brought an alternative for those who sought meaning and religious experience and did not find it in traditional religious institutions. New Age spirituality offers a smorgasbord of religious possibilities. Considering them collectively, one does see some common themes. One is the connection between ecology and spirituality. Take, for example, a decision by some New Age watchers who believed—based on Mayan astrology—that the date of a new spiritual consciousness would emerge on August 16–17, 1987. That weekend, tens of thousands of people gathered at such places as Mount Shasta, California, and Stonehenge, England. They danced, sang, chanted, and opened themselves to what they hoped would be greater cosmic consciousness. The event was dubbed the "Harmonic Convergence." Though nothing much happened, the event represented a belief that spiritual awakening was available—and perhaps only accessible—outside of mainstream religions, which are often rendered as harbingers of the status quo and part of the problem of the West's spiritual emptiness.

A second theme of New Age spirituality is the rejection of traditional religion while retaining an eclectic combination of traditional and esoteric teachings. For example, Joseph Chilton Pearce argues in *The Death of Religion and the Rebirth of Spirit* that conventional religion robs the soul. What one finds in Pearce's book is a collection of claims from fields as wide as neuroscience, Zen, Gnostic Gospel sayings of Jesus, an evolutionary theory of consciousness, and so on (none of which evidences deep research). In Steven Foster and Meredith Little's *The Roaring of the Sacred River: Wilderness Quest for Vision and Self-Healing*, one finds Native American spirituality mixed with world mystical texts, the wisdom of the I Ching (an ancient Chinese divination practice), Buddhist scriptures, poems by the Islamic mystic Rumi, and sayings from the Gnostic gospels—all in one theoretically seamless presentation. Finally, in Eckhart Tolle's *The Power of Now* and *A New Earth*, we find combinations that include the Christian mysticism of Meister Eckhart, Hindu Vedanta, personal esoteric interpretations of the Bible, Islamic mysticism, *Dao De Jing*, Zen, and the philosophies of Krishnamurti and Ramana Maharishi. On scrutiny, the result is something metaphysically incoherent.

A third theme of New Age spirituality is that institutional religions are irrelevant. While they are often not overtly critiqued, they are rarely mentioned as important. What is crucial is one's personal, spiritual awakening. In a two-year study of journalistic databases on prayer in the 1990s, the term *prayer* appeared 55,000 times. Yet, in only 2,500 of these appearances (less than 5 percent) was there any mention of a religious organization or historical tradition. One might also look at the famous spiritual guidebook of the 1990s by Thomas Moore, *The Care of the Soul*. While this is a thoughtful book, interestingly, it offers little specific mention of God and none of religion. Virtually all New Age books are devoted to discovering personal meaning outside of formal religious communities.

Collectively, one might say that New Age spirituality is both a rejection and an affirmation. On the one hand, it rejects dry, seemingly pointless religiosity. It rejects normative expressions of truth, and challenges highly rational, abstract expressions of meaning. In contrast, New Age spirituality strives to affirm one's inner life, intuitive knowledge of the truth, and self-authorization. It also seeks a holistic approach to life in the spirit that integrates body and soul, human and animal life, and this world and the next. There are some strange and problematic expressions of New Age spirituality, some of which will be addressed in what follows. Nonetheless, mainstream religion would be arrogant to imagine nothing relevant is going on in New Age spirituality. In addition, it would be smug and superficial for mainstream religion to think it could simply demand that Church members fall back into line. Something about New Age spirituality resonates with the cultural paradigm shift that is under way. One needs to pay attention.

INTERESTING CONTRIBUTIONS AND STRANGE PERMUTATIONS
Explosion of New Religious Movements

New religious movements have been addressing spiritual malaise in the West, and particularly in America, for more than a century. As shown in chapter ten, there have been numerous predictions of the second coming of Christ. William Miller (1782–1849), for example, gained followers when he proclaimed that Christ's second coming was to occur in 1843 and then revised that to 1844. After Christ did not return—a nonevent known as the Great Disappointment—Miller's ideas were continued by Ellen G. White (1827–1915), who founded the Seventh Day Adventist Church in 1861 on the premise that Jesus indeed had returned, but invisibly. Charles Taze Russell (1852–1916), founder of the Zion's Watchtower Society in 1874, also taught of Christ's invisible return. His successor, Joseph Franklin Rutherford (1869–1941), declared the official date of Christ's return as 1914 and renamed the community the Jehovah's Witnesses.

Both the Seventh Day Adventists and Jehovah's Witnesses promised a new era of spiritual transformation; they were not alone. In 1920, Paramahansa Yogananda, a well-regarded Hindu guru, started the Self-Realization Fellowship, a philosophy and spiritual practice based on the Hindu Yoga Sutras. Maharishi Mahesh Yogi popularized a form of Hindu meditation, Transcendental Meditation (TM), in the 1960s. At that same time, the International Society for Krishna Consciousness (ISKCON) came to the West. One of the more extravagant movements arrived with the advent of the Unification Church under Sun Myung Moon, who claimed that Jesus appeared to him and commanded him to complete Christ's mission by starting a church. He also claimed to have met periodically with Abraham, Moses, the Buddha, and God. The Unification Church began formally in 1959 and became widespread in the 1970s.

Along with such new religious movements, other spiritual and psychological trends have emerged in recent decades as well. The Human Potential Movement grew in the 1970s and 1980s. It sought to unleash repressed or untapped spiritual and psychological power in its followers. Those decades and the years since also have seen an accelerated interest in the Holistic Health Movement, Native American shamanistic spirituality, and Deep Ecology, as well as an increase in spiritualism, which includes practices such as channeling spirits, healing with crystals, astrology, and fortune telling with tarot cards.

In short, over the past century, and particularly over the past several decades, a barrage of new spiritual philosophies and practices have appeared, all claiming to be able to fill the void of the postmodern world.

Strange Permutations: Two Examples

Neopaganism and Wicca

Neopaganism is a collective term designating a religious movement that seeks to return to the religious practices and insights of premodern societies. Many neopagans align these practices with Native American wisdom—a wisdom that respects nature and cultivates a heightened sense of the inner-connectivity of all created things. It sees the world ordered by sacred forces that are celebrated, as neopagans strive to harmonize their lives to, and be charged with, such forces. One example of neopaganism is the revival of **Druidism**, an ancient nature religion in Europe that was especially prevalent in the British Isles and was suppressed by the Roman Empire in the first two centuries CE. Perhaps the most influential proponent of modern Druidism was Philip Ross Nichols (1902–1990). Druidism had already been reconstituted by Nichols's time, but he orchestrated a popular expression that developed Druid celebrations and orders of rank within the Druid community. Druids are generally polytheistic, believing in both male and female gods. They see nature as divine in its own right, and they celebrate that divinity particularly with rites at agrarian festival times, such as sowing and harvesting, as well as during lunar and solar periods of note, such as full moons, equinoxes, and solstices.

The most popular form of neopaganism is **Wicca**. *Wicca* is a medieval Anglo-Saxon word that can be translated as *witch*, though most members of Wicca move away from that term, given its false associations with devil worship or casting evil spells. Wicca is anything but that. Rather it sees itself as a form of the Old Religion that was particularly interested in goddess worship. One could imagine Wicca as the ultimate feminist critique of patriarchal religions. While patriarchy is seen to represent hierarchy, domination, dogma, suppression of the feminine, suppression of the body and sexuality, and abstract rationality, Wicca celebrates egalitarianism, a unified web of life, the divine feminine and women's participation in it. Starhawk, one of the most important articulators of Wiccan theology and practice, describes Wiccans and the Goddess:

> In the Craft, we do not *believe* in the Goddess—we connect with Her; through the moon, the stars, the ocean, the earth, through trees, animals, through other human beings, through ourselves. She is here. She is within us all. She is the full circle: earth, air, fire, water, and essence—body, mind, spirit, emotions, change. . . . The earth Goddess is also air and sky, the celestial Queen of Heaven, the star Goddess, ruler of things felt but not seen: of knowledge, mind, and intuition. She is the Muse, who awakens all creations of the human spirit. . . . The celestial Goddess is seen as the moon, who is linked to women's monthly cycles of bleeding and fertility.
>
> *The Spiritual Dance*, 91–92

The beginnings of Wicca can be traced back to 1940 and the writings of Gerald Gardener, who claimed to be an initiate of a Wiccan coven. A coven is ideally a group of twelve to thirteen members who act as a self-contained religious congregation. Two of Gardener's students brought the practice to the United States in 1960, and in 1965, an official Church of Wicca was institutionalized. Much of the inspiration for the modern expression of Wicca came from Sir James George Frazer's *The Golden Bough: A Study of Magic and Religion*, first published in two volumes in 1890. Like Druidism, Wicca is, by and large, a modern expression of an imagined past with no real textual

246 • E<small>NCOUNTERS IN</small> F<small>AITH</small>

or archeological data. Some Wiccans, for example, date their Old Religion back to Paleolithic times in the worship of the god of the hunt and the goddess of fertility. Further, some Wiccans assert that in pre-Bronze Age Europe, the goddess was worshipped and known through the mediation of shaman priestesses. This claim is based on a few stick drawings in recently excavated caves. Other influential works that have attempted to reconstruct and incorporate ancient goddess worship into neopagan/Wiccan rituals are Merlin Stone's *When God Was a Woman* (1976) and Carol Christ's *The Laughter of Aphrodite* (1987).

Wiccan covens gather regularly in ceremonies called *esbats*. Their main rituals involve the creation of a sacred space by casting a circle through purification rituals involving the four elements of fire, water, earth, and air. They also ritually attend to the four directions. The circle becomes a sacred world in which they chant, dance, and strive to realize the collective energy of the group as well as invite the divine energy of the goddess. This "drawing down" of the energy of the goddess is understood variously, from the coven at large experiencing divine power to the power entering the priestess of the coven, who makes the goddess's spiritual power tangibly present. This instantiation of the goddess's power should not be imagined like the possession of the *Iwa* in voodoo rituals discussed in chapter ten. Rather, it expresses a particular presentation of the universal presence of divinity—something similar to what Catholics at Mass celebrate in the presence of Christ in the Word being preached, the community gathered, and in the priest who acts in *in persona Christi*.

More important solemnities are called *sabbats*, which typically number eight: (1) Yole—winter solstice, December 20–23; (2) Brigid—dedicated to the Goddess of fire, February 2; (3) Eostar—spring equinox, March 20–23; (4) Beltane—fertility, April 31; (5) Litha—summer solstice, June 20–23; (6) Lughnasad—harvest, August 1; (7) Mabon—fall equinox, September 20–23; and (8) Samhain—New Year, October 31. Because Wicca has no united orthodoxy or structured leadership, the rituals and practices have a kind of extemporaneous quality. If there is any continuity in Wiccan rituals, it comes from influential writers. Margot Adler's *Drawing Down the Moon* (1986) presented a virtual manual on Wiccan practice that is extensively used. Starhawk's *The Spiritual Dance* (1979) has also been widely adopted as a ritual book. Starhawk, however, recommends that each coven make and remake rituals, leaving behind what does not seem to work well and creating rituals that are personally meaningful.

Neopaganism, like much of New Age spirituality, has an eclectic quality. Sarah Pike, an expert on neopagan religious expression, describes a neopagan gathering called the Rites of Spring. This several-day conference and celebration included a workshop on "Tantric Ecstatic Breath Ceremony." A brochure for the event described the ceremony this way:

> Breathe the Breath of the Goddess, awakening the sacred snake of Kundalini, purifying and opening your vessel to the Divine Chalice. Breathe the Breath of God, and fill with the light of manifestation. Bathe in the ecstasy of their Sacred Union. In this snake magic tantric ceremony, be prepared to move through what stands between you and ecstasy.
>
> —*New Age and Neopagan Religions in America*, 139

The brochure language shows a mix of religious practices and sensibilities. Kundalini Yoga attempts to recognize and open inner energy centers through meditation and breath control. Tantric Yoga might be associated with energy centers but is a very different yogic practice—one that is reserved for the most spiritually advanced and that might in rare circumstances involve channeling sexual energy, though making it nonerotic. Note that both Kundalini and Tantric yogas require long apprenticeships with spiritual masters. A description of the workshop points to the medieval imagery of the Holy Grail or a possible allusion to Catholic Eucharist and what might be an invitation to sexual intercourse, or at least a spiritualized version of it. All of this is accomplished in a weekend workshop session and with the promise of spiritual ecstasy.

One of New Age spirituality's most important contributions to the modern world is also one of its greatest problems. That is, in identifying with deep ecology and the interconnectedness with all of life, it draws on Native American spirituality. Starhawk makes it clear that the Old Religion is highly aligned with native shamanism.

The asset, as shown in chapter ten, is that culture is rightly challenged to revise dramatically its disconnection from, and exploitation of, Earth. New Age spirituality aligns with the native wisdom in inviting one to engage the world with respect and harmony and in a sacred manner. The liability in such an alignment is that by identifying with and drawing on native traditions, the nonnative and New Age practitioner can easily become little more than a native Indian dilettante at best and a cultural exploiter and religious thief at worst. Co-opting native spiritual traditions is one of the most popular attractions of New Age spirituality. For example, Ted Andrews's book, *Animal-Speak: The Spiritual and Magical Powers of Creatures Great and Small*, has sold more than three hundred thousand copies. Other titles include, *The Sacred Dance, The Way of the Shaman, Soul Retrieval, The Dancing Healers, Teachings around the Sacred Wheel, Mother Earth Spirituality, Rainbow Tribe, Mayan Vision Quest*, and the list goes on. In *Mother Earth Spirituality: Native Paths to Healing Ourselves and the World*, Ed McGaa teaches how to perform Lakota rites and encourages the reader to practice them. This would be similar to a book encouraging non-Christians to regularly perform a Catholic Mass. One prolific writer is Wolf Moondance, whose ritual book *Spirit Medicine* teaches the reader to take a shamanic journey. She is not alone. In New Mexico's Heyokah Center, for example, programs in shamanism are offered for training individuals and groups.

Kabbalah for the Masses

The Kabbalah, as noted in chapter three, was originally an esoteric, mystical interpretation of the Torah and indeed a description of the spiritual substructure of the entire universe. The Kabbalah is subtly part of mainstream Jewish thinking. Historically, pious Jews who wanted to deeply investigate Kabbalah needed to already be well advanced in the Jewish faith, at least forty years old, male, and have a spiritual master to guide his soul skillfully. In contrast, the contemporary Kabbalah Centre's mission is to spread the message of Kabbalah far and wide with no such requirements.

The Kabbalah Centre began in Los Angeles and now has twenty-seven locations throughout the world, including in New York, Tel

Aviv, and London. Philip Berg, an insurance salesman turned rabbi, and his wife Karen founded the Kabbalah Centre. Berg was briefly a student of an influential Hasidic scholar and community organizer, Rabbi Avraham Brandwein, who was a student under a well-known Kabbalist scholar, Rabbi Yehuda Ashlag.

The Kabbalah Centre of Los Angeles is an excellent example of New Age spirituality. First, it is a mass-marketed esoterica— that is, it takes highly mystical or secretive teachings and brings them to a large audience. Second, it aligns itself with other psychological and transpersonal growth initiatives. Recent Centre offerings included not only courses on Kabbalah, but also other classes, such as Fears & Phobias, 12 Steps to Lasting Love, and Mastering Negativity. Third, it tends to distance itself from any traditional, organized religion. One may be surprised to discover that one does not have to be Jewish to practice Kabbalah at the Kabbalah Centre. Even more surprising is that the Bergs intentionally downplay its Jewish associations. At the Kabbalah Centre, in fact, the word *God* is rarely used, because it is seen to have negative, patriarchal connotations. Rather, the terms *light* and *sharing* represent the Divine.

These are not necessarily criticisms of New Age or the Kabbalah Centre. Proponents consider the qualities just described as strengths. Kabbalistic sensibilities are very much part of Jewish mainstream, and the Bergs are passionate about providing a forum for investigating Kabbalistic insights and discovering how to incorporate them in day-to-day life. Further, the Bergs might defend the other classes being offered at the Centre as holistic, arguing that the spiritual journey is not simply an isolated inner search but involves the need to attend to everything in one's life, including psychological trauma and healthy relationships. Finally, the tradition of Kabbalah already is filled with jargon; that is, God is *Eyn-Sof* (Endless). Thus, if understanding God in Kabbalah is more accessible through the term *light*, then why not use it?

Other aspects of New Age spirituality represented in the Kabbalah movement are, however, clear weaknesses. First, its spirituality seems to demand little. This is particularly shocking given Kabbalah's background and that it promises to provide a forum for profound spiritual transformation. New Age spirituality in general tends to require little from its adherents, even as it promises extraordinary experiences and deep, lasting renovations of the soul.

A second and typical expression of the New Age movement that appears at the Kabbalah Centre is what one could call crass consumerism. At the Centre, one can, for two dollars a bottle, buy Kabbalah Water, which is supposed to be so charged with positive energy that it changed the molecular structure of the water at Chernobyl. One is also encouraged to purchase, for twenty-six dollars, red string to wear as a bracelet in order to protect one from the Evil Eye. Finally, they also sell Kabbalah Energy Drink. This is an example of one of its ads:

> *Kabbalah Energy Drink* is a delicious citrus fusion which contains essential vitamins and amino acids that pick you up and keep you going. . . . Whether you need to take your dog for a walk, study for finals, bar-hop with friends, or just need a second wind at the office, reach for *Kabbalah Energy Drink*. Also available in low-carb Sugar Free variety!
>
> —Cited in Mara Einstein, *Brands of Faith*, 160

Accepting the Incredible

Why would intelligent persons accept religious claims that are simply incredible? Why is one willing to follow a leader who seems to make outlandish statements or act in obviously dubious ways? Consider Jim Jones's People's Temple in Jonestown, Guyana, where, on his orders, more than nine hundred people committed suicide in 1978. In the early 1990s, Shoko Asahara, a prophet of the apocalypse, began a new religious movement called Aum Shinri-kyo. In 1995, he ordered his adherents to attack the Tokyo subway with sarin gas, killing twenty-seven people. That same year, seventy-four members of the Order of the Solar Temple committed suicide. Its founder, Joseph di Mambro, taught them that they were descendents of the medieval Knights Templar and that he was receiving communications from superhuman "Masters of the Temple."

Perhaps one of the most outlandish modern religious communities was Heaven's Gate, begun by Marshall Applewhite and Bonnie Nettles. They taught that souls were imprisoned in human bodies but that the souls had an opportunity to be released and transformed. When the Hale-Bopp comet approached Earth, Applewhite told believers that Nettles, who had died earlier, was on an alien spaceship trailing behind the comet's tail. If they committed suicide together on March 26, 1997, they would be beamed up to the spaceship and carried to TELAH, a form of existence above humanity. Thirty-nine members gladly ended their lives that day, believing such a claim. It should be noted that Applewhite had a history of mental illness. Why was he credible to his followers?

One might ask the same thing of the followers of L. Ron Hubbard (1911–1986), the founder of the Church of Scientology. Hubbard had been a science-fiction writer early in his career. This writing profession morphed into a self-help health system known as Dianetics. This system became the foundation for his theory of Scientology. Yet, the Scientology myth stays close to his science fiction. Based on the teachings of Hubbard, this is what Scientologists believe: Seventy-five million years ago, Earth was part of a galactic planetary confederation ruled by the despot Xenu. To solidify his power and control this population, Xenu captured billions of beings and froze them. He then transported them to Earth and threw them into volcanoes. Their souls, called *thetans,* eventually entered human bodies and have forgotten that they are, in fact, not humans at all. Scientology, at its spiritual heart, is a form of mental training (auditing) that enables people to recognize their thetan truth and thus become "clear." There are currently eight levels of "clear," each level requiring deeper and financially more expensive investment. Ultimately the goal is for the thetan to cross the bridge to total freedom and escape MEST (matter, energy, space, and time).

Much has been written about Scientology, including the sordid history of Hubbard, the contradictions in his teachings as his religion developed, the exorbitant costs required of believers to take classes if they are to grow spiritually, the cultlike control Scientology exerts on its believers, and so on. When one adds the religion's overtly preposterous claims, one must wonder about the current cultural milieu and what is really going on. It could simply be that Americans are hungry for something other than the status quo, that something is not working in traditional religion, and that spiritual hunger is so great people are willing to believe virtually anything different.

CULTS

The word *cult* originally and technically refers to any religious practice. Today, it is typically used to describe a destructive religious group. Cults are not merely poorly conceived or non-normative religions. They share general disturbing characteristics. First is control. Cults manipulate by progressively taking away one's ability to choose essential things for oneself. Second is separation. Cults physically or psychologically work to keep one from friends and family who might tempt one away from the group. Third is group domination. There is a culture of *us vs. them.* This creates a high degree of exclusivity. Fourth, usually there is an authoritarian power structure, either a charismatic leader or team. From this leadership there is a lack of transparency and no appeal process. Some religious groups are not cults in themselves, but have unhealthy cultlike qualities to them. To discern whether one is involved in a cult, one should ask oneself: If I say no to a demand, will I be seen as a bad follower? Am I told not to question, and is questioning not respected? Does my association feel like lack of freedom? Was what is being asked or demanded of me now hidden from me when I first came into the group? If the answer to *any* of these questions is yes, then this is a dangerous religious group.

Christian Reflection

As mentioned at the beginning of this chapter, our examination of New Age spirituality is less interested in generating insights that spark our religious imagination than in exploring how one ought to respond skillfully to the New Age movement. New Age spirituality is both a symptom and a response and needs to be taken seriously. It is a symptom of a spiritual hunger and rootlessness experienced by many in the West. As a response, it is one way to feed that hunger and reground modern religious believers.

The Status Quo Is Unacceptable

One clear message of the New Age movement is that the status quo simply does not suffice to hold and inspire many Christians. (Post)modern Americans believe that they have the right and the duty to choose what kind of faith to practice. Threats of hell or demands from on high will not motivate American Christians to remain in their traditional religious communities. In 2008, the Pew Forum on Religion and Public Life released the results of a massive study of religious practices in America. It discovered that more than 25 percent of Americans had left the religion of their childhood. If one includes Protestant Christians changing denominations, then that figure climbed to 44 percent. Americans feel quite free to find different forms of faith.

One reason for these shifts is that at times religious organizations simply provide poor ministry. Sometimes the cause is the personal lethargy of a given pastor or community, which can be addressed locally. Some of the lethargy, however, is much larger and institutionalized. For example, American Catholicism devotes fewer resources to youth ministry than any other Christian denomination. Not surprisingly, Catholic adolescents and young adults are the least knowledgeable and least devout among American Christians. For traditional institutions to turn a blind eye to such a gap is to risk losing large swaths of the next generation.

New Age sensibility challenges communities to take religious experience seriously. People are hungering for an experience of the divine, and Christian communities need to embrace this challenge. Happily, some are. The last twenty years have seen a great increase in retreats and workshops on prayer. Faith-sharing initiatives, such as those that come from the New Evangelism, have provided opportunities for Christians to gain spiritual insights into both themselves and others. It could very well be that some of the most energizing initiatives in American Christianity have something to do with this larger New Age spiritual impulse.

Nevertheless, many Christian communities are not receiving the message. One can reflect on some confirmation programs. Sixteen-year-old students meet on Wednesday nights for the better part of an academic year and hear lectures on such things as the nature of the Trinity, Jesus as human and divine, the sacraments, Luther's *Small*

Catechism, and so on. At some point, they do a modest service project, and then they are confirmed. For many, the experience is flat and lifeless; ironically, it turns into something that might fuel restlessness or dissatisfaction more than it grounds the candidates deeply in their faith. The New Age religious ethos tells us that religious meaning must be charged with experiences of transcendence. An emotional, experiential component is crucial.

The Cost of Discipleship

This book has regularly raised the issue that authentic Christianity demands real transformation. One dies to oneself in order to live for and through Christ. Biblical faith has less to do with what one believes, though this is important, than it does with completely entrusting one's life to God and living a new life in the Spirit. One of the great weaknesses of New Age spirituality is that it promises so much and demands so little. Wicca promises the power of the Divine Goddess and ancient shamanic mediations of the spirit-world. What is required is little more than monthly gatherings to celebrate nature. Many religious scholars have also wondered why intelligent, well-educated people would believe in astrology, a practice that has been debunked countless times. One possible answer is that it promises a kind of cosmic care while demanding nothing of its adherents.

This charge of "cheap grace" or "transformation on the cheap" is not isolated to the New Age. Christianity can be swept up in the same dynamic of low expectations as well. Robert Wurthnow's *After Heaven* analyzes several interesting Christian fads. One was an imagined challenge to greater Christian discipline in the 1970s and 1980s. James Dobson's book *Dare to Discipline* (1971), for example, sold more than two million copies. When one investigates this particular spiritual agenda, however, one finds that what was really meant was adjusting one's attitude more than one's behavior. Often spiritual discipline was sold as a way to adjust emotionally to life's situations, but it did not challenge people to live much differently than they might otherwise.

The spiritual fad of the 1990s was **angels**. This fad involved both mainstream Christian consciousness and broad American spiritual sensibilities. Sophie Burnham's *A Book of Angels* (1990) sold a half-million copies. Joan Wester Anderson's *Where Angels Walk* (1993) was even more successful at a million copies. During the first half of the 1990s, at least twenty other popular books on angels appeared at the same time, collectively selling more than five million copies. During that time, national surveys revealed that one-third of Americans claimed to have had a personal encounter with angels. Why angels? Why now? The proliferation of angels corresponds to something in the New Age spirit and is part of our entire religious culture: spiritual comfort with no real cost to one's self.

While a belief in angels is certainly standard in the Christian tradition, angels became a spiritual fad in the 1990s.

In *Soul Searching*, author Christian Smith concludes that Christian teenagers and adults functionally have the following faith: moralistic, therapeutic deism. That is, their actual operative understanding of religion is that God exists; God wants people to be nice and fair; the goal of life is to be happy and feel good about oneself; God is not involved much in our lives unless we need him to resolve a problem; and nice, non-evil people go to heaven when they die. This, he claims, they get tacitly from their parents, and all religions fundamentally boil down to this.

At the end of *Soul Searching*, Smith offers advice regarding how adults might assist adolescents in developing a truly integrated faith. First, adults need to be more involved with their own faith and more serious with the religious development of their children's. Second, adults should demand a faith that expects a lot. (Society does not hesitate to demand a good deal in terms of school and sports, but it flounders in things religious.) Third, adults need to help youth practice talking about their faith. Fourth, adults should challenge youth to examine culture's messages of individualism and consumerism. Fifth, adults should spend time with youth discussing faith and values. Sixth, youth need to be given daily spiritual practices that go beyond congregational meeting time.

Shallow Traditions

Some of the most fascinating imagined strengths of New Age spirituality is that it purports to be nonauthoritarian, nondogmatic, and outside of institutional religious traditions. These imagined strengths are fascinating for several reasons: First, New Age spirituality's permutations ironically appeal to ancient traditions. Even as it dismisses Judaism and Christianity for being locked into old and worn-out traditions, its variations usually draw on something older and more worn out, such as the Egyptian cult of Isis, ecstatic Dionysian dance, or the supposed Old Religion of Europe. Thus, New Age has the aura of something primordial while it claims to be new and original. As Starhawk lauds and identifies Wicca with Paleolithic shamanism, one wonders if she would readily embrace the hunter-gatherer society on which she claims it was based, surely a patriarchal structure.

A second fascinating point is that virtually all New Age religions claim to be antidogmatic. Such a claim suggests that dogmas, or central, nonnegotiable religious claims, are problematic. Are they? Every religious tradition discussed in this text has some nonnegotiable, core, first-principle beliefs. To lack them is to fail from the start. Take Christianity, for example. If Christianity taught, "Whatever you want to believe about Jesus is okay around here, we don't really care," why would anyone want to join such a community?

An additional problem with the New Age claim of being antidogmatic is that many New Age expressions are, in fact, more dogmatic than anything one would find in most religions. In addition, they are so without paying their dues. When Pope Benedict XVI published his first encyclical, *Deus Caritas Est* ("God Is Love"), his teaching was based on the Bible, traditional and modern theological authorities, ancient and contemporary philosophers, and modern culture and science. While Catholic theologians were typically solicitous to the encyclical, they also evaluated it according to its methodology, use of texts, internal coherency, and so on. In contrast, many New Age teachers simply make pronouncements with absolute authority and typically with little argument or methodological support.

One reason that New Age spirituality claims to be antidogmatic is that it encourages one to claim one's power, intuition, and spiritual knowledge, a lesson not without value. As discussed in chapter three, a spiritual master's main goal is to become obsolete, that is, to empower disciples to become masters themselves. Recall also that the Catholic Ignatian and Salesian spiritualities are very much focused on helping the Christian discover what the Holy Spirit is doing uniquely in one's soul. It is crucially important that religions work to empower and help self-authorize those who believe in them.

However, there is something dangerous about wholesale trust in one's intuitions, particularly when intuitions have not been fully developed. Malcolm Gladwell, in his book *Blink: The Power of Thinking without Thinking*, demonstrates that one's intuitions can know things that one's rationality cannot. A central argument in the book, however, is that this superintuition comes only after long, hard, deeply invested, and intentionally developed expertise in a given field. Gladwell also shows how trusting one's intuitions without doing the work usually ends in disaster. Ignatian or Salesian spiritualities assume that one is working within a tried-and-true religious context. The Christian tradition provides the lens of traditional wisdom and practice in order to help Christians interpret the movements of the Spirit. One becomes spiritually mature with reliable intuitions only over time and with mentoring. No one becomes holy or wise in a day. Dogma, authority, form, and tradition need not be seen as impediments to spiritual growth. Typically, they are the conditions for great growth. That New Age spirituality tends not to be embedded in a long-standing tradition is considered by many adherents to be an asset. According to the world's religious witnesses we have encountered in this book, it is a dangerous liability. Additionally, it invites would-be adherents to trust their intuitions long before such intuitions are cultivated wisely.

Review Questions

1. New Age religious expressions are utterly varied yet share common characteristics. What are those characteristics?
2. What are the reasons that have led up to the proliferation of new religious movements in the twentieth century?
3. What are the lessons that New Age spirituality brings to Christianity?

In-Depth Questions

1. What do you think are the greatest strengths and greatest weaknesses of New Age spirituality in general?
2. What do you think are the greatest strengths and greatest weaknesses of neopaganism?
3. Do you think that the author is too dismissive or unfair regarding New Age spirituality?
4. Do you think that the author is too dismissive or unfair about the way that much of mainstream Christianity expresses itself?

Select Bibliography

Bloch, Jon. *New Age Spirituality, Self, and Belonging: How New Agers and Neo-Pagans Talk about Themselves.* Westport, CT: Praeger, 1998.

Button, John, and William Bloom, eds. *The Seekers Guide: A New Age Resource Book.* London: Aquarian/Thorsons, 1992.

Carr-Gomm, Philip. *The Elements of Druid Tradition.* Longmead, UK: Elements Books, 1991.

Chadwick, Nora. *The Druids.* Cardiff, UK: University of Wales Press, 1997.

Chryssides, George. *The Advent of Sun Myung Moon: The Origins, Beliefs, and Practices of the Unification Church.* New York: St. Martins' Press, 1991.

Einstein, Mara. *Brands of Faith: Marketing Religion in a Commercial Age.* London: Rutledge, 2008.

Feldmeier, Peter. *The Developing Christian: Spiritual Growth through the Life Cycle*. Mahwah: Paulist Press, 2007.

Ferguson, Duncan, ed. *New Age Spirituality: An Assessment*. Louisville, KY: Westminster/John Knox Press, 1993. This is a fine, balanced assessment of New Age spirituality by a number of advocates and critics, all of whom are Christian.

Hawkins, Craig. *Witchcraft: Exploring the World of Wicca*. Grand Rapids, MI: Baker Books, 1996.

Hutton, Ronald. *The Triumph of the Moon: A History of Modern Pagan Witchcraft*. New York: Oxford University Press, 1999.

Jenkins, Philip. *Dream Catchers: How Mainstream America Discovered Native Spirituality*. Oxford: Oxford University Press, 2004. This text takes the reader through the history of Western culture's experience of Native American religion and describes the current exploitation of native themes and practices in popular spirituality.

Lewis, James, ed. *The Oxford Handbook of New Religious Movements*. Oxford: Oxford University Press, 2004. This is a scholarly investigation of new religious movements, from sociological and psychological dimensions to descriptions of major new religious practices.

Ness, Peter H. Van. *Spirituality and the Secular Quest*. New York: Crossroad Herder, 1996.

Pearce, Joseph Chilton. *The Death of Religion and the Rebirth of Spirit: A Return to the Intelligence of the Heart*. Rochester, VT: Park Street Press, 2007.

Pike, Sarah. *New Age and Neopagan Religions in America*. New York: Columbia University Press, 2004. This is an excellent sociological study of the context and rise of New Age spiritual values and neopagan religious beginnings.

———. *Earthly Bodies, Magical Selves: Contemporary Pagans and the Search for Community*. Berkeley: University of California Press, 2001. This excellent study of neopaganism focuses on practices and beliefs. It also includes a disturbing look at New Orleans voodoo.

Smith, Christian, with Melinda Lundquist Denton. *Soul Searching: The Religious and Spiritual Lives of American Teenagers*. Oxford: Oxford University Press, 2005.

Starhawk. *The Spiritual Dance: A Rebirth of the Ancient Religion of the Great Goddess*, revised. San Francisco: HarperSanFrancisco, 1989. Slightly revised and expanded, this book was originally published in 1979 and is one of the most utilized and cited texts in the Wicca movement.

———. *Truth or Dare: Encounters with Power, Authority, and Mystery*. San Francisco: Harper & Row, 1987.

Wessinger, Catherine. *How the Millennium Comes Violently: From Jonestown to Heaven's Gate.* New York: Seven Bridges Press, 2000. The text analyzes how apocalyptic religious sensibilities can manipulate believers into extreme behavior.

Wurthnow, Robert. *After Heaven: Spirituality in America Since the 1950s.* Berkeley: University of California Press, 1998. This is a superb sociological assessment of the shifts in Christian religious ethos in America during the last half of the twentieth century.

CHAPTER TWELVE

Interreligious Encounters

Backward and Forward

LOOKING BACK

Encountering Others

As this investigation comes to a close, it might be helpful to reconsider its original intent. The simplest and most important interest was to meet other traditions sympathetically. To love others is to want to listen to them, to pay attention to what is meaningful and sacred in their lives, and to honor that. Such solicitude does not demand that one always agree, but it does demand that one recognizes that one is walking on sacred ground. We saw such a witness with Pope John Paul II, who was cited in chapter one. After meeting with religious leaders from dozens of venerable traditions in Assisi, Italy, to pray for peace, he asserted, "There are undeniably differences [in religions] that reflect the genius and spiritual 'riches' that God has given to the peoples." This book strives to mine some of those riches.

One reward from encountering others is that by appreciating the gifts in other traditions one can deepen one's religious life. For example, the more deeply one appreciates the Daoist principles of yin and yang and their interrelationship, the more sensitive one will be to the present moment and the more attentive to the subtle movements of the Spirit. One does not have to embrace a full-fledged Chinese

A Trappist monk and a Buddhist nun engage in conversation at the Second Gethsemani Encounter in 2002.

worldview to learn that *wu-wei*, the practice of nonimpositional action, is profoundly wise. Buddhism's incisive sensitivity to the relationship between the ego's delusions and one's suffering can help a Christian learn to listen to Jesus' parables with new ears. Now instead of judging the judgmental Pharisee—the very trap that the Pharisee was caught in—one can recognize better how self-inflation is toxic to one's own soul. Remember that some expressions of Buddhism are so invested in compassionate action that Buddhists will take on the bad karma of others that it might be purified by love. This is exactly what Christianity teaches Jesus did on the cross. Could it be that some Buddhists are practicing Christian principles better than Christians?

Another gift from encountering traditions other than one's own is that of critique. Other religions may simply be engaging in wise spiritual practices, and one can learn from that. For example, Native Americans pay attention to and profoundly love the natural world. This trait can prompt a Christian to recognize that some forms of Christian theology can support damaging the environment or harming other creatures. Jewish devotion to the Sabbath challenges one to rethink time and space and to consider one's Sabbath commitment with greater religious intentionality. Even as Christian prayer is different in some respects from Muslim prayer, Islamic spirituality challenges a Christian to ensure against becoming too casual with a conception of God.

A number of instances exist in which Christianity compares well with other religions. For example, some of the most profound expressions of religious depth witnessed in other religions are also witnessed in Christianity. Christianity can, for example, witness to the possibilities in relating to God with great intimacy.

Finally, this text presents some forms of religion as comparatively weak, such as New Age, or seriously problematic, such as voodoo.

It would be both unfortunate and unnecessary to leave this comparative project as relativists. On the one hand, **relativism** respects that sincere, intelligent people have different beliefs and that no one can objectively prove that one religious belief is the best. On the other hand, relativism is ultimately disrespectful because it does not take religious claims seriously. Relativism flattens all differences as if they do not matter, and it invites one to give up without the hard work of serious investigation. Perhaps the worst way to leave this project would be with the attitude that the encounter does not really matter much. To do so would be to listen with respectful curiosity, perhaps gain a little information, but be unchanged. This book has attempted to inform, inspire, challenge, and renew one's religious sensibilities, so that regardless of one's religious affiliation, one returns to that religion a better person, respectful and grateful for the religious other and all the more enlivened to reengage with one's religious tradition.

Lessons from the Experience

Without tediously recapping every insight or lesson from this book, there are some particular lessons that appear regularly. One repeated theme is that Christians may know less than they think they know about spiritual reality. While Christianity is steeped in revelation, much of the faith is embedded in mystery. Christians still know little about the nature of heaven and what and whom it will include. They know little about what happens after death and before the final resurrection. They know little about the nature of the soul or its relationship to the body. Above all, they affirm that God is ultimately beyond conceptualization.

Faith can be posited in simplistic terms but only by disregarding its profound mystery. It took Christianity four centuries to hammer out the dogmas regarding Jesus Christ and the Trinity. These explain the mystery of the Christian faith less than they provide a kind of theological boundary for investigation within the realm of orthodox doctrine. Jesus never exactly explained what he meant by the "kingdom of God." In fact, he used images and themes that cannot be synthesized, as Jesus preaches the reconstitution of the time of the Judges when God was king (Isaiah 1:26; Luke 22:28–30), the reconstitution of a spiritualized version of David's dynasty (Isaiah 7—11; Jeremiah 23:2–6; Matthew 21:9; Luke 1:32, 69), and an apocalyptic messiah (Daniel 7:1—12:13; Matthew 24:30; Mark 14:62; John 1:51). Surely, Jesus did not intend to be incomprehensible. Rather, the kingdom is something transcendent, something that can only be described by metaphors. It is not a political, religious, or spiritual manifesto with a specific description and action plan. The kingdom is ultimately beyond description.

This insight is expressed in many religions. *Dao* can be given metaphors, and one can be told about the kinds of behavior that represent skillful living in *dao*, but the eternal *dao* cannot be named. Likewise, the Buddha limited his teachings to what was helpful to attain Nirvana. Much was mysterious to the Buddha himself. Concepts, images, metaphors, similes, and paradoxes can fire one's imagination regarding transcendent things. Yet they cannot, by the very nature of transcendence, describe in a linear way what transcendence is and means.

A second lesson or theme is that most religions describe life as unnecessarily hard because of humans' ignorance and sin. Humans foolishly enslave themselves and compromise their possibilities for gaining the very freedom and fulfillment they seek. That is, they regularly undermine their own happiness. As the Buddha says, "Whatever an enemy would do to an enemy, a hater to one hated, worse than that is the harm a wrongly directed mind can do to oneself" (*Dhammapada*, no. 42).

There is a Hindu story of a wandering holy woman who had an interesting way of financing her lifestyle. When she was in need of money, she would take a bowl, put in dirt and water, and then stir. Periodically, she pulled out a small piece of gold. One day, a shopkeeper saw her and begged to know the secret of her magic bowl. It is not magic and there is no secret, she assured him; she just put in these ingredients and stirred. He bought her bowl for an extraordinary price and went back to his shop. She took her extra money, gave it to the local orphanage, and was off. For months, this shopkeeper spent hours daily stirring mud and striving to make gold but to no avail. About a year later, the holy woman was wandering through the marketplace of this same town and he accosted her. "You lied to me," he said. "There is a secret to the magic that you did not tell me." She assured him that she did not lie or trick him, but then she said, "Well, there is one condition I may have forgotten. To get the gold, you have to completely renounce all greed."

This story is wonderful on many levels. First, because the gold is a metaphor for spiritual richness and a flourishing life, the very thing that keeps one from being rich is oneself. If one lives only for self, one cannot have the kind of wealth that will make one happy. Second, the kind of paradox that exists in this story is found in most religions. That is, there is a kind of dying to self unto rebirth of self, or an emptiness that simultaneously is fullness. To live for oneself as if one is the center of the universe is to guarantee great suffering. To live for God is to guarantee that the self flourishes. However, one really has to live for God. One cannot say, "Because I want to be happy and God will give me happiness, I'll align myself to God and his kingdom." In this instance, the self remains at the center, while God is conceived as merely the happiness resource. One would still end up being the greedy shopkeeper with nothing but a bowlful of mud. Finally, this parable points out that spiritual flourishing or wealth is right before everyone. Jesus teaches that the kingdom is at hand. Zen teaches that Nirvana and samsara are one. Daoism states that all one needs to do is pay attention and the wisdom of Dao will emerge right before one. Native wisdom instructs that the whole world is *waken* (sacred) and that every step can really be a holy experience.

Another story, this one about the holy man Nasrudden. Always riding on a mule, Nasrudden kept going back and forth between one state and another. The constancy of his crossings convinced the border guards that he was smuggling something. Every time he crossed,

266 • Encounters in Faith

they would fastidiously search his packages, clothing, and even the mule's mouth to see what was being smuggled. They never found anything and were always obliged to let him pass. Many years later one of the former border guards, now long retired, asked Nasrudden to come clean as to what he was smuggling. He smiled and simply said, "Mules." The truth is right before us.

A third lesson that one can take away from these encounters is that it is obvious the theologies and religious practices of various traditions are many-layered. Without this realization, one can all too easily imagine them as superficial. Consider the following caricatures:

— *Jews:* The Orthodox are such legalists that they cannot turn on a light switch on the Sabbath.
— *Muslims:* They believe that if they follow the five pillars, they are guaranteed to go to heaven, and if they die in jihad, they will have seventy-two virgins in a heavenly harem.
— *Hindus:* They believe in reincarnation and that is why they are vegetarians.
— *Buddhists:* They believe that everything is suffering and that there is no-self, so they are escapists and nihilists.
— *Native Americans:* They are animists and believe that the spirits are part of everything, including animals, plants, and the sun and wind.

What is interesting is that these stereotypes do reflect something that is actually true about these traditions. However, they are posed flatly, superficially, and without the internal context that makes such teachings intelligible. Another way to address the above claims would be the following:

— The Jewish Sabbath is so sacred that it anticipates heaven; this is never a time for *melachah*, an act of domination.
— For Muslims, the essence of heaven is closeness to God, something they practice throughout every day. Such closeness demands the "greater jihad," utter purity of heart.
— Hindus recognize that violence has great karmic consequences, and they honor the holy core of all beings as Atman, which shares the same truth as Brahman.

— Buddhists see the conditioned self as dominated by greed, hatred, and delusion. They seek freedom from this imprisoned state in order to be compassionate toward all living beings.

— Native Americans recognize the one God of creation and worship him alone. Wondrously, this God has filled all created things with holy significance and intrinsic spiritual value.

A final lesson is that religions make extraordinary claims that may seem far-fetched to those who do not belong to the religion. In his classic essay, "The Will to Believe," William James points out that what one believes has everything to do with one's will, experience, expectations, and worldview. A religious—or any other—belief cannot simply be assessed as if it were an abstract claim set on a table for analysis. Rather, one's openness to accepting it has to do with one's history. Highly intelligent Islamic scholars take it for granted that there are jinn (genies), while most Christians dismiss such a belief as mere myth. A Native American might find the Christian belief that God has assigned each person a guardian angel pretty strange, even egotistical. Thus, one should not be quick to dismiss strange sounding claims outright. Their newness to one's ears may be what makes them easy to disparage. Could it be, as Zen teaches, that emptiness is form and form is emptiness? Could it be that some shamans really do know how to enter spiritual levels of the cosmos that are incomprehensible to Western science? At least before simply dismissing such claims, one should consider one's own claims of faith and how other religions might experience them.

LOOKING FORWARD: THE FUTURE OF INTERRELIGIOUS DIALOGUE

Interreligious Practice

In 1984, the Vatican's Pontifical Council for Interreligious Dialogue published a document titled, "The Attitude of the Church towards the Followers of Other Religions." This document describes several kinds of dialogue. One is a dialogue of life, which focuses on a greater appreciation for common humanity and seeing one's faith anew. Another is a dialogue of deed and collaboration, which focuses on humanitarian initiatives. A third is theological dialogue, which seeks greater mutual theological and philosophical understanding. A fourth is dialogue of religious experience, which includes sharing one's spiritual life and opens the possibility for corporate religious experience, such as prayer. It should be obvious that this book has focused on the third and fourth kinds of dialogue, at least on a conceptual level.

The dialogue of religious experience is currently considered the most interesting and potentially fruitful of the four types of dialogue. Because this also typically includes engaging in some forms of religious experience of the other, this kind of dialogue is also the more problematic. One would not want to become a dilettante in another sacred tradition, which is a problem in the New Age mentality. One also would not want to participate in a practice that would somehow compromise one's faith life. Still, interreligious practice can be fruitful. Some argue that one cannot really understand the theologies of others without some sense of the experience that their religious language and categories intend to convey. Thus, to teach Buddhism without experiencing Buddhist meditation would be something like teaching swimming without ever going into the water; it cannot be done. In a class that I teach on world religions, the students and I enter a three-week Spiritual Engagement Experience. We commit ourselves to highly restricted use of technology and entertainment, we follow a vegetarian diet and consume no alcohol, tobacco, caffeine, processed sugar, or pre-servatives, we include days of monastic silence, and we commit to praying one-and-a-half hours a day. The prayer portion includes two forms of Buddhist meditation, neither of which would com-promise any other religious commitment. Students regularly report that this project is the most eye-opening and important part of the class, and some say, even of their college careers.

Some scholars of interreligious dialogue argue that the essence of dialogue is spiritual practice. One great pioneer in Christian–Hindu dialogue was the Benedictine Father Henri Le Saux (1910–1973), better known as **Abhishiktananda**. He never left Christianity but was deeply involved in Hindu Vedanta philosophy and meditation. Some have argued that in many religions the theology is merely a backdrop to practice. Thus, to truly be in dialogue, one has to engage the practices of the religion. This would certainly be true with Zen, in which concepts have a relative utility and get in the way.

One might consider two fundamental limitations for interreligious practice. The first is a theoretical limitation. Religions, as has been shown, exist in paradigms. They provide ways of thinking about the world, oneself, transcendence, and so on. This thinking suggests that one cannot fully embrace two religious paradigms simultaneously. Here, the biblical dictum seems appropriate: "One cannot serve two masters" (Matthew 6:24). Even if a religious path is conceived as relative, one needs to embrace it wholeheartedly for real transformation. The Christian path habitually cultivates an awareness of grace and reliance on God. One looks for God in life and seeks a personal relationship with God. The Buddhist path, for example, seeks self-reliance and a way of deconstructing the self. These two paths have very different spiritual agendas.

A second limitation is practical. Do not the constraints of one's time, energy, community affiliation, necessary focus, and so on, limit the thoughtfulness with which one can embrace two (or more!) different religious traditions? Some Hindus, for example, have striven intensely to seek Brahman and have meditated in Hindu forms and culture and with a profound faith in Hindu philosophy. To imagine that one could jump into some Hindu practices and really obtain something substantial out of them may trivialize the depth needed for such a venture.

However, one need not be completely daunted in imagining the possibility of interreligious practice. It can provide a forum for spiritual growth that a Christian or Buddhist or Muslim may otherwise miss or fail to integrate to the same degree. Even in the modest Spiritual Engagement Experience, students acquire a small sense of how spiritual practice works and thus gain access into others' faith life. Just listening to other religious traditions can help one's faith, as can engaging in another's religious practice. Buddhist *vipassana*, or insight practice, for example, can help a Christian to become freer from reactivity to experience. Interreligious practice can complement one's own faith life. In the Spiritual Engagement Experience, my students and I practice a loving-kindness Buddhist meditation strategy that has helped us love more freely and universally and has proven a great asset in healing wounds with more difficult persons in our lives.

Multiple Belonging?

There is little question that the future of interreligious dialogue will focus on spiritual practice more than it has in the past. This means that those most involved will have to be particularly careful how they conceive interreligious practice and its relationship to one's home religion. One of the most dramatic and controversial topics currently in interreligious dialogue involves the possibility of belonging to Christianity and another religion simultaneously.

The idea of mutual belonging has already been encountered twice in this book. Recall that Black Elk, in chapter ten, believed in the myth of the White Buffalo Cow Woman and the sacred rituals she brought to the Sioux as well as his vision in which spiritual grandfathers taught him how to become a healer. Black Elk was also a Roman Catholic catechist for his tribe. In chapter eight, one read that some Christians claim never to have left Christianity and yet seemed to have utterly integrated Zen into their lives. Recall that Father Robert Kennedy is also a Roshi, a Zen Master.

IMAGE: © VITTORIANO RASTELLI/CORBIS

Native Americans participate in a celebration in St. Peter's Basilica in January 1981 for the canonization of Kateri Tekakwitha, the first North American Indian to be canonized by the Roman Catholic Church.

Other scholars believe that Buddhism and Christianity bring to each other what is fundamentally lacking in the other. Jesuit Father Aloysius Pieris argues that Christians have love (*agape*) and Buddhists have wisdom (*gnosis*), and that collectively, they form the fullness of the spiritual life. Benedictine Brother David Steindl-Rast has argued that Buddhism represents silence while Christianity represents Word, and this is how they complement and complete each other. Silence (Buddhism) represents the transcendent foundation from which Word (Christianity) speaks. Speech then takes one to silence, which supports more wisdom to speak, and so on. It is not surprising that these positions have been challenged. The most obvious question would be why Christianity is presented as if lacking wisdom or silence. To be fair to Pieris, he is referring to a kind of wisdom (*prajna*) that represents seeing deeply into the fundamental truth of created reality. Even so, why would a Christian imagine that Jesus' preaching needed Buddha's silence to be wise, or that as eternal *Logos*, Jesus did not have sufficient wisdom?

Another way to consider the complementary nature of other religions, and the need for a kind of mutual belonging, is exemplified by Benedictine Father Bede Griffiths, a friend of Abhishiktananda. Griffiths taught that all valid religious impulses and truths need to be subsumed under Christ, who is the final and complete revelation of Divine Mystery and whose cross is the ultimate and supreme symbol of salvation. Thus, Griffiths argues, it is imperative that the Church integrate the valid insights of Hindu Vedanta if it is to remain faithful to its universal mission and the universal savior it proclaims. This is really an interesting idea: if other religions have unique insights and Christianity is the completion of all revelation, would it not need to incorporate what is true in all of them? Others have pointed out that such a position then would demand that Christianity would have to incorporate all authentic insights from everywhere—why stop at Vedanta?—including Buddhist, Jainist, Daoist, Jewish, Muslim, and Native spiritualities. This is an impossible task.

Others who support the possibility of multiple belonging are more modest in perspective. They simply argue that one cannot help but be affected by serious engagement with another. That is one of the aims of this text. Another major figure in interreligious encounter is Jesuit Father Francis Clooney. Clooney's specialty is Hindu devotional

272 • Encounters in Faith

texts. In studying them, he describes being informed by the truths that they reveal: truths about God, experience of God, and insights into the nature of prayer. These insights affect how he then reads his own Christian tradition, particularly the spirituality of Saint Ignatius of Loyola, the founder of the Jesuit Order. These new insights into Ignatius's spirituality then make Clooney ask different questions of Hindu texts, which re-influences his return to his home tradition. Ultimately, some of the truth of the other religion becomes part of one's psyche. If asked, "Are you a Hindu or a Christian-Hindu?" Clooney would say that he is not, that he is a Christian, particularly a Roman Catholic Jesuit. Then he might say, as he has in public conferences, something like, "But, in a way, I am a kind of Hindu-Christian. It has become part of me."

DOES WHAT YOU BELIEVE MATTER?

Translation or Transformation

Addressing the question of whether it matters what one believes may surprise the reader, but it is a question worth investigating. If one were to compare religious traditions or spiritualities, then it matters a great deal. Say a friend was considering joining either a version of the Heaven's Gate community or Lutheran Social Services or participating in either *zazen* or a voodoo possession ritual, the wiser choice in either comparison is obvious. Even the most relativistic pluralist knows that some religious expressions are more wholesome than others.

Another answer might be that it matters a great deal if one takes one's religious beliefs seriously. Thus, if one believed in the Trinity, the Lordship of Christ, and that his Gospel brought universal salvation, then everyone would do better being a Christian. Even if one conceded that all articulations of transcendence are relative and never actually do justice to divinity, this would still be the closest version. Therefore, for the Christian, the image discussed in chapter one of the elephant and the blind men does not completely work. Recall that six blind men, representing six traditions, authentically encounter an elephant, representing God. Could it not be that Christ reveals the whole elephant?

Another answer to the question might be that it depends on who one is and what speaks deeply to one's soul or what would be the forum for the deepest religious life. Could it be that a given religion simply speaks to someone dramatically and, thus, that religion is best for that particular person? There are many accounts of people who were otherwise minding their own business and who all of a sudden felt compelled to enter a church or a mosque or a temple. Immediately, they find that they are home and have no doubt that this is where they should be. They experience great meaning and spiritually flourish in obvious ways.

Possibly the most sobering response is that, to judge from an objective look at the majority of religious believers, the exact nature of one's belief doesn't seem to be all that decisive. This book does not advocate such a position, but one ought to take it seriously. There seems to be little evidence that what people believe makes all that much difference in their spiritual life. Rather, it is having a religious faith that matters. People who go to church, synagogue, mosque, temple, and so on, are demonstrably healthier, more moral, more stable in their families, and experience themselves as happier than those who do not. It does not seem to matter which religious building one enters; it is believing in something that matters. This is not to suggest that merely having any belief at all makes the difference. It seems far more reasonable to suggest that a tremendously wide variety of believers are really experiencing God in various ways in their respective communities.

Nonetheless, one might also wonder just how profoundly people are being transformed in those various religions. While religiously observant people do live better lives, the differences are not dramatic. So whether one goes to church on Sunday morning as a Lutheran or sits at home and reads the paper as an agnostic, the difference is only modestly significant for most.

One particularly interesting religious theorist is Ken Wilber. Wilber asks if taking on a new religion is little more than changing furniture in a house. He calls this *translation* as opposed to *transformation*:

> The self is simply given a new way to think or feel about reality. The self is given a new belief. . . . The self then learns to translate its world and its being in terms of this new belief or language or new paradigm. . . . This function

of religion does not usually or necessarily change the level of consciousness in a person; it does not deliver radical transformation. Nor does it deliver a shattering liberation from the separate self altogether. Rather, it consoles the self, fortifies the self, defends the self, promotes the [narcissistic] self.

—Ken Wilber, *One Taste*, 27–28

In his earlier works, Wilber theorized a spectrum of consciousness. In many ways, the spectrum is similar to psychological theories on ego or moral development. Wilber's categories describe various stages of transformation: (1) Undifferentiated Self—the infant's mind; (2) Primitive Self—the toddler's sense of self as separate from the world; (3) Membership Self—one has internalized rules that tell one to do things one does not want to do but knows one should; (4) Egoic Self—one has a superficial sense of one's soul that is defined by culture and training, with little availability with one's unconscious or critique of what one believes; (5) Unified Self—this represents an expanded sense of identity that is integrated and self-authorizing; (6) Transpersonal Self—this represents the expansion of one's consciousness so as to experience divinity directly and realign one's identity within the divine; (7) Mind—this is the level of utter awakening so that all dualisms disappear, even that between self and Ultimacy.

Wilber suggests imagining an apartment complex with seven floors. On every floor, representatives of various religions are located. The furniture and decorations in any given apartment reflect the specifics of a given religion. On the surface, and in terms of the furniture, the Jew on the sixth level will look like the Jew on the second level. Regarding the specifics, both go to synagogue, study Torah, and have menorah candles lit in their windows. However, Wilber says, look at how they experience themselves and the world, look at why they have the faith they have and what kinds of transformation such faith has on their souls. If you compare them this way, then these Jews do not look so much alike. Rather, the Jew on the sixth floor looks like the Christian, Buddhist, Hindu, Native American, and Muslim on the sixth floor.

Do different religions matter, according to Wilber? Yes, he says, because some religious practices tend to bring the soul to different levels. He recommends, for example, working with Jungian psychoanalysis to help achieve the Unified Self, and he recommends Kundalini Yoga for beginning work on the Transpersonal Self. The Christian contemplation tradition would support the full possibilities of the Transpersonal Self, although it would not allow one to enter Mind, given its belief in a personal God. For the stage of Mind, Wilber recommends Hindu Vedanta meditational practices and Zen. (No one should be surprised that his particular tradition is Zen.)

This book does not recommend this schema wholeheartedly, and the method Wilber uses in his work has been exposed by scholars as problematic. Still, there is something important in Wilber's vision. Different people do engage their religious traditions differently. The kind of engagement has more to do with how transformed one becomes. One might convert from a highly fundamentalist Christian perspective to, say, Islam. However, if one does not really grow interiorly, then one simply becomes a fundamentalist Muslim. The words and practices are a bit different, but one's consciousness really is not transformed at all. One form of Christianity could also be much better at addressing one spiritual level than another form of Christianity. For example, perhaps Pentecostal or charismatic spirituality strongly supports a vibrant and wholesome expression of the Egoic Self. Yet, this very kind of spirituality may undermine the possibility for the Transpersonal Self. Perhaps exactly which religious tradition one embraces really does not matter for most people. Wilber believes that most people do not advance beyond the level of Egoic Self. He does believe, however, that many (not most) sincere religious practitioners achieve a version of the Unified Self. As for the Transpersonal or Mind levels, these would be much more rare in any religion.

Are Holy People Alike?

I once asked a Hindu swami if holy people are similar even as they represent very different religions, something like what Ken Wilber believes. He quickly replied, "Oh yes, they are all the same." I then asked him how he knows that. He paused and then replied, "They all have the same inner vibration." While I am not certain of this claim, or exactly what it means, the swami may have proposed a wise insight. There is a story of a Buddhist Zen master and a Muslim Sufi master who argued all day about the nature of religion, God, and the soul. They could not agree. At the end of their conversation and while having tea, the Buddhist said, "What intrigues me is that all day long I've been looking at you and I cannot help but to think that you seem like a Roshi." To this the Muslim replied, "I've had the uncanny feeling that all day long I was talking to a Sufi shaikh."

To be sure, the more deeply one invests in a religious community, the more profoundly one takes on the personality of that community. A Zen way of being feels very different from a standard Christian way of being. Native American consciousness is not like consciousness one would have by deeply following Daoism. Still, there seem to be common themes among religions, particularly as their best representatives express them. One such theme is that the life and self that most people seem to think they have are not their real self. There is a great shift from a self that looks at the world through its own interests, and one that seems to become reoriented. Holy people relocate their personal truth within the Ultimate Dimension. A second common theme is great inner freedom. Once the self is released from its delusion, one's life is extraordinarily free. Obviously, this is not the freedom to do what one wants if what one wants is selfish. That is the ultimate form of slavery. Real freedom is an expression of spiritual authenticity. Holy people are typically joyful and spontaneous. A third common theme is moral rigor. An axiom states that a morally ordered life is foundational for religious development. Intimacy with God is virtually impossible if one is also cultivating greed, anger, and so on. As one's spirituality progresses, one's moral sensitivities also become deeper and more acute when one finds subtler layers for moral refinement. A fourth common feature is that the road to holiness is long and arduous. Typically, one needs mentors and guides who are holy, as discussed in chapter three. To desire what a given religion fully offers is to dive in wholeheartedly and at great cost. The common approach to the spiritual life is as though it was merely part of one's many interests and with little real intention to expose the ego's deluded, grasping nature. What is seen in every religion is that, on the contrary, holiness does not come cheaply.

Qualities of Spiritual Maturity

Jack Kornfield, a wise contemporary spiritual writer, has suggested a list of ten qualities of spiritual maturity in his book *A Path with a Heart*. These points do not necessarily imply profound holiness, but collectively they do reflect a wise, seasoned soul.

- *Nonidealism:* The mature heart is not perfectionist; it rests in compassion instead of ideals of the mind. It is not romantic about some spiritual stage but takes on a spacious heart to all that is. This heart can turn suffering and imperfection into an occasion for compassion.

- *Kindness:* One's spiritual posture has to be gentle and loving, particularly toward oneself. Spiritual maturity is naturally generous and gentle.

- *Patience:* Spiritual maturity understands that the process of awakening goes through many seasons. Patience is constancy, that capacity to be with what is true moment after moment after moment.

- *Ordinariness:* A seasoned soul allows the divine to shine through day-to-day activities. One becomes less interested in the dramatic or exotic and more interested in being wholly present to the moment.

- *Integrated:* The truly mature soul does not compartmentalize one's life, mind, or heart. The spiritual life includes one's work, relationships, and creativity and it integrates the universal with the personal.

- *Uniqueness:* Spiritual maturity accepts different paths and expressions, and in doing so, it honors one's creative uniqueness. There is a story that Leo, a friend of Francis of Assisi, was bemoaning that he could never be like Francis. Francis replied, "Leo, on the last day God will not ask, 'Have you been a good Francis?' but rather, 'Have you been a good Leo?'"

- *Questioning:* Questioning and doubt are not a lack of faith but an expression of faith. When one becomes so confident that one is loved and held in God's hands, then challenging questions can be asked of one's self, world, church, and even God. Maturity allows one an expansive heart and mind to investigate truth without fear.

- *Flexibility:* Mature spirituality has a kind of flexible stability. One stands stably for the deepest self, and yet engages in the complexity of life with a skillful fluidity. One also becomes more respectful of other ways of being spiritual.

- *Relationship:* The mature soul focuses less on *what* one experiences in relationships, more on *how* one experiences them. One sees that one's relationships to self, family, sexuality, money, community, and all else can be known in a sacred manner.

- *Embracing Opposites:* Maturity becomes increasingly comfortable with paradoxes in life and more appreciative of life's ambiguities. One develops a sense of irony, metaphor, and humor and the capacity to embrace the whole, with its beauty and outrageousness.

PERSONAL LAST WORD BY THE AUTHOR: WHY I AM A CHRISTIAN

This book was written from various Christian perspectives. Sometimes my lens has been inclusivist, in which I have imagined the Holy Spirit working through other religious people. From such a position, I have also suggested looking critically at some forms of religion that seem to me unhealthy, such as voodoo or New Age spiritualities. At other times, I have implicitly taken a pluralist position. Here I have assumed that there is only one possible Ultimate, Divine reference and that this is what religions are wrestling with in different ways. Further, I have assumed that God is bigger than concepts about God and that there are various ways to speak about and engage the Divine. At still other times, I have taken on a kind of postmodern mutualist posture and simply allowed very different ways of thinking about religiosity to be unique. This approach was most obvious with Zen and the Chinese religious spirit.

From all these various postures, I write as a Christian. Surely one reason that I am Christian and not, say, Muslim, is because I was raised in a Christian home. This formed my religious imagination, and my religious experience was interpreted through the lens of that imagination. Having encountered other religions and studied some in depth, I can also say that I am an intentional Christian as well.

That is, I have warranted Christian faith that goes beyond merely accepting what I had been taught. I believe in Christianity because I experience Christianity as intellectually and spiritually compelling. Interestingly, my very engagement with other religions has reinforced my Christian faith—in part because I see how Christianity illuminates and fulfills core impulses in many of those religions.

Christianity addresses the confounding relationship between humanity and divinity in a decisive way. Many religious traditions recognize that there is an Absolute Reality. They also recognize that the soul has a transcendental quality and was made for some kind of oneness or union with the Divine. This recognition was expressed profoundly in chapter two on mysticism. So profound is such association that mystics from many traditions frequently embrace one of two perspectives. One perspective is utter identity whereby the soul becomes God or discovers that it always was divine in the first place. The other is an intense I–Thou relationship of love, a metaphorical marriage between the soul and God. In the first, one flirts with monism in which everything is God, or self-deification, as though the true nature of the soul is divinity. In the second, the soul is obviously different from God and cleaves to God in love. Christianity formally teaches a kind of deification that is a radical participation in God's life as well as a mystical marriage, in which the soul attains a profound union of love. Both, at the same time, are held in a kind of paradox. If the soul were God in an unqualified way, then one would have a metaphysical problem that blurs Creator and creature. One would also have the problem of how to be in loving relationship with God if one were God. Yet if the soul were only in relationship with God, as if from the outside, then heaven would not be an ultimate experience but a relative one. Such an exterior knowledge of God would be a fantastic expression of the life one is leading now, but it would not constitute radical salvation. Christianity proclaims that salvation is paradoxically both, and it points to Jesus Christ the God-man as the model.

The dogmas about Jesus Christ provide the context for Christianity to speak to both forms of union. To some non-Christians, the idea that Jesus had a relationship with God and was divine as well (two natures in one person) seems a ridiculous leap of faith and sacrifice of the intellect. To others, such as Muslims, the idea is nothing short of blasphemy. However, Christianity sees in the doctrine the conditions for the very unification that is attested to by mystics around the world. As Augustine writes, "The Son of God, divine by nature, became human, so that 'sons of man' by nature [might] become the sons of God by grace, and dwell in whom alone and from whom alone the blessed can be made sharers of His immortality" (*On the Trinity*, 13.9.12).

Zen proclaims the Ultimate Truth of things as the unification of samsara and Nirvana, the relative and the Absolute. Paradoxically, these two are truly distinct reference points even as they are indistinguishable from each other and mutually imply each other. Again, one can look to Jesus Christ. One need not blur the distinctions between Zen and Christianity. Nonetheless, it is uncanny that Jesus embodies the unification of self-emptiness and divine fullness.

Some critics of Christianity point out that Christianity is not alone in asserting a god-man. Krishna, for example, is an incarnation (avatara) of Vishnu. We can also see a god-man attested to in mythologies, such as Hercules who is son of the god Zeus and the human Alcmena. Other associations, such as the hero making a sacrificial death to appease the gods, appear in some mythologies. Therefore, some argue, Christianity is just one myth among others. It seems far more reasonable, however, to interpret the evidence in the exact opposite way: to see these traditions as having tapped into core, primordial religious truth, something that God has placed in the soul. What Christianity celebrates is that these authentic religious impulses are historically actualized in Jesus Christ. He is the fulfillment of religious truth anticipated in these other communities, and in their best myths.

As noted in chapter three, Christians claim Christ as savior, typically in three different ways. By his **Incarnation**, God has united Creator with creation, and provided the means for human nature to participate in the divine. By the cross, God has affected atonement for our sins. By the Resurrection, God has broken the bonds of death and provided the means of immortality. I see in Christ that the three great human religious problems are solved, or divisions are bridged: the ontological one; the moral one; and the mortal one. All great religions deal with these problems, and they do so in various ways. Christianity celebrates a Savior who did so utterly, decisively, and historically. The historical piece is crucial because humans exist in time. For God to save humanity, it seems necessary that this salvation happen in time. A mythic expression of salvation could articulate salvific truths but could not yet instantiate them or make them real in the world. Salvation, for it to be actual and relevant, had to be both on God's terms and on human terms. Christianity proclaims Christ has achieved both in himself. For me, Christianity is not a sacrifice of the intellect but a confirmation of the divine mystery to which the intellect decisively points and a mystery reflected broadly in the religious world.

Finally, I am convinced of the primacy of love, which is the centerpiece of Christianity. Love is the means of union with God and the principal expression of what it means to be a Christian. I believe that only love has the power to transform a soul completely, because it grabs the soul from its very center. Every great religion recognizes the power and importance of love, but Christianity has made it core: "God is love" (1 John 4:8). Even the most confounding Christian dogma, the Trinity, expresses this Ultimate Truth. By Trinity, Christianity does not say that God is three separate beings with the same nature or three expressions of a single God. Rather, Christianity teaches that the very nature of Divinity is dynamic love (relationality in singularity). The reason that I feel confident to give my life over to God, with all the unnerving paradoxes that this entails, and the reason that I do not fear death is because I know myself to be utterly loved by God. Jesus represents for me (and Christianity) love incarnate.

Review Questions

1. Why is relativism ultimately insulting to others' beliefs even as it appears to be respectful?

2. What are the three lessons seen repeatedly in Christianity and other religions?

3. What are the various positions put forward for mutual belonging?

4. How does Ken Wilber imagine the relationship between members of the same religious tradition and members of the same level of spiritual transformation?

In-Depth Questions

1. This book frequently addresses and affirms relativity, that is, all articulations of truth are culturally conditioned and that truth is beyond all conceptual categories. In this chapter, relativism is roundly criticized. Do you think that *relativity* and *relativism* have been persuasively distinguished?

2. This chapter raised the possibility that one religion may help one person spiritually flourish while a different religion may help someone else spiritually flourish. How do you respond to this suggestion?

3. Do you believe that it is possible to be a Christian and identify with another religious tradition? Could one have an association or a secondary affiliation with another tradition, and if so, how would that work? How do you respond to Francis Clooney's belief that serious interreligious encounter cannot help but to have some of another tradition become part of one's consciousness and thus religious identity?

4. This chapter claims that religion typically makes only a small difference in people's lives. Do you agree? If so, how can this problem be addressed or solved? If you disagree, provide evidence that religion actually makes a substantial difference.

5. The author ends this chapter by describing why he holds the religious faith that he does. How would you share with others what makes your religious faith compelling to you?

Select Bibliography

Abhishiktananda, Swami [Henri le Saux]. *Saccidananda: A Christian Portrait to Advaitic Experience*. Delhi: I.S.P.C.K., 1974.
———. *Prayer*. Philadelphia: Westminster Press, 1973.
Cornille, Catherine, ed., *Many Mansions? Multiple Religious Belonging and Christian Identity*. Maryknoll, NY: Orbis Books, 2002.
Griffiths, Bede. *Return to the Center*. Springfield, IL: Templegate, 1977.

————. *Vedanta and Christian Faith.* Clearlake, CA: Dawn Horse Press, 1973. This book also has essays by Swamis Paramanda and Abhishiktananda.

Kornfield, Jack. *A Path with a Heart.* New York: Bantam, 1993.

Wilber, Ken. *One Taste: The Journals of Ken Wilber.* Boston: Shambhala Publications, 1999.

————. *Up from Eden.* Garden City, NY: Anchor Press/Doubleday, 1981.

————. *The Atman Project.* Wheaton, IL: Theosophical Publishing House, 1980.

————. *No Boundary: Eastern and Western Approaches to Personal Growth.* Los Angeles: Center Publications, 1979.

Glossary

abba From Aramaic for "father." A spiritual father, typically describing a spiritual master in the desert monastic tradition or a monastery's abbot.

Abhishiktananda (Henri Le Saux; 1910–1973) Benedictine priest who lived in India for decades and strove to integrate the truths of Hindu Vedanta with Christianity.

amma From Aramaic for "mother." A spiritual mother, typically describing a spiritual master in the desert monastic tradition or a monastery's abbess.

Analects Chinese for "sayings." The collected sayings of Confucius.

angel From the Greek *angelos*, "messenger." A being created by God to mediate divine messages and to provide access to God's graces in various ways.

annihilation This word, or like terms, are often used by mystics to refer to a kind of loss of a separate self in the context of reconfiguring an identity that is lost in union with God.

apophatic From the Greek *apophatikos*, "negative." Approaching theology or experiencing God by removing concepts or leaving behind the normal functioning of the brain.

Atman Sanskrit for "self." The immortal, unchanging, ultimate entity in a living thing. The Atman is understood as beyond thought, body, or mundane consciousness. It is intricately related to, or sometimes identified with Brahman as an eternal, absolute being.

avatara Sanskrit for "crossing over." A deity's descent into the world of human experience.

Bhagavad Gita A classic Hindu text that is part of an epic story, the *Mahabarata*, and represents central themes in Hindu theology and spirituality.

baptism of desire The phrase is applied to Thomas Aquinas's theory that anyone seeking God's grace and salvation—even implicitly—in their hearts were on some level already baptized by God in terms of their will, because they were already responding to, and living in, God's saving grace.

bhakti Sanskrit for "devotion." Hindu piety focused on one's personal, emotional relationship to a deity. It also represents a major Hindu discipline, or yoga.

Black Elk (1853–1950) Lakota medicine man and Roman Catholic catechist whose life story and description of the sacred rites of the Lakota Sioux have created an indispensable source of insight into the life of Native American traditions.

Bodhidharma (sixth century CE) Reportedly the son of an Indian prince and the twenty-eighth patriarch in a direct line from the Buddha. He traveled to China and introduced a new form of Buddhism, *Ch'an,* or Zen, that focused on meditation and realization of the universal Buddha-nature.

Brahman Sanskrit for "great" or "infinite." Refers to Ultimate Reality and the core truth that underlies the phenomenal universe. Brahman is often distinguished between Nirguna-Brahman (without qualities or conceptualization) and Saguna-Brahman (with qualities).

Brahmin The priestly caste in Hinduism.

Buddha Sanskrit for "awakened one." The standard reference is to Siddhartha Gautama, who began the religion of Buddhism. It also refers to all the Buddhas who have preceded or will follow the historical Buddha throughout the universe's history.

Buddha-nature The foundational reality and pure truth in all beings in Mahayana Buddhism.

comparative theology A theological discipline that seeks to perform Christian theology in the context of interreligious dialogue. Here, one crosses over into the texts, theologies, practices, and imagination of another tradition, and returns with a new perspective to engage Christian doctrine.

Confucius (551–479 BCE) The founder of an academy in China who later traveled from state to state trying to persuade political leaders that the means for social and political order as well as human flourishing were through appropriate relationships. His *Analects*, or "Sayings," were collected a century after his death and have become the cornerstone of Asian culture.

cosmology When used in theology, it represents one's understanding of the structure of the spiritual universe, including the relationship between spiritual and physical beings, or levels and qualities of spiritual beings, that is, angels.

dao Chinese for "way" and "way-making." Refers to the way the universe works as well as the most skillful way one should proceed in the world.

Dao De Jing (*Tao Te Ching*) The book, reportedly written by Laozi in the sixth century, represents the earliest strata of Daoist philosophy.

dependent coarising A Buddhist descriptive of the interconnected arising of all physical or mental formations. Each part of the person depends on the arising of every other part. In order to break the chain of rebirth (Samsara), one has to conquer the ignorance that perpetuates the mutual dependence.

deva A godlike being in Hinduism and Buddhism.

dharma Sanskrit for "carrying," it has three principal meanings. It can refer to one's duty, particularly regarding the obliga ions of one's Hindu caste, to the cosmic law, and to the Buddha's collective teachings.

divinization A Christian term used to describe radically participating in God's life in heaven such that, while one never changes one's nature, one lives the divine life through God's grace.

doctor of the Church A designation of the Roman Catholic Church meaning a particular theologian has produced theological insights of great depth and perennial value.

Druidism An ancient nature religion, particularly in the British Isles. Druid religious sensibilities have reemerged in modern neopagan religions.

dukkha Pali for "suffering" or "dissatisfaction." The pain or dissatisfaction that is endemic to all of life. That life is *dukkha* is also the first of the Four Noble Truths.

Eightfold Path The last of the Four Noble Truths, constituting the path to enlightenment. The Eightfold Path represents (1) Right Understanding, (2) Right Thought, (3) Right Speech, (4) Right Action, (5) Right Livelihood, (6) Right Effort, (7) Right Mindfulness, and (8) Right Concentration.

Eucharist This term (from the Greek noun *eucharistia*, "good grace," and verb *eucharisteo*, "to thank") refers to the Church's celebration of Communion. For Roman Catholics and Eastern Orthodox Christians, it expresses a ritual embodiment of the sacrifice on Calvary, a celebration of victory over sin and death, the ratification of the new covenant, and a feast of communion with Christ.

exclusivism The position among some Christians that in order to be saved one must explicitly be a Christian.

five pillars The fundamentals of Islam: confession of faith, prayer, charity, Ramadan, and pilgrimage.

Four Noble Truths The Buddha's fundamental message: (1) life is dissatisfying; (2) the cause of dissatisfaction is craving; (3) there is an end to craving, which is Nirvana; (4) the way to Nirvana is the Eightfold Path.

grace From the Greek *charis*, "favor." God's favor, love, and saving presence in our lives.

guru Sanskrit for "teacher." A spiritual guide in the Hindu tradition.

Hasidism From the Hebrew *hasidut*, "piety." A popular Jewish religious movement tinged by mysticism. Founded by Israel Baal Shem (1700–1760 CE), it spread through the Ukraine and other Slavic territories as a corrective to the excessively intellectual approach to Jewish piety. Its leaders were charismatic rabbis called rebbes.

Incarnation The belief that God took on human existence in Jesus Christ.

inclusivism The position among some Christians that Christ saves non-Christians who implicitly cooperate with his saving grace.

Iwa The spirits venerated by voodoo practitioners. *Iwa* participate in human life through possession and are considered responsible for boons and curses on communities.

Kabbalah Hebrew for "receiving." A collective term for the most widespread form of Jewish mysticism. Of particular note is the belief that the structures of the soul, of the universe, and of God as manifest follow the sefirot pattern, and that the way to union with God is to master this pattern.

karma Sanskrit for "action." The universal law of cause and effect in Hinduism and Buddhism. Unless one is fully enlightened, every action has karmic consequences that affect one's current life situation or that of one's future life, for good or ill.

kataphatic From the Greek *kataphatikos*, meaning "affirmative." It refers to approaching theology or experiencing God as mediated with concepts.

koan Chinese for "public document." *Koans* are seemingly impossible questions or puzzles on which Zen practitioners reflect in order to break away from linear thinking.

lama Tibetan for "teacher." A spiritual guide and master in Tibetan (Vajrayana) Buddhism.

Laozi (Lao Tzu; b. 600 BCE) According to legend, Laozi spent most of his life as a state archivist or librarian in China. At the end of his life, he produced the *Dao De Jing* (*Tao Te Ching*) that formed the framework of the philosophy of Daoism.

Mahayana Buddhism Sanskrit for "great vehicle." A school of Buddhism that arose in the first century CE that emphasizes the possibility of liberation for a great number of people in various lifestyles. Mahayana is a collective term referring to various schools of Buddhism, including the Madhyamika and Yogachara schools in India, Tibetan, Zen (Chan), and Pure Land Buddhism.

maya Sanskrit for "illusion." The deceptive apparent solidity or value of things in the phenomenal world. It sometimes references the apparent duality of the phenomenal world in contrast to universal Brahman, the true reality that underlies all things.

mediator One who guides or provides access to the divine or one who sacramentally embodies a particular spiritual gift.

mitzvot (plural for *mitzvah*) Acts that express Jewish faithfulness and allow Jews to participate in the holiness of God. Mitzvah, Hebrew for "commandment," is an act that either fulfills a Torah requirement, or one that is particularly sacred or meritorious.

moksha Sanskrit for "release." The liberation from the cycle of rebirth. For most Hindus, it marks the self's union with Brahman, and for all Buddhists, it marks attaining Nirvana.

mutuality model An emerging model in the theology of religions that highlights the uniqueness of various traditions. One does not seek out universals that all religions might share or make proclamations about other religions from one's religious perspective but allows other religious expressions to be truly other.

mysticism From the Greek *mystikos*, "secret." The study of extraordinary states of spiritual consciousness and/or union with God.

Nagarjuna (c. 150–250 CE) Considered the most influential Buddhist philosopher in the Mahayana tradition, particularly on his insistence that Nirvana and Samsara are one.

Nirguna-Brahman Sanskrit for "Brahman-without-qualities." Brahman as understood beyond any conceptualizations.

Nirvana Sanskrit term for "blowing out." The goal of Buddhism, it refers to the extinction of all karmic formations and breaking the chain of the cycle of rebirths (Samsara).

no-self Buddhism's claim that there is no eternal, unchanging core, or self (Atman), by which one might identify oneself.

original sin The Christian belief that from the time of Adam and Eve's fall from grace, humans have had a fundamental disorder of their will that requires God's grace to be fully healed and reordered.

pluralism The position among some Christians that no religion can speak of an absolute revelation and that God saves others outside of Christian understandings of salvation.

polytheism The belief that there are many gods.

postmodern A cultural and philosophical reference that argues that no single way of interpreting reality can account for all of it. It rejects meta-narratives, or large pictures, stories, or explanations that answer or address all of reality. It further argues that every interpretive lens is culturally and historically conditioned.

Qur'an Arabic for "recitation" or "proclamation." Islam's sacred text, believed to be perfectly preserved, unmediated revelation directly from God.

rabbi Hebrew for "master" or "teacher." A Jewish teacher and community leader.

rebbe Yiddish for "master" or "teacher." A community spiritual leader and holy man in Hasidism.

relativism A theory or position that asserts there is no absolute truth or moral norms but rather that all truths and morality are relative to the groups that hold them.

Rinzai Zen A tradition of Zen developed from the Southern School in China, particularly known for its emphasis on sudden experience of enlightenment and for the use of *koans*.

Sabbath From the Hebrew *shabbat*, "to cease." The Jewish day of rest, reflection, prayer, and study that begins at sundown Friday evening and ends at sundown Saturday evening.

Saguna-Brahman Sanskrit for "Brahman-with-qualities." Brahman as understood in a way that is describable or takes on form. Many Hindus believe that Vishnu or Shiva represents Saguna-Brahman.

samsara Sanskrit word for "wandering." The succession of rebirths that all beings go through within various modes of existence until they become fully enlightened and achieve moksha or escape.

Satan Hebrew for "accuser." The figure, traditionally believed in Christianity to be the archangel Lucifer, who rebelled against God and was cast out of heaven along with those angels who followed him. In Islam, Satan (also known as Iblis) is a spiritual being made from fire who refused to bow before Adam and Eve and was thus cast out of heaven.

satori Japanese for "understanding." A dramatic experience of insight or even enlightenment in Zen Buddhism, particularly in the Rinzai tradition.

sefirot Hebrew word for "numbers." The qualities that make up the spiritual structure of God as manifest, the universe, and the human soul in Jewish Kabbalah.

serviteur Devout voodoo practitioner who claims a particular *lwa* as a kind of mystical spouse.

shaman An important member of a native tradition who acts as an intermediary between the visible and spiritual worlds.

Shankara (788–820 CE) One of the most influential philosophers of Hindu Vedanta, who argued for radical nonduality in which the self (Atman) was identical to Ultimate Reality (Brahman).

Soto Zen A tradition of Zen developed from the Northern School in China, particularly known for its emphasis on a step-by-step approach to spiritual enlightenment.

sutra Sanskrit for "thread." An authoritative spiritual teaching, particularly one in either the Hindu or Buddhist canon.

sympathetic magic The practice of taking an item that represents an object or person and ritually infusing the object, with the result that the curse or blessing proceeds to the object and then to the person represented by it.

Talmud Hebrew for "instruction." A compendium containing debate and interpretation of biblical law. The Talmud is a history of the national and religious experience of the Jews from the sixth century BCE to the fourth century CE (Palestinian Talmud) and sixth century CE (Babylonian Talmud). The Babylonian Talmud is considerably longer and more authoritative and continues to dominate Jewish theological sensibilities.

theology of religions A discipline in theology that seeks to give definition and shape to Christian reflection on the nature of other religions and the status of non-Christians.

Theravada Buddhism Pali for "teaching of the elders." The only surviving school from the early period of Buddhism, sometimes known as the "Hinayana," or little vehicle, which today is experienced pejoratively. Theravada Buddhism is widespread in the countries of Southeast Asia, such as Thailand, Burma, Sri Lanka, Cambodia, and Laos.

Tibetan Buddhism A form of Mahayana Buddhism practiced in Tibet and neighboring Himalayan countries since the eighth century CE, also known as Vajrayana or "Diamond Vehicle."

Torah Hebrew for "teaching," "way," or "law." A central theme in Jewish theology, Torah can refer to God's commandments, the first five books of the Bible (Pentateuch), or even the Bible and the entire biblical commentarial tradition in the Talmud.

Upanishads Sanskrit for "sitting near." A collection of Hindu sacred scriptures that built upon and expanded the Vedas. They are preoccupied with the relationship between the self (Atman) and Ultimate Reality (Brahman), and how one might escape endless rounds of rebirth.

Vedas Sanskrit for "knowledge." The four collections of sacred scripture in early Hinduism.

voodoo This term represents a Haitian religion that focuses on venerating supernatural beings that protect and often possess practitioners.

Wicca Old English for "witch." A modern neopagan nature religion that particularly celebrates the divine feminine.

yin/yang Chinese terms that represent interconnected, complementary forces. Yin represents the principles of receptivity, silence, contemplation, femininity, darkness, and so on, while yang represents the principles of assertion, vocalization, action, masculinity, light, and so on.

yoga Sanskrit for "union" or "discipline." A particular practice or path in Hinduism. Major yogas are jnana (transcendent knowledge); **karma** (selfless action); bhakti (devotion); raja (meditation); and kundalini (energy release).

Zen Buddhism Zen Buddhism in Japan or Ch'an in China is a school of Mahayana Buddhism that developed in China in the sixth and seventh centuries. While Buddhism had been in China since the end of the first century CE, the great Buddhist saint Bodhidharma brought a form of it that became most influential. The essential nature of Zen can be summarized as (1) transmission of the dharma by a teacher, (2) nondependence on sacred writings, (3) direct pointing to the heart, and (4) realization of one's Buddha-nature.

Zhuangzi (or Chuang Tzu; fourth century BCE) The second most important figure in Daoism, whose writings complement Laozi's Dao De Jing.

Index

Page numbers in italics refer to illustrations.

A

abbesses/abbots, 57, 66, 285
Abhishiktananda, 271, 285
ablutions, 109, 111
Abraham, 101, 110–11, 243
absence of God, 131–33, 134–35
Absolute (Eternal, Ultimate). *See also* God; inclusivism; mediation; relativism; Truth; universality
  Aristotle and, 207
  basics, 8, 11, 216, 278, 279
  Buddhism and, 9, 11, 62, 143, 216 (*See also* Buddha-nature)
  Chinese spirit and, 208, 216
  Christianity and, 5, 9, 11, 24, 182–83, 192, 216, 271, 279–81, 290
  Confucianism and, 210
  Daoism and, 11, 203, 206, 207
  Hinduism and, 9, 11, 15, 41–42, 121–22, 131 (*See also* Brahman)
  indigenous traditions and, 223
  Islam and, 9, 11, 107, 117
  Judaism and, 11, 73, 88
  mysticism and, 27–30, 31–32, 206, 279
  pluralism and, 11
  relationship and, 279
  science and, 17

Wilber on, 274
Zen Buddhism and, 171, 172, 176, 177, 178, 185, 191, 192, 280
Abulafia, Abraham, 29
acceptance of reality, 153–54, 155
actions (deeds, works). *See also* karma
  Chinese spirit and, 199, 204–5, 208, 262, 293
  Christianity and, 116, 190, 191
  Daoism and, 203–4, 204–5
  dialog and, 267–68
  Hinduism and, 60, 293
  importance of, 273
  Islam and, 96
  Judaism and, 85, 88–91
  nonimposing, 204–5, 208, 262
Adam and Eve, 102, 103–4, 127, 290, 291
Adler, Margot, 246
adoration, 49, 61
Aelred of Rievaulx, 116
aesthetics. *See* beauty
After Heaven (Wurthnow), 254
agape, 271
aggadah, 75
Aggivacchagotta Sutta, 158
Agni, 120, 121
Agwe, 231

Akiva, 89
Alan of Lille, 55
al-Bistami, Abu Yazid, 29
Al-Fatihah, 95, 109
al-furquan, 107
al-huda, 107
Allah, 11, 101–2
allegorical interpretation of the
    Bible, 24
al-ma'ruf/al-munkar, 102–3
al-mi'raj, 100, 101, 113
Al-Suyuti, Jalal al-Din, 100
Alvalokishvara, 62
Amazon, 224, 235
Americans, x–xi, 10–11, 105, 241,
    242, 251–53, 254–55
amisa dana, 161
ammas, 57, 285
Analects (Confucius), 210, 285
anamnesis, 79–80, 84
anatta, 145, 156, 175
ancestors, 199, 206, 212, 231
Andal, 132–33
Anderson, Joan Wester, 255
Andrews, Ted, 248
angels. *See also individual angels*
    arch-, 55
    basics, 285
    Christianity and, 37, 40, 53–56,
        57, 102, 103, 232, 234,
        254–55, 291
    indigenous traditions and, 267
    Islam and, 99–100, 102, 112, 234
    Judaism and, 234
    mediation and, 49, 50
anger, 187
Anglicanism, 10, 48, 129
anicca, 145, 156

anima, 53
animals (creatures). *See also* nature
    Christianity and, 226, 227, 228
    indigenous traditions and, 221,
        222–23, 225, 263, 266, 267
    New Age and, 242
    Animal-Speak (Andrews), 248
    animism, 266
animus, 53
annihilation, 31, 285
anthropocentrism, 221, 228. *See also*
    animals; nature
apophatic experiences, 25, 27–31,
    32, 35–36, 42, 203, 285
appearances, 201. *See also* delusions
Applewhite, Marshall, 250–51
apprentices. *See* aspirants
Aquinas, Thomas, 7, 286
Arabi, Ibn, 29
Aranyakas, 120
archangels, 55
Areopagus, 1, 15
arguments. *See* dialogue (interreli-
    gious encounters)
Arianism, 88
Aristotle, 207
Arjuna, 138
Aruni, Uddalaka, 126
Asahara, Shoko, 250
asceticism, 144
Ashlag, Yehuda, 249
Ashvaghosha, 143, 146
aspirants (apprentices, disciples). *See
    also* mediation (guides, masters);
    specific types of aspirants
    Buddhism and, 62–63
    Christianity and, 66–67, 254–56
    Hinduism and, 59–61

New Age and, 247, 254–56
Zen Buddhism and, 185–86
Assisi Day of Prayer, 18
astrology, 240, 241, 254
atakkavacara, 158
Atharva Veda, 120
Atman, 9, 42, 122, 142, 285, 292, 293
attachments (clinging), 148, 155, 163, 188, 204. *See also* desires (cravings); detachment
Augustine, 5–6, 25, 31, 103, 280
aum, 122
Aum Shinri-kyo, 250
Aurobino, Sri, 30
authority, 257
avatara, 130, 280, 285
avisayasmim, 158

B

Baal Shem Tov, 63
Babylonian Talmud, 29, 292
Banyacya, Thomas, 224–25, 235
baptism of desire, 7, 286
Barlaam, 19
Barth, Karl, 26
beauty (aesthetics)
Buddhism and, 63
Chinese spirit and, 197, 211, 212
Christianity and, 278
Hinduism and, 131
Islam and, 100, 113
Judaism and, 52, 53, 77
Plotinus and, 28
Zen Buddhism and, 184
Being-Bliss-Consciousness, 42
belaghah, 106

beliefs, importance of, 272–75. *See also* faith
Benedict XVI, 116, 227, 256
Berg, Philip and Karen, 249
Bernard of Clairvaux, 25, 28, 134
Bhagavad Gita, xii, 20, 138, 285
Bhagavan, 130
Bhagvata Purana, 130–31
bhakti, 60, 61, 129–30, 138, 286, 293
Bible, the, 24, 93, 107–8, 234, 242. *See also specific books*
Binah, 52, 53
bishops, 56–57, 66, 67
Black Elk, 220, 222–24, 229, 233, 235, 270, 286
Black Jaguar, 235–36
blind monks and elephant, *13*, 272
Blink: The Power of Thinking without Thinking (Gladwell), 257
bliss. *See also* joy
Buddhism and, 171
Hinduism and, 41, 42, 55, 127, 131
mysticism and, 41, 42
yoga and, 60, 61
Zen Buddhism and, 172, 189
Bloom, William, 240
bodhi, 177. *See also* enlightenment
Bodhidharma, 173–75, 286, 293
bodhisattvas, 62, 164–65, 166
bodhi tree, 144, *145*
bodies, human. *See also* sexuality
Buddhism and, 154
Christianity and, 160, 264
Hinduism and, 60, 124–25
mysticism and, 40
New Age and, 250–51

Soto Zen and, 177
bodies of buddhas, 62
Body of Christ, 6–7. *See also*
    Incarnation
Bonaventure, 25, 182
Bondye, 230
A Book of Angels (Burnham), 255
bowing, 113
Brahman
    Absolute and, 201, 292 (*See also*
        Absolute (Eternal, Ultimate),
        Hinduism and)
    Atman and, 122, 216, 266, 292,
        293
    basics, 9, 11, 42, 266, 286, 289
    Buddhism and, 143, 156
    Christianity and, 15
    Daoism and, 203, 206
    gods and, 123, 129–30
    multiple belonging and, 269
    mysticism and, 43
    Nirguna-, 42, 203, 286, 290
    Saguna-, 129–30, 291
    self and, 45, 125–27, 143, 156
    universality and, 9, 127
Brahmanas, 120
Brahmanda Purana, 136
brahmas, 51
Brahma Sutras, 127
Brahmins, 126, 286
Brandwein, Abraham, 249
bride metaphors. *See* wedding
    (marriage) metaphors
Brihadratha, 124–25
Brunner, Emil, 26
Buck, Pearl S., 199
Buddha, the, 62, 142–47, 149, 164,
    165, 243, 286

Buddhacarita (*Acts of the Buddha*)
    (Ashvaghosha), 143
Buddhaghosa, 153
Buddha-nature. *See also* Absolute
    (Eternal, Ultimate), Buddhism and
    basics, 286, 293
    Christianity and, 191
    koans and, 180
    lamas and, 62
    Ox-herding pictures and,
        185–86, 188, 189
    Zen Buddhism and, 174–75,
        176, 178–79
Buddhas, 164, 286
Buddhism. *See also* the Buddha;
    dependent coarising; karma;
    Nirvana; *specific types of*
    Buddhism
    basics, xiii
    caricature, 266
    China and, 197, 214
    Christianity and, 20, 149–53,
        154–55, 159–60, 165–66,
        262, 271
    Four Noble Truths, *145*, 147–48
    Golden Rule and, 72
    meditation, 153–54
    mysteries and, 264
    mysticism and, 43
    New Age and, 242
    non-Buddhists and, 17–18
    pluralism and, 11, 12–13
    self and, 156–59, 267
    shifts in, 161–65
    souls and, ix–x
    spiritual guides, 61–63
    sutras, 292
    universality and, 9

Buddhist nun, *262*
Bultmann, Rudolf, 26
Button, John, 240

C

Calvin, John, 7
Canticle of Zachariah, 114
Care of the Soul, The (Moore), 242
caricatures of religions, 266–67
"Caring for Creation" (Evangelical
    Lutheran Church of America),
    227
Cassian, John, 189–90
Catechism of the Catholic Church, 81,
    115–16
Catherine of Siena, 26, 33, *34*, 39
Catholicism, 5–8, 10, 27, 49, 92, 129,
    267–68. *See also* Christianity;
    Eucharist; patristic Church
    (second-fifth centuries)
celibacy, 143, 232
challah, 78
Ch'an, 173. *See also* Zen Buddhism
Chandogya Upanishad, 30, 126
change, 148
Chang Tsai, 212
de Chantal, Jane, 215
chants, 114, 120, 122
charismata, 232
charismatics, 34, 232, 275
Charity, 96
charoset, 79
cherubim, 54
Chinese spirit. *See also* Confucian-
    ism; Daoism; Rinzai Zen
    basics, 196–97
    Christianity and, 214–16

cosmology, 199–200
    language and metaphysics,
        197–99
    modern, 212–14
    New Age and, 242
Ch'ing-yuan, 177
Christ, Carol, 246
Christian and Religious Pluralism
    (Race), 9
Christianity. *See also* Jesus Christ;
    under other religions; *specific branches*
    author and, 278–81
    cosmology, space and time and,
        51, 53–56, 81–84
    doctrine and, ix
    experiences and, 32
    Golden Rule and, 72
    heaven and, 159–60
    mediation and, 48–50, 56–57,
        56–59, 65–67
    modern, 8–9, 26 (*See also*
        postmodernism)
    open-mindedness and, 87
    pluralism and, 12
    souls and, 133
    war and, 99
christification, 40
Chrysostom, John, 5
Chuang Tzu (Zhuangzi), 204–5,
    206, 293
Chuang Tzu, The (*The Zhuangzi*),
    201–2
Chu His, 210
Clement of Alexandria, 5, 24, 30–31
Climacus, John, 58, 190
climate change, 227
Clooney, Francis, 271–72
coarising, dependent, 162–64, 171

communion
basics, 30
Buddhism and, 63
Christianity and, 116, 117, 166
(*See also* Eucharist)
indigenous traditions and, 223,
230
Islam and, 109
mediators and, 63, 66
Communism, 213
comparative theology, 18, 19–21,
286
compassion. *See also* Golden Rule
Buddhism and, 62, 152, 153,
155, 156, 161, 163, 262, 267
Christianity and, 38, 40, 55,
91–92, 139–40, 152, 191, 262
Hinduism and, 139
Islam and, 95, 96, 109, 111–12,
116
Judaism and, 29, 53, 71, 74, 75,
76, 85–87, 89, 90–92
Soto Zen and, 178
spiritual maturity and, 277–78
Zen Buddhism and, 39, 178,
188, 189
complementarity, 270–72
compline, 114
comprehension, 31
concepts. *See* language
Confessions (Augustine), 103
Confucianism, 72, 197, 198, 209–14,
286–87
consciousness, 127, 162, 228, 241,
242, 274. *See also* minds, human
consumerism, 227, 250, 256
contemplation. *See also* meditation
Buddhism and, 154

Chinese spirit and, 293
Christianity and, 40, 55, 59, 82,
190–91, 276
Daoism and, 203
Judaism and, 77
mysticism and, 24, 26
context, historical, 6, 15–16, 37,
280–81
control, 205, 252
conventionality, 137, 156, 163, 206
coolness, 121, 122–24
cosmology. *See also* time
basics, 287
Buddhist, 62
Chinese spirit and, 199–200
Christianity and, 51, 53–56, 234,
280
Hinduism and, 119, 129, 146
indigenous traditions, 50,
228–30
Islam and, 113
Judaism and, 76–78, 86–87,
88–91, 234, 289, 291
mediation and, 50–56
Council of Florence, 6
covenants, 83, 84, 116, 225
covens, 245, 246
cravings. *See* desires
creation. *See also* nature and
environment
Christianity and, 81, 92, 225–26,
280
Daoism and, 203
Islam and, 102
Judaism and, 51, 77, 78, 79,
88–89
creativity, 204, 215, 277
Creator, 223

credibility, 250–51, 254, 267, 279, 281
crown, 52
Crucifixion, 83, 84
cults, 252, 256
culture
Chinese spirit and, 196–97, 209
Christianity and, 39–40, 108, 261
Hinduism and, 119
importance of, ix
Islam and, 107, 108
Judaism and, 74
postmodernism and, 290
religious experience and, 37
spiritual paths and, 58–59
truth and, 201
Zen Buddhism and, 173
Cyprian, 5
Cyril of Jerusalem, 28

D

Dahbala Wedo, 231
Dalai Lama, *62*
Dao De Jing (*Tao Te Ching*) (Laozi), 198, 201, 202–3, 205, 210, 242, 287
Daoism. *See also* Lao Tzu (Laozi)
basics, 197, 201–8
Christianity and, 206–9, 261, 264
dao, 197, 198, 202–6, 210, 264, 287
Golden Rule and, 72
pluralism and, 11
spiritual path of, 265
21st century and, 213, 214
yin and yang and, 19

Dare to Discipline (Dobson), 254
"The Dark Night" (John of the Cross), 134
David, 90
Day of Judgment, 91, 95, 96, 113
death of humans. *See also* heavens; Hell; judgment; resurrections; salvation
Buddhism and, 144, 146–47, 158–59, 162–63
Christianity and, 83, 263–64, 280, 288
indigenous traditions and, 230
New Age and, 240
Death of Religion and the Rebirth of Spirit, The (Pearce), 241–42
de Chantal, Jane, 215
Deep Ecology, 244
deism, 255
delusions, 148, 163, 176. *See also* appearances
dependent coarising, 162–64, 171, 287
de Sales, Francis, 58–59, 215
desires (cravings). *See also* attachments (clinging); detachment
Buddhism and, 147, 151, 153, 157, 158, 161–64, 162, 288
Daoism and, 202, 203, 204, 208, 213
Hinduism and, 124–25, 131
Zen Buddhism and, 176, 178
detachment, 185, 191, 203. *See also* attachments (clinging); desires (cravings)
Deus Caritas Est (Benedict XVI), 256
devas, 51, 142, 164, 234, 287

Devil (Satan), 54, 102, 150–51, 233, 291
devotion
Buddhism and, 63, 153, 155, 165, 185
Christianity and, 49, 58–59, 134, 135, 139, 155
Confucianism and, 212
Hinduism and, 61, 121, 123, 135, 136, 137, 271–72 (*See also* bhakti)
Islam and, 97, 109, 115
Judaism and, 263
voodoo and, 231–32
dhamma dana, 161
dharma, 62, 143, 157, 178, 188, 287, 293
dharmakaya, 11, 62
dhyana, 173
dialogue (interreligious encounters). *See also* open-mindedness
basics, 18–21, 261–63
Christianity and, 263–67, 278–81
comparative theology and, 18, 286
future of, 267–72
holiness and, 276
holy people and, 275–76
importance of, x
Judaism and, 87
spiritual maturity and, 277–78
transformation/translation, 272–75
universality and, 9
Dianetics, 251
dignity. *See also* respect
Christianity and, 68, 103, 150

Daoism and, 207
indigenous traditions and, 221
Islam and, 101
Judaism and, 53, 65
direct experience, 31, 33
directions (north, east, south, west), 223, 246
directors, spiritual, 56, 59
discernment, 55, 57, 59, 107, 232, 233
disciples. *See* aspirants (apprentices, disciples)
diversity. *See also* multiple belonging; pluralism; universality
caricatures and, 266
Hinduism and, 119
holiness and, 275–76
John Paul II on, 261
mysticism and, 43
relativism and, 263
spiritual paths and, 58–59, 67
theology and, 8
Divine Abiding meditations, 153, 155
divine eye, 138
Divine Feminine, 137, 293. *See also* goddesses
divine manifestation, 62
divinity. *See also* mysticism
basics, 278
Buddhism and, 62
Christianity and, 49, 87–88, 92, 185, 246, 272, 279, 280, 281, 287
Daoism and, 206
emptiness and, 183
Hinduism and, 123, 124, 130, 138, 139

Islam and, 100, 101
Judaism and, 47, 48, 53, 64, 65, 74, 81 (*See also* Torah)
mediators and, 54–55, 56, 59, 60
New Age and, 244, 245, 246, 249
Wilber on, 274
Dobson, James, 254
Docetism, 87
doctor of the church, 26, 33, 287. *See also individual doctors*
doctrine, ix, xi, 62, 87
Dogen, 175–76, 178
dogmas, 88, 256, 257, 264, 279
dou, 230
Drawing Down the Moon (Adler), 246–47
Druidism, *240*, 244, 287
dualisms, 171, 174–75, 176, 177–78, 200, 275
dukkha, 148, 151–52, 155, 156, 287
Dumoulin, Heinrich, 170
dye of Allah, 101–2

E

Earth. *See* nature and environment
Earth in the Balance: Ecology and the Human Spirit (Gore), 239
Eastern Orthodox Church, 10, 26, 48, 49, 83, 129, 288. *See also* Christianity
Eckhart, Meister, 182–83, 242
eclecticism, 240, 247
ecofeminism, 240
ecology. *See* nature and environment
ecumenism, 26
egos. *See* self (egos)

Eightfold Path, 147, 288
elephant and blind monks, *13*
Eliade, Mircea, 219
ben Eliezer, Israel, 63
Elijah, 81
Elizabeth, 149
empowerment, 66, 257
emptiness
    Christianity and, 182–83, 184, 192, 280
    Confucianism and, 212
    Daoism and, 203, 205
    Hinduism and, 265
    Jesus and, 182
    New Age and, 241
    Zen Buddhism and, 171, 176, 178, 179, 188, 192, 267
encounters with other faiths, 18–21, 261–84
engagement, 275, 276, 279
enlightenment
    Buddhism and, *145*, 62, 153, 157, 188–89
    Confucianism and, 212
    Rinzai Zen and, 178
    Soto Zen and, 175–76, 177, 178
    Zen Buddhism and, 172–73, 174–75, 185, 186
Enoch, 54, 104
Enomiya-Lassalle, Hugo, 170
environment. *See* nature and environment
Ephesians, 228
equanimity, 153, 155
equilibrium, 205
Eros, 130–31
esbats, 246
essence, 156

Esther, 79
Eternal. *See* Absolute
eternity, 77, 83, 171
Eucharist, 24, 81, 83–84, 247, 288
Evagrius Ponticus, 58, 189, 232
Evangelical Christianity, 9, 14, 15, 88, 91–92, 226
Evangelical Lutheran Church of America, 227, 228
evil
 Buddhism and, 151
 Chinese spirit and, 200
 Christianity and, 54, 55, 57, 133, 151, 232–33, 255
 Hinduism and, 137
 indigenous traditions and, 234, 235–36
 Islam and, 107, 111
 Judaism and, 89, 90
 New Age and, 245, 250
exclusivism, 9, 11, 13–14, 197, 252, 288. *See also* inclusivism
Exodus, Book of, 139
exorcists, 233
experiences. *See* religious experiences
eyn-Sof, 51, 88, 89, 249
Ezekiel, 104, 133

F

faith, 72–74, 96, 160, 255–56, 264, 273, 279. *See also* beliefs, importance of
Father, 116
Feast of Booths, 79
Feast of Tabernacles, 90
feelings, 162, 166, 208

femina religiosa, 57, 67
feminine side, 53, 245
feminism, 240, 245. *See also* goddesses
festivals
 Christianity and, 83–84
 Judaism and, 78–81
 time and, 82–83
fire, 122–24, 157–59, 160
five pillars of Islam, 96, 288. *See also* *specific pillars*
flexibility, 278
forgiveness, 79, 111
form, 171, 176, 178, 188
Foster, Steven, 242
foundation, 52
Four Noble Truths, *145*, 147–48, 287, 288
Fourth Lateran Council, 6
Francis de Sales, 58–59
Francis of Assisi, 37–40, 277
Frazer, James, George, 245
freedom. *See* liberation
free will, 5–6, 7
fufu, 198

G

Gabriel, 99–100, 106, 149
Gallup Poll, 23–24
Gandhi, Mohandas, 20
Ganesha, 129
Gardener, Gerald, 245
Gautama family, 143, 286
Genesis, 76, 127, 226
genies, 112, 234, 267
Gevurah, 52
ghosts, 234

Gladwell, Malcolm, 257
global warming, 227
gnosis, 271
Gnostic Gospels, 242
God. *See also* Absolute; *alternative
names*; divinity; God, glory of;
gods
absence of, 131–33, 134–35
basics, 51, 124
Christianity and, 1–5, 103–4,
115–16, 127–28, 139, 171,
182–83, 190, 206, 226, 255,
263, 264, 269, 272, 275
Daoism and, 203, 206–7
Hinduism and, 124–27
indigenous traditions and, 222,
224, 230–31
Islam and, 95–96, 98, 102,
108–13, 116–17, 263
Judaism and, 29, 51–53, 72, 75,
289
Moon and, 243
mysticism and, 24–28, 31, 34–37,
43, 104–6
New Age and, 242, 249
pluralism and, 11–13, 15, 18, 278
word of, 5, 107, 114, 115, 246,
271
God, glory of
Christianity and, 14, 25, 27, 28,
91, 104, 149, 160
Islam and, 29–30, 101
Judaism and, 29, 77
goddesses, 240, 244, 245, 246,
247. *See also* Divine Feminine;
individual goddesses
"God is Love" (Benedict XVI), 256
"God is Love" (John), 281

god-men, 279, 280
gods. *See also* divinity; polytheism;
individual gods
Buddhism and, 146, 287
Chinese spirit and, 199
Hinduism and, 120, 123,
129–30, 138–39, 287
New Age and, 244, 246
*Golden Bough, The: A Study of Magic
and Religion* (Frazer), 245
Golden Rule, 72, 91
Good Earth, The (Buck), 199–200
goodness, 183, 211
Gore, Al, 239
Gospels, 83, 242
grace. *See also* baptism of desire
angels and, 285
basics, 50, 288
Christianity and, 3, 5, 6, 7, 8, 10,
84, 171, 183, 184, 287, 288,
290
inclusivism and, 10–11, 12
Judaism and, 77
mediation and, 55
mysticism and, 27
Graham, Billy, 14
Grandfather, 223, 235–36
Great Disappointment, 243
Great Spirit, 224
greed, 96, 188, 225, 227, 267. *See
also* wealth
Greeks, 1–4, 28, 207
Greeley, Andrew, 23, 24
Greening of America, The (Reich),
239
Gregory of Nyssa, 5, 24–25
Gregory the Great, 25
Griffiths, Bede, 271

guides, spiritual. *See* mediation
gurus, 59–61, 63, 125, 138, 288
guru yoga, 63

H

Habakkkuk, 73
hadith, 111
hadith qudsi, 111
Haitian voodoo, 51, 230–32
hajj, 96, 97, 97
halakah, 75
Hale-Bopp comet, 251
Haman, 79
Hammuna, 86
Hanabusa, *13*
Hanukkah, 79
happiness, 164, 264, 265, 273. *See
also* desires (cravings)
Haram Mosque, *97*
Hari, 60
Harmonic Convergence, 241
harmony
  Chinese spirit and, 207, 213
  Christianity and, 207
  Confucianism and, 210, 211
  Daoism and, 206, 213
  indigenous traditions and, 221,
    224, 225
  New Age and, 239, 244
Hasidic Judaism, 63–65, 288
Havdalah, 78
healings
  Buddhism and, 269
  Christianity and, 232
  indigenous traditions and,
    229–30, 233–34, 235–36
  Judaism and, 89, 90

New Age and, 244
Zen Buddhism and, 189
health care, 227
heaven
  Buddhism and, 143
  Chinese spirit and, 197, 199
  Christianity and, 159–60, 255
  Confucianism and, 212
  Daoism and, 206
  Islam and, 266
  New Age and, 245, 251
Heaven's Gate, 250–51
Hebrews, Letter to, 103
hell, 100
Hercules, 280
Herod, 150
Heschel, Abraham Joshua, 77
Hesed, 52
Heyokah Center, 248
Hillel, 71, 74–76, 90
Hilton, Walter, 190
Hinayana Buddhism, 292
Hinduism. *See also* Bhagavad Gita;
  Brahman; gurus; karma
  basics, xiii, 119–24
  Buddha and, 142, 144
  caricature, 266
  Christianity and, 20, 127–28,
    133–34, 139–40, 271–72
  cosmology, 51, 129–30
  Daoism and, 201, 203, 206
  dialog and, 269
  God and self, 124–27
  Golden Rule and, 72
  greed and, 264–65
  iconography, 136–39
  inclusivism and, 15
  mysticism and, 30, 43

New Age and, 242
non-Hindus and, 18
passion and, 129–33
pluralism and, 11, 12–13
religious movements and, 243
scriptures, 293
spiritual guides, 59–61
sutras, 292
universality and, 9
vegetarianism of, 266
Wilber on, 275
wildness of God, 136–39
historical context, 6, 15–16, 37, 280–81
history, ix
Hod, 52
Hokmah, 52, 53
holiness, 47–48, 88, 89, 162, 189,
    257, 275–76
Holistic Health Movement, 244
holy days. *See* festivals
Holy Grail, 247
holy people, 275–76
Holy Spirit, 4, 25, 58, 67, 128,
    215–16, 232, 257. *See also* Trinity,
    Holy
homoousia/homoiousia, 87
homo religiosus, 220
Hopi people, 224
Hosea, 133
host, Communion, *84*
hozeh, 48
Hsun Tzu, 210, 212
Hubbard, L. Ron, 251
Hui-k'o, 174
Huineng, 177
human beings, 101–2, 103, 226, 279,
    280. *See also* death of humans;
    minds, human; resurrections

Human Potential Movement, 244
humility, 36, 65, 149, 152, 160, 189,
    191
Hung-jen, 176–77
hyper-douleia, 49

I

Iblis, 102, 291
I Ching, 242
icons, 136–39
identity, 126–27, 154, 229, 279. *See
    also* individuality
idols, 1, 2
Ignatius of Loyola, 58, 257, 272
ignorance, 161, 162, 163, 164, 188,
    287
illusion, 121–22, 192, 289. *See also*
    reality, human
ill will, 148, 158
imagination, 36, 62
impermanence, *145*, 153, 154, 155,
    171
Incarnation, 280, 288
inclusivism, 10–11, 14–15, 278, 288.
    See also exclusivism; universality
incredibility, 250–51, 254, 267
indifference, 155
indigenous traditions (Native
    traditions). *See also* shamanism;
    individual Native persons
anthropocentrism *versus*, 221–25
basics, xiii
caricature, 266
Christianity and, 225–28,
    232–36, 262–63
cosmology, 50, 228–30
culture and, ix

importance of, 219–21
shamanism and, 228–30
voodoo, 230–32
individuality, 126, 139, 163, 198,
199. *See also* identity
Indra, 120, 121
ineffability, 31
infant death, 14
infatuation, 158
insight meditation, 154
integration, 277
interdependence (interrelatedness).
See also relationships
Buddhism and, 163–64, 165
Chinese spirit and, 293
Christianity and, 165–66, 227
Daoism and, 201
indigenous traditions and,
220–22, 228
New Age and, 242, 244, 245,
247–48
Zen Buddhism and, 171, 178
Interior Castle (Teresa of Avila),
190–92
International Society for Krishna
Consciousness (ISKCON), 243
interpretation, 32, 37, 75, 86–87,
106, 290. *See also* culture
interreligious encounters, 18–21,
261–84
intuitions, 257
Irenaeus, 5
Isaiah, Book of, 3–4, 90, 104, 133
Isamannaphala Sutta, 161
Ishaq, Muhammad Ibn, 98
ISKCON (International Society for
Krishna Consciousness), 243
Islam. *See also* Muhammad; Qur'an

basics, xi, xii, 95–98
caricature, 266
Christianity and, xi, 103–6,
107–8, 114–17, 263, 279
cosmology, 51, 113
credibility and, 267
experiences and, 32
five pillars of, 96, 288 (*See also*
specific pillars)
Golden Rule and, 72
human condition and, 98–103
jihad of, 266
mysticism and, 29–30
New Age and, 242
non-Muslims and, 17
pluralism and, 11
prayers, 95, 108–13
Satan and, 291
spiritual path of, 265–66
universality and, 9
Zen Buddhism and, 276
Israel, 5, 27, 47–48, 52. *See also*
individual Israelites
I-Thou relationships, 279
Iwa, 51, 231–32, 236, 288

J

Jable Nur, 99
Jäger, Willigis, 170
jahil, 96
James, 49
James, William, 220, 267
Japan, 209, 212
Jehovah's Witnesses, 225–26, 243
Jerome, 88
Jesus, 150
Jesus Christ

birth of, 149
bodhisattva vow and, 166
Body of, 6–7 (*See also*
   Incarnation)
Buddhism and, 262
compassion and, 91
Daoism and, 203
glory of, 105, 106, 107, 128, 165,
   174, 182
heaven, on, 159, 160
interrelatedness and, 165
Judaism and, 91
Kingdom of God and, 181
mediation and, 48, 67–68
mysticism and, 25
Qur'an and, 107–8
religious movements and, 243
Sabbath, on, 81
seders and, 83
sorcerers and, 234
truth and, 150–51
union and, 183–84
universality and, 280
Zen Buddhism and, 192
Jesus of Nazareth (Benedict XVI),
   116
jihad, 266
Jinn, 234
jinn, 112, 267
jinn, 51
jnana yoga, 61, 293
jnana yoga, 60
John, Climacus, 58
John, First Letter of, 10
John, Gospel of, 9
John of the Cross
   mediators, on, 67
   mysticism and, 25, 26, 28, 30, 33

wedding metaphors of, 135
Zen Buddhism and, 183
John Paul II, 18, 207, 261
Johnston, William, 170
Jokin, Koin, 179–80
Jones, Jim, 250
Jonestown, Guyana, 250
Josaphat, 19–20
Joshua (Rabbi), 74
Josiah, 234
joy, 153, 155, 164, 172, 191. *See also*
   bliss
Jubilees, 54
Judaism. *See also* Hasidic Judaism;
   rabbis; Sabbath; Torah
   basics, ix, xii, 71–76
   caricature, 266
   Christianity and, 5, 91–92, 263
   compassion and, 86–87
   cosmology, space and time,
      51–53, 76–78, 81–84, 85–87,
      88–91, 234
   festivals, 78–81, 82–84
   idols and, 2
   Kabbalah, 51–52, 56, 88, 248–50
   mediation and, 47
   mitzvot, 289
   mysticism and, 27, 28–29
   New Age and, 240, 249
   non-Jews and, 17
   open-mindedness and, 87
   pluralism and, 11
   Sabbath and, 76–78, 81–82, 266
   scriptures, 292
   spiritual guides, 63–65
judgment, 9–10, 91, 95, 96, 113,
   155, 178, 190. *See also* dualisms
judgmentalism, 152–53, 190, 262

Julian of Norwich, 34–35
Jung, Carl, 208, 275
justice, 7, 74, 90, 91–92, 96, 139, 140
justice, social, 74

K

Kaaba, 97
Kabbalah, 51–52, 56, 88, 248–50,
    289, 291
Kali, 41, 42, 136, 137
kami, 51
karma, 120–21, 124, 140, 153, 162,
    163, 262, 293
    basics, 289
    Bodhisattva vow and, 164
    Nirvana and, 290
karma, 60
Karma Chagme Rinpoche, 62
kataphatic experiences, 26, 33–37,
    36, 37, 203, 289
Katz, Steven, 32
kenjo, 179
Kennedy, Robert, 170, 270
Kether, 52, 53
Khadijah, 99
Khetuvim, 85
Kiddush, 78
King, Jr., Martin Luther, 20
kingdom of God, 150–51, 181–82,
    264, 265
Kings, Books of, 81
Kings II, 234
kneeling, 113
Knights Templar, 250
knowledge
    Buddhism and, 145, 142, 158–59
    Christianity and, 160, 190

Confucianism and, 209
Daoism and, 204
Hinduism and, 31, 60, 119–20,
    123, 126, 293
Islam and, 102, 107
    New Age and, 242, 245
    postmodernism and, 15
    Zen Buddhism and, 172, 185
koans, 179–81, 182, 289
Kong Fuzi (Master Kong), 209–10
Korea, 209, 212
Kornfield, Jack, 277–81
Krishna, 130–31, 131–33, 138–39, 280
Krishnamurti, 242
kuffar, 103
kundalini, 60, 247
Kundalini Yoga, 247, 275
Kuoan, Master, 186, 188, 189

L

Lakota tribe, 220, 248, 286
lamas, 61, 63, 66, 289
language (concepts,words). See also
    dualisms; prayers; recitations
    Buddhism and, 159, 175
    Chinese spirit and, 197–99
    Christianity and, 275
    Daoism and, 202, 203, 204
    inclusivism and, 15
    Islam and, 101, 106, 275
    silence and, 271
    Soto Zen and, 178
    Zen Buddhism and, 175,
        177–78, 188
Lankavatara Sutra, 174–75
Laozi (Lao Tzu), 198, 201–2, 206,
    210, 211, 289. See also Dao De Jing

last judgment, 91
Last Supper, 83
Late Great Planet Earth, The
    (Lindsey), 226
Laughter of Aphrodite, The (Christ),
    246
laws
    Christianity and, 103, 104, 207
    Daoism and, 201
    Hinduism and, 120 (*See also*
        dharma; karma)
    Islam and, 98
    Judaism and, 72, 73, 77, 292 (*See
        also* Talmud; Torah)
Laylat al-mi'raj, 100
leadership, 214
learning. *See* study
"Lecha Dodi Likrat Kallah" (hymn),
    77
Leclerc, Jean, *38*
lectio divina, 114
Left Behind series, 226
Legba, 231
Leisure, the Basis of Culture (Pieper),
    82
le-kadesh, 77
Le Saux, Henri, 268, 285
levitation, 33
Lewis, C.S., 31
li, 197, 212
liberation (freedom). *See also* salva-
    tion (redemption)
    beliefs and, 273–74
    Buddhism and, 154, 155, 156,
        159, 161, 264, 266, 267, 289,
        290
    Christianity and, 83, 149, 191
    cults and, 252

Hinduism and, 127, 290
Judaism and, 79, 80
New Age and, 240–41, 251
Soto Zen and, 178
universality and, 276
Zen Buddhism and, 187
Life of Moses, The (Gregory of
    Nyssa), 24–25
light, 88–89, 101, 138, 247, 249
Lin-Chi, 179
Lindsey, Hal, 226
lingams, 136–37
Lin Zhao-en, 214
Little, Meredith, 242
Liturgy of the Hours (Divine
    Office), 114
Liu Mi, 214
locutions, 33, 35–36
Logos, 5, 271
logos, 201, 203
Lord of Rama, 130
Lord of Yoga, 130–31
Lord's Day, 81–82
lotus flower story, 172
love. *See also* lust
    Christianity and, 67, 68, 128,
        133–35, 155, 160, 166, 183,
        184, 191, 271, 279, 281
    Hinduism and, 42, 129–33, 138
    Judaism and, 52, 53
    listening and, 261
    mysticism and, 279
loving-kindness, 153, 155, 269,
    277
l'shaym shamayim, 87
Lubavitch sect, *64*
Lucifer (Satan), 54, 102, 150–51,
    233, 291

Luke, Gospel of, 82, 149
Lurianic tradition, 88
lust, 148, 158
Luther, Martin, 7

M

Madyamika Buddhism, 289
Maggid, Israel, 64–65
magic, 236
Magnificat, 114
Mahabarata, 285
Mahakashyapa, 172, 189
Mahara-ji, 61
Maharishi, Ramana, 242
Maharishi Mahesh Yogi, 243
Mahayana Buddhism, 62, 162, 163,
    164, 170, 171, 188, 192, 286
    basics, 289, 290, 293
    Daoism and, 202
Maimonides, Moses, 73–74
Maitreya, 146
majesty, 52
Malachi, 81
Malkuth, 52, 53
Malunkyaputta, 157
di Mambro, Joseph, 250
Mao Zedong, 212
Mara, 144–45, 150
marga, 60
Markandeya Purana, 137
maror, 79, 80
marriage metaphors. *See* wedding
    (marriage) metaphors
Martha, 82
Martyr, Justin, 5
Mary, mother of Jesus, 149
Mary and Martha, 82

masculine side, 53
Mass, the, 246
Massau'u, 224
masters, spiritual. *See* mediation;
    specific titles
materialism, 225
materiality, 162
matins, 114
Matthew, Gospel of, 149–50
matzot, 79, 80
maya, 122, 289
Mayayana Buddhism, 161–62
McGaa, Ed, 248
Mecca, 97, 98
mediation (guides, masters). *See also*
    aspirants (apprentices, disciples);
    specific types of aspirants; *specific
    types of mediators*
    basics, xii, 47–48, 289
    Buddhism and, 61–63, 269
    Christianity and, 5, 48–50,
        56–59, 65–68, 84
    cosmology and, 50–56
    Hinduism and, 59–61, 63, 125,
        138, 288
    Islam and, 107
    Judaism and, 63–65
    kataphatic experiences and, 289
    universality and, 276
medieval Church (sixth-fourteenth
    centuries), 6–7, 10, 40, 190
medieval Judaism, 73
Medina al-Nabi, 98
meditation. *See also* contemplation
    Buddhism and, 62–63, 142, 144,
        153–54, 163–64
    Christianity and, 134
    dialog and, 268

Hinduism and, 60, 121, 122, 124, 243
New Age and, 247
Wilber on, 275
zazen, 178, 180
Zen Buddhism and, 173–74
Meister Eckhart, 242
melachah, 78, 266
men, 207–8. *See also individual men*
Mencius, 210, 212
mentors, xii, 276
menuha, 76, 78
mercy
   Christianity and, 8, 91, 151
   Islam and, 101, 116
   Judaism and, 52, 74, 90
merit, 29, 107, 124, 164–65, 173, 289
Merton, Thomas, 28
Messiah, 81, 89
metaphors, 181–82, 264. *See also* symbols; *specific metaphors*
metaphysics, Chinese, 197–99
Meyer, Bundula, 170
Micah, Book of, 90
Milinda, 156
Miller, William, 243
mimesis, 79–80, 84
minds, human. *See also* consciousness; enlightenment; meditation; self (egos)
   apophatic and, 285
   Buddhism and, 141, 142, 148, 153, 155, 156, 158, 162
   Christianity and, 24–25
   dialog and, 269
   God and, 289
   Hinduism and, 125

mysticism and, 33, 37
New Age and, 245
Rinzai Zen and, 179
Soto Zen and, 176, 177–78
Zen Buddhism and, 171, 175, 180, 185, 187–88
Ming Dynasty, 214
Mirabai, 132
miracles, 39, 55, 106
mi'raj, 113
Mishnah, 85
missionaries, 15
mitavoth, 85
Mitra, 120
mitzvot (plural for *mitzvah*), 87, 89, 91, 289
moksha, 122, 142, 290
monasticism, 57, 143, 161, 215, 285
monks, 57, 59, 114, *115*
Monophysitism, 88
monotheism, 86, 123
Moon, Sun Myung, 243
Moondance, Wolf, 248
Moore, Thomas, 242
morality, 96, 121, 206–7, 210, 213, 276, 280
Moses, 243
Mother Earth Spirituality (McGaa), 248
motherhood, 215
mountains and waters, 177–78
movements, religious, 243–44
Muhammad, 96, 98–101, 106, 111–12, 113
multiple belonging, 270–72, 286
multireligious world, 1–22
Munan, Shido, 176
mutuality model, 16, 290

mysteries, 48, 160, 203, 204, 263–64,
271, 281. *See also* paradoxes
mysterion, 24
mysticism. *See also* visionaries/
visions
Absolute and, 27–30, 31–32,
206, 279
annihilation and, 285
apophatic, 27–31
basics, xii, 23–24, 290
Christianity and, 24–28, 37–40,
104–6, 134, 279–80
conclusions, 43
Confucianism and, 212
criteria for, 35–36
Daoism and, 202–3, 206–7
God and, 279
Greek, 28
Hindu, 30–31, 41–42
Islam and, 29–30, 100, 104–6
Judaism and, 28–29, 51–53, 87,
289
kataphatic, 33–37
New Age and, 242, 249
souls and, 279
universality of, 31–33
wedding metaphors and, 131
myths, 280

N

nabi, 48
Nagarjuna, Acharya, 171, 172, 176,
188, 290
Nagasena, 156
Nahmanof Braslav, 29
Naphtali of Ropshitz, 65
Nasrudden, 265–66

Native American spirituality
animism and, 266, 267
basics, 219
caricature, 266
Christianity and, *270*
New Age and, 240, 242, 244,
247–48
Native traditions. *See* indigenous
traditions
nature and environment. *See also*
animals; creation
Christianity and, 226–27, 228,
262–63
indigenous traditions and, 220,
223–24, 225, 262–63
New Age and, 239, 241, 244,
245, 247–48
Neebkatori baba, 61
neopaganism, 244, 246, 247, 287,
293
Neoplatonism, 26
Nesah, 52
neshmah yeterah, 77
neti-neti, 127
Nettles, Bonnie, 250–51
Nevi'im, 85
New Age
basics, xiii, 239–43
Christianity and, 242–43, 246,
247, 252–57, 253–54, 255
credibility and, 250–51
cults, 252
Kabbalah and, 248–50
neopaganism, 244
weaknesses, 249, 256–57, 268
Wicca, 245–48
New Culture Movement, 212
New Earth (Tolle), 242

New Evangelism, 253
New Jerome Biblical Commentary, The, 226–27
Newman, John Henry, xii
New Testament, 54, 127–28, 139.
   See also Paul; *specific books*
Newton's laws, 17
Nichols, Philip Ross, 244
Night of Ascension, 100
Night of Power and Excellence, 99
nihilism, 158
Nirguna-Brahman, 42, 203, 286, 290
nirmanakaya, 62
Nirvana
   basics, 143, 288, 290
   bodhisattva vow and, 164–65
   Christianity and, 159–60, 185
   meditation and, 153, 154
   mysticism and, 43
   philosophical questions and, 157
   samsara and, *145*, 265, 280, 290
   self and, 156–59
   suffering and, 156
   universality and, 9
   Zen Buddhism and, 171–72, 265, 280
nomos, 201
non-Christians, 5, 7, 28–31, 292.
   See also universality; *specific non-Christian religions*
none, 114
nonimposing action, 204–5, 208, 262
non-Jews, 89
non-Muslims, *97*
no-self, 163, 290. *See* self, Buddhism and

numerology, 86
nuns, 57

O

Ocean of Consciousness, 41
Ogou, 231
old age, 158
Old Testament, 54, 139, 149, 150.
   See also prophecies/prophets; Torah; *specific books*
open-mindedness, 108, 214–15, 277.
   See also dialogue (interreligious encounters)
Order of the Solar Temple, 250
ordinary life/mind, 172–73, 178, 277
Origen, 5, 24, 27–28, 134
original sin, 102, 103–4, 290
orthodoxy, 74
orthopraxy, 74
Other, the , 19–21, 191, 290
Oxford Bible Commentary, The, 227
Ox-herding pictures, 185–89

P

pagans, *240*
pain. *See* suffering
Palestinian Talmud, 292
Pali canon, 142
pantheism, 212
paradigms, 37, 269
paradoxes. *See also* koans; mysteries
   basics, 264, 265, 278
   Buddhism and, 56–57
   Christianity and, 25, 182, 184, 279, 281

Daoism and, 205
Hinduism and, 42
maturity and, 278
Zen Buddhism and, xiii, 182,
    280 (*See also* koans)
Paramahamsa, Ramakrishna, 41–42
paramattha-sacca, 156
Parjanya, 120
Passover, 79–81, 82, 83
pastors, 56
A Path with a Heart (Kornfield),
    277–78
paticca samupadha, 162
patience, 277
patriarchy, 245, 249, 256
patristic Church (second-fifth
    centuries), 5–6, 24, 39–40, 57,
    67, 114
Paul
    angels and, 54
    Athens and, 1–3, 5, 15
    bishops and, 56
    bodhisattva vow and, 166
    Body of Christ image and, 6–7
    God and, 182
    heaven, on, 159–60
    interrelatedness, on, 165
    mediation and, 49
    Muhammad and, x
    mysticism and, 24, 27, 105–6
    open-mindedness and, 215
    redemption, on, 228
    self-emptying and, 182
    sin, on, 104
    sorcerers and, 234
    souls and, 128
    spirits and, 57
peace (tranquility), 91, 191, 224

Pearce, Joseph Chilton, 241–42
Pentateuch, 292
Pentecostals, 232, 275
perfection, 277
Persians, 79
Peruvians, 224
pesach, 79, 80
Peter, 11, 27
Peter the apostle, 9
Pew Forum on Religion and Public
    Life, 253
Pharisee and the Publican, 152–53,
    262
Philo of Alexandria, 28
physics, 17
Pieper, Joseph, 82
Pieris, Aloysius, 271
Pike, Sarah, 247
pilgrimages, 96, 97
Pio, Padre, 39
pipe, sacred, 223–24
pity, 155
Plato, 30–31, 201
platonism, 40
Plotinus, 28, 30, 32
Plotkin, Mark, 235–36
pluralism, 9, 11–13, 15–16, 119, 240,
    278, 290. *See also* relativism
polytheism, 290
Ponticus, Evagrius, 58, 189, 232
poor people, 140
possessions (trances), 231–32, 235,
    236, 288
postmodernism, 15, 16–18, 290
power, 52, 53, 55, 128, 149, 150
Power of Now, The (Tolle), 242
practice, 268–69, 274–75
Prajapati, 120

prajna, 271
Prashna Upanishads, 30
prayers
  Christianity and, 115, 154–55,
    190–91, 263
  dialog and, 268
  Hinduism and, 120
  humility and, 152
  indigenous traditions and, 225
  Islam and, 95, 96, 98–99,
    108–13, 114, 263
  mysticism and, 33
  New Age and, 242
predestination, 6, 7–8
presence, 52, 184–85
prie, 114
priests, 56, 57, 231, 246
principalities, 55
proclaimers, 48
prophecies/prophets, 48, 56, 140,
  150, 224, 226, 232, 233. *See also*
  individual prophets
propriety, 212
Protestantism, 7–8, 10, 11,
  26, 48–49, 92, 129. *See also*
  Christianity
Psalms, 114
psychology
  Chinese spirit and, 208
  Hinduism and, 144
  mysticism and, 35
  New Age and, 240, 244, 249,
    274
  religious movements and, 244
  shamanism and, 229, 232
  stigmata and, 39
psychosomatic phenomena, 39
Publican and the Pharisee, 152–53

purification
  Buddhism and, 163
  Christianity and, 135
  indigenous traditions and, 223,
    225
  Islam and, 96, 109, 111
  New Age and, 246
  Zen Buddhism and, 174–75
Purim, 79

Q
questioning, 277
quidquid recipitur, principle of, 37
Qur'an
  basics, 95, 100, 106–7, 108,
    109–10, 290
  inclusivism and, 17
  prayers and, 109, 111
  recitation of, 112–13, 115
  revelation and, 106–7
  universality and, 9

R
rabbis, 64, 291. *See also* rebbes;
  individual rabbis
Race, Alan, 9
rafraf, 100, 101
raft and snake metaphor, 157
Rahula, 143
raja yoga, 61
raja yoga, 60
rak'ah, 108–9
Rama, Lord of, 130
Ramadan, 96
Ramadan, 97
Ramakrishna, 60

Ramakrishna Paramahamsa, 41–42
Ramana Maharishi, 242
Ramanuja, 59
Ram Dass, 61
Raphael, *3*
Rasa Lila, 130–31
Reality. *See also* Absolute (Eternal,
    Ultimate)
    Buddhism and, 156
    Christianity and, 160, 263
    Daoism and, 201–2, 203, 206
    Hindu, 121, 124
    silence and, 271
    Soto Zen and, 176, 177–78
    symbols and, 83
    Zen Buddhism and, 171, 172,
        175, 180–81
reality, human, 285, 287. *See also*
    dukkha; illusion; karma
reason (science), 233, 234, 236, 267
rebbes, 52, 63–65, 66, 288, 291
rebirth, 121–22, 125, 142, 162, 163
receptivity, 104, 114
reciprocity, 212
recitations
    Hinduism and, 120
    Islam and, 99, 106, 107, 109–10,
        111–12, 113, 114, 115, 290
    Judaism and, 78, 81
redemption. *See* salvation
Reformation, 7–8
Reich, Charles, 239
reincarnation, 121–22, 287, 290,
    291, 293. *See also* samsara
relationships. *See also* interdepen-
    dence (interrelatedness)
    Chinese spirit and, 197, 198–99
    Christianity and, 281

Confucianism and, 211–12, 287
maturity and, 277, 278
New Age and, 249
relativism, 240, 263, 272–732, 291.
    See also pluralism
relativity, 16, 172, 178, 183, 280. *See
    also* samsara
religious experiences. *See also* mysti-
    cism; retreats; visionaries/visions
    basics, xii, 12–13, 15, 228, 273
    dialog and, 268
    indigenous religions and, 265
    interreligious practice and, 269
    multiple belonging and, 272
    New Age and, 254
    Wilber on, 274
ren, 212
repair, 89, 90
respect. *See also* dignity
    basics, 20, 21, 216
    Buddhism and, 146
    Chinese spirit and, 208, 211, 214
    Christianity and, 216, 227
    indigenous traditions and, 220,
        222
    Judaism and, 65, 87
    maturity and, 278
    New Age and, 244, 248
    relativism and, 263
resurrections, 83, 160, 280
retreats, 253
Revelation, Book of, 133, 160
revelations
    Christianity and, 115
    exclusivism and, 9–10
    Hindu, 137
    Islam and, 100, 111, 115
    Judaism and, 75, 76, 87, 88

Richard of St. Victor, 58
righteousness, 197, 210
Rig Veda, 120
Rinzai Zen, 178–81, 291
rita, 120
rites and rituals. *See also specific*
  rituals
  basics, 82–83
  Chinese spirit and, 197, 199
  Confucianism and, 210–11, 212
  Daoism and, 210
  Hindu, 120–21
  indigenous traditions and, 223,
    229–30, 231, 233, 235, 236
  New Age and, 244, 246, 247,
    248
Rites of Spring, 247
rituals. *See* rites and rituals
*Roaring of the Sacred River, The:
  Wilderness Quest for Vision and
  Self-Healing* (Foster and Little),
  242
Roberts, Oral, 226
Robertson, Pat, 226
roeh, 48
Roman Catholicism, 7, 10, 11, 26,
  48, 83, 88
Rosh Hashanah, 79, 91
Roshi, Robert Kennedy, 192
Roshi, Yamada, 192
Roshis, 170, 270
Rudra, 120
rulers metaphor, 204
Rumi, Jalal ad-Din, 30, 242
Russell, Charles Taze, 243
Rutherford, Joseph Franklin,
  243
Ruysbroeck, Jan, 190

S
Sabbath, 76–78, 81–82, 85, 263,
  266, 291. *See also* Lord's Day
sabbats, 246
sacrifices, 47–48, 83, 84, 120–21,
  140, 288. *See also* fire
sadhana, 60
Saguna-Brahman, 42, 123, 129, 203,
  286, 291
saints, 49–50. *See also individual
  saints*
salat, 96, 108–13, 114
Salesian spirituality, 215, 257
salvation (redemption). *See also*
  liberation (freedom); resurrections; soteriology
  Christianity and, 4, 7, 83–84,
    149, 166, 279, 280–81
  creation and, 227–28
  exclusivism and, 9
  inclusivism and, 14–15
  Judaism and, 80
samadhi meditations, 153
Sama Veda, 120
samghogakaya, 62
samkhya, 144
sammuti-sacca, 156–57
samsara
  basics, 265, 287, 291
  Buddhism and, *145*, 216
  Hinduism and, 121, 123, 124
  Nirvana and, 171–72, 185, 265,
    280, 290
Sangha, 62
Satan (Lucifer), 54, 102, 150–51,
  233, 291
satchitananda, 42, 127
satori, 178, 291

Sawm (Ramadan), 96, 97
Scale of Perfection (Hilton), 190
schisms, 6
Schneerson, Menachem, *64*
scholars, *75*
Schuller, Robert, 226
science, 17, 233, 234, 236, 267
Scientology, 251
scotosis, 151
Seattle (Chief), 221–22
second coming of Christ, 243
Second Gethsemani Encounter, *262*
Second Vatican Council, 129
Seders, 79–81, 82, 83
Seeker's Guide, The: A New Age Resource Book (Button and Bloom), 240
seers, 48
sefirot, 51, 52, 53, 88–89, 291
self (egos). *See also* Atman; no-self; Transpersonal self
  basics, 124
  beliefs and, 273–74
  Buddha and, *145*, 142, 143, 148, 264
  Buddhism and, 154, 155, 156–57, 163–64, 165, 171, 262, 269
  Charismatics and, 275
  Christianity and, 128, 152, 153, 182, 192
  Hinduism and, 42, 43, 45, 122, 124–27, 143, 265
  maturity and, 278
  mysticism and, 31
  Soto Zen and, 175–76, 178
  universality and, 276
  Wilber on, 274, 275–76

Zen Buddhism and, 180, 186, 187–88, 192
self-help, 257
self-intoxication, 146
self-knowledge, 190
self-righteousness, 155
seraphim, 51, 54, 55
serviteurs, 231–32, 291
Seven Steps of the Ladder of Spiritual Love (Ruysbroeck), 190
Seventh Day Adventists, 225–26, 243
sext, 114
sexuality
  Buddhism and, 143
  Christianity and, 133
  Hinduism and, 130–34, 136–37
  maturity and, 278
  New Age and, 245, 247
  voodoo and, 232
Shahadah, 96
Shakalya, Vidagdha, 123
Shakayana, 124
shakti, 42
shamanism
  basics, 50
  Christianity and, 232–36
  credibility and, 267, 291
  indigenous traditions and, 228–30
  New Age and, 240, 244, 246, 247, 248, 256
Shammai, 71, 74–76
Shang-Ti, 199
Shankara, 42, 123, 292
Shantideva, 163–64
She, Israel Baal. *See also* Hasidic Judaism
Shinshu, 176

Shintoism, 51

Shiva, 123, 136–37, 291

shofar, 79

shou, 202

showings, 34–35

shu, 202, 212

Shubun, *187*

shunyata, 188

Shvetaketu, 126, 128

Siddhartha Gautama, 143–44, 146
286

silence, 157, 173, 271

Simlai (Rabbi), 72–73, 89–90

sins. *See also* original sin; *specific sins*
Buddhism and, 151, 264

Christianity and, 83, 103, 104,
280, 288

Hinduism and, 264–65

Islam and, 102

Judaism and, 79, 89, 111

Sioux culture, 220, 224

skillfulness
Buddhism and, 153, 155, 161

Chinese spirit and, 197, 203–4,
208

Christianity and, *209*

Daoism and, 197, 202, 203, 287

maturity and, 278

New Age and, 248

religion and, xiii, 17, 20, 151

Zen Buddhism and, 185, 189

Smith, Christian, 255

snake and raft metaphor, 157

snakes, 247

Soma, 120

soma pneumatikos, 160

Song of Songs, 134

soteriology, 119

Soto Zen, 175–78, 292

souls
basics, ix–x

Chinese spirit and, 196–97

Christianity and, 103, 104, 116,
127–28, 133, 135, 171, 190,
191, 228, 264

Hinduism and, 123, 131–32, 133

indigenous traditions and, 230

Islam and, 102, 104

Judaism and, 77

mysticism and, 26, 27

New Age and, 250–51

Soul Searching (Smith), 255

space, 85–87

sparks, 89

Spirit, Holy, 4, 25, 58, 67, 128, 215–16,
232, 257. *See also* Trinity, Holy

Spirit Medicine (Moondance), 248

spirits, 57, 199–200, 228–29,
229–32, 232–33, 244. *See also*
Holy Spirit

Spiritual Canticle (John of the
Cross), 135

Spiritual Dance, The (Starhawk), 247

Spiritual Exercises (Ignatius of
Loyola), 58

spirituality. *See also* spiritual paths
Christianity and, 40, 55–56

courses, xii

doctrine *versus*, xi

mysticism and, 26, 36–37

Paul and, 3

spiritual maturity, 277–81

spiritual paths. *See also* mediation
(guides, masters); spirituality

Buddhism and, 147, 159,
161–62, 163, 269, 288

Christianity and, 55–56, 58,
189–91, 192, 254, 269
Daoism and, 202, 265
dialog and, 269
Hinduism and, 60, 265
indigenous traditions and, 223,
224–25
Islam and, 96, 98, 111, 265–66
Judaism and, 85, 289
maturity and, 277
New Age and, 241, 242, 248,
249–50, 251
Soto Zen and, 176
universality and, 276
Wicca and, 254
Zen Buddhism and, 171,
172–73, 175, 185–89, 192,
265
spontaneity, 204
Sribhasya, 59
Starhawk, 245, 247, 256
status quo, 253–54
Steindl-Rast, David, 271
Steinsaltz, Adin, 29
stigmata, 37–39
stillness, 212
Stone, Merlin, 246
Stonehenge, *240*
study (learning), 75, 85, 87, 88, 126,
211
submission, 95–96, 98, 101
suffering. *See also* desires (cravings)
Buddhism and, 144, 146–47,
147–48, 155, 156, 163,
164–65, 287, 288
Christianity and, 40, 135
delusion and, 153
heart and, 277

Hinduism and, 131–32, 265
Judaism and, 89
Sukkot, 79
Sun Myung Moon, 243
sunnah, 98
Surat al-fatihah, 111–12
sutras, 292
Svetasvatara Upanishads, 30
symbols. *See also* metaphors
Buddhism and, 143
Christianity and, 104, 116, 150,
160
Islam and, 100–101, 101–2, 104,
113
Judaism and, 85
rituals and, 83
Zen Buddhism and, 172
sympathetic magic, 236, 292
sympathy, 212
synergy, 116
Synoptic Gospels, 83

T

Talmud, 72, 73, 75, 77, 292
"Tantric Ecstatic Breath Cer-
emony," 247
Tantric Yoga, 247
Tao Te Ching (Lao Tzu), 198
tea, 174
technology, 82
Tekakwitha, Kateri, *270*
Tenakh, 85
Ten Commandments, 72
ten perfections, 164
terce, 114
Teresa of Avila, 25, 26, 33, 58,
190–92

Thérèse of Lisieux, 115
Testament of the Twelve Patriarchs, 54
theology. *See also* cosmology
   basic positions, 9, 16
   Christianity and, 287
   comparative, 18
   dialog and, 268
   Islam and, 96
   mysticism and, 32
   pluralism and, xii, 8, 292
   practice and, 268–69
   religious experience and, 37
theology of religions, 8, 292
theos, 201
Theravada Buddhism, 161, 162,
   164, 292
Thérèse of Lisieux, 184–85
thetans, 251
thought. *See* minds, human
Three-Body Mentor Yoga, 62–63
thrones, 54, 55
Ti, 199
tiaren heyi, 210
Tibetan (Vajrayana) Buddhism, 61,
   62, 289, 292
tien, 197, 199, 212
Tifereth, 52, 53
time, 76–78, 79, 81, 82–83, 85–87, 281
Timothy I, 4
tiqqun, 89
TM (Transcendental Meditation),
   243
Tolle, Eckhart, 242
Tolstoy, Leo, 19–20
Torah. *See also* Kabbalah
   action and, 88–91
   basics, 71, 73, 75–76, 289, 292
   Christianity and, 116

mediation and, 47, *64*
time and space and, 85–91
tradition, 256–57
trances (possessions), 231–32, 235,
   236, 288
transcendence
   Buddhism and, 62–63, 271
   Christianity and, 2, 127, 182
   Confucianism and, 212
   Daoism and, 201
   Hinduism and, 15, 122, 127
   indigenous traditions and, 223
   Islam and, 102, 117
   Judaism and, 88
   mediation and, 47–48
   mystery and, 264
   mysticism and, 25
   New Age and, 254
   pluralism and, 13, 15
   Zen Buddhism and, 188
Transcendental Meditation (TM), 243
transformation
   Buddhism and, 146, 155
   Chinese spirit and, 205, 210
   Christianity and, 28, 65–66,
      105–6, 128, 134, 155, 191,
      254, 269, 272–78, 281
   Hinduism and, 137
   inclusiveness and, 15
   indigenous traditions and, 220, 224
   Islam and, 96
   Judaism and, 79
   mediators and, 60, 61, 62, 66
   mysticism and, 35, 36
   New Age and, 243, 249, 251
   Wilber on, 273–74
   Zen Buddhism and, 188
Transpersonal self, 275

Trappist monk, *262*
trikaya, 62
Trinity, Holy, 11, 14–15, 281
Truth. *See also* Absolute (Eternal,
    Ultimate); open-mindedness
    Buddhism and, 63, 147, 151–52,
        154, 156–57, 164
    Christianity and, 108, 150–51,
        191, 192, 281
    Confucianism and, 210
    conventionality and, 163
    culture and, 201
    Hinduism and, 125, 126
    Islam and, 103, 107
    Judaism and, 85
    multiple, 272
    New Age and, 242
    postmodernism and, 15–16, 17
    Soto Zen and, 177, 178
    Zen Buddhism and, 175,
        188–89, 192, 280
tsa'aq, 74
tusita heaven, 143
tzadik, 64

U

Ultimate. *See* Absolute (Eternal,
    Ultimate)
umm al-kitab, 107
underworld, 50, 54
Unexcelled Yoga, 62
Unification Church, 243
union/unity
    Chinese spirit and, 214
    Christianity and, 183, 191, 279,
        281
    Confucianism and, 212

Hinduism and, 127, 130–31, 293
indigenous traditions and, 223
mysticism and, 279, 280
New Age and, 247
sexual metaphors, 134
Wilber on, 274
Zen Buddhism and, 280
uniqueness, 277
United Nations, 224
United States Council of Catholic
    Bishops, 227
universality. *See also* diversity;
    inclusivism; multiple belonging
    basics, xiii
    Buddhism and, 171
    Christianity and, 3–4, 3–9, 271,
        272
    Daoism and, 201
    holy people and, 276
    indigenous traditions and, 222
    Judaism and, 90–91
    mutuality model and, 290
    mysticism and, 32–33, 43
    physics and, 17
Upanishads, 30, 32, 121–23, 124,
    125, 127, 293
Ushigua, Gloria, 224, 229, 235
Uzzah, 139

V

Vaccha, 158, 159
Vajrayana (Tibetan) Buddhism, 61,
    62, 289, 292
van Ruysbroeck, Jan, 28
Varieties of Religious Experience, The
    (James), 220
Varuna, 120

Vedanta, Hindu, 271, 275, 292
Vedas, 119–20, 122, 293
vegetarianism, 227, 266, 267
veneration, 49, 199
vespers, 114
Viet Nam, 209
Vimalakirti, 161–62
vipassana, 269
vipassana meditation, 154
virgin births, 143
vir religiosus, 57, 67
virtues, 55, 207
vir venerabilis, 57, 67
Vishnu, 123, 129, 130, 137, 280, 291
visionaries/visions
    Christianity and, 33–34, 37–38,
      105
    Hinduism and, 41, 138
    indigenous traditions and, 229, 233
    Islam and, 100–101
    Judaism and, 48
Visitation of Holy Mary, 215
Vivekananda, 60
Vo, 230
voodoo, 51, 230–32, 288, 293

W

Wakan-Tanka, 223, 224
war, 99
washing rituals, 109, 111
Watchtower Society, 243
Way, the, 197
Wayana tribe, 235
Way of the Bodhisattva, The
    (Shatideve), 163–64
wealth, 96, 264–65. *See also* greed
wedding (marriage) metaphors

Christianity and, 84, 133–35,
    191, 279
Hinduism and, 130–31, 132–33
indigenous traditions and,
    231–32, 236
Judaism and, 77
mysticism and, 279
wen, 212
When God Was a Woman (Stone), 246
Where Angels Walk (Anderson), 255
White, Ellen G., 243
White Buffalo Cow Woman, 223
Wicca, *240*, 245–47, 254, 256, 293
Wilber, Ken, 273–74
"The Will to Believe" (James), 267
Wirthnow, Robert, 254
wisdom
    Buddhism and, 163, 271
    Chinese spirit and, 207
    Christianity and, 191
    Confucianism and, 211
    Hinduism and, 127
    Islam and, 107
    Judaism and, 52, 85, 88
    New Age and, 248
    Zen Buddhism and, 173, 186, 188
women, 52, 207, 208, 212, 215, 246.
    See also goddesses; *individual*
    women
word of God, 5, 107, 114, 115, 246,
    271
words. *See* language
works. *See* actions
world, 162, 163
World Council of Churches, 227
worship, 49, 123
woundedness, 89, 92, 103, 132, 135,
    283

wu forms, 203–5, 208
wu-wei, 203, 205, 208, *209,* 262
wu-yu, 204, 208
wuzhi, 204

X

xiao, 212

Y

Yajnavalkya, 123
Yajur Veda, 120
Yakut, North Asian, 51, 229
Yashoda, 138
Yasodhara, 143
Yathrib, 98
Yesod, 52
YHWH, 11
y'i, 197
"*Yigdal*" hymn, 73
Yiguandao, 214
yin and yang, 19, 200, 205, 207–8,
    261, 293
yoga, 60–63, 144, 243, 247, 275,
    286, 293
Yogachara Buddhism, 289
Yogananda, Paramhansa, 61, 243
Yohanan ben Zakkai, 74
Yom Kippur, 79
young adults, 253–54, 255
Yukteswar, 61
yuzchou, 201

Z

Zaehner, R.C., 32
Zakat, 96

Zapara people, 224, 229
zazen, 178, 180
Zechariah, Book of, 4
Zen Buddhism (Ch'an). *See also*
    Bodhidharma; *koans*; Rinzai
    Zen; Soto Zen
    Absolute and, 171, 172,
        176, 177, 178, 185, 191,
        192, 280
    basics, xiii, 170–73, 289, 293
    Christianity and, 170–71,
        181–85, 189–92, 270,
        280
    Daoism and, 202
    dialog with, 269
    historical notes, 173–75
    Islam and, 276
    mutuality model and, 16
    New Age and, 242
    scriptures, 293
    spiritual path of, 265
    spiritual progress, 185–89
    Wilber on, 275
Zeus, 280
Zhou Zhongzhi, 213
Zhuangzi (Chuang Tzu), 204–5,
    206, 293
Zhuangzi, The (*The Chuang Tzu*),
    201–2
Ziaozong, 214
zimzum, 88
Zion's Watchtower Society, 243
ziran, 204
zizi, 198
Zohar, 87
Zoroastrianism, 72
z'roa, 79
Zusya, Rebbe, 65